Praise for
Finding the Kingdom Within

"Brian's new book, *Finding the Kingdom Within*, is an inspiration for the emerging New Reality. This latest masterpiece brings an abundance of helpful, healing words from The Prince of Peace himself to assist you in waking to your true spiritual potential."

–Owen K. Waters, Spiritual Dynamics Academy.

". . . *Finding the Kingdom Within* is a rare find, and I am happy for the world that Brian chose to recount more of his life-long relationship with Brother Jesus, and to share what he has learned from that relationship so that we could all benefit from it."

–Rev Myron Jones, author of *Hey, Holy Spirit, It's Me Again* and *Healing Family Relationships*.

"I love Brian's writing style. It is very clear and poetically in-touch and in-tune with the Divine. The Inner Voice messages Brian shares here are extremely lucid, as though one is seeing from a higher dimension – indeed, from the perspective and authority of Eternity. He speaks endearingly of the Healed Mind of Papa's beloved Son. That would be you and me – Jesus, Brian and all of us together as One Holy, Healed Mind."

–Jon Mundy, Ph.D., author of *Eternal Life and A Course in Miracles*.

"I truly am impressed by Brian's ability to explain deep esoteric and mystical reality in a way that is so easy to understand. As I read *Finding the Kingdom Within*, I was drawn deeply into the precise, simple, easy-to-understand explanations that he offers to his readers.

". . . Brilliant, Brian, you have done it again! This is an exceptional book that will feed the hungry with the Truth that just as Christ is within us, so we are within Christ. No one could possibly make this more clear than Brian Longhurst."

–Michael J. Roads, author of *Through the Eyes of Love, Journeying with Pan* trilogy, and *Stepping . . . Between . . . Realities*.

Finding the Kingdom Within

Awakening to Eternity

Brian Longhurst

Six Degrees Publishing Group
Portland • Oregon • USA

Six Degrees Publishing Group
5331 S.W. Macadam Avenue, Suite 258
Portland, Oregon 97239 USA
ISBN: 978-1-942497-17-2
Library of Congress Control Number: 2016935273

(Ebook ISBN: 978-1-942497-18-9)

Enquiries may be made by emailing Permissions@SixDegreesPublishing.com
Cover image of Orion Nebula courtesy of ESA/Hubble

Printed simultaneously in the United States of America and the United Kingdom.

Unless otherwise indicated, all Scripture quotations are extracts from the Authorized Version of *The King James Bible,* the rights in which are vested in the Crown.

Author's note: In quoting portions of *A Course in Miracles*, or other sources, I have bracketed words added by me, and have underlined, emboldened and italicised some words for emphasis.

Amazon Edition

PUBLISHED BY SIX DEGREES PUBLISHING GROUP
IN COLLABORATION WITH
(6)   HONEST TO GOODNESS   (h†g)

www.SixDegreesPublishing.com   www.honest2goodness.org.uk

For Clara

3   5   7   9   10   8   6   4   2

ALSO BY BRIAN LONGHURST

"Seek ye First the Kingdom ..."
One man's journey with the living Jesus

Contents

Acknowledgements   *xi*

Introduction   *xiii*

1: Darkness or the Light: Our Free Choice   1

2: Leavening the Mind: an Operation of Hiddenness   9

3: The Ease of Overcoming the Ego World   17

4: Distraction by Detail   23

5: Mind-to-Mind Communing   31

6: True Forgiveness   39

7: Responding to Opportunities   48

8: Reflections on Our Eternal Reality   52

9: The Great Leavening   57

10: Shining Away the Veil   65

11: The Open Door to the Most Holy Place   70

12: Karmic Tug of War   76

13: Entering-in to the Real World   82

14: Identity Discernment   88

15: On Grace   94

16: Opening to Greater Awareness of Brotherhood   100

Contents

17: Forgetting-not to Laugh 106

18: Restoration to Oneness Through Forgiveness 111

19: How to Save the World 117

20: The Oneness of Every Living Thing 123

21: Choosing Between Reality Within and Illusion Without 129

22: Two Sides of the Same Coin 134

23: Moving from Bodily Sight to True Vision 139

24: Letting Technology *Serve* the Awakening 146

25: Engaging the Creative Process 151

26: Waking from Slow Suicide to Eternal Life 157

27: The Polarity Switch 163

28: Transforming Enmity into Amity 169

29: Soul Mates 175

30: Adversity: Opportunity in Disguise 180

31: Love Believeth *All* Things 185

32: Communing with the Mind of Christ 191

33: Exchanging Thinking for Being 197

34: Accessing Help in Escaping the Carousel 202

35: Who am I? Why am I Here? 208

36: Our Greatest Joy and Blessing:
Communing with Universal Mind 213

37: Qualities that Connect Us to Eternity   218

38: Becoming Like Jesus   222

39: To Fear or to Love: Our Only Choice   227

40: Freedom through *Self*-Forgiveness   232

41: Attuning Our Mind and Life with Truth   237

42: Taking Advantage of Opportunities   243

43: Inner Peace through Forgiveness   249

44: Unburdening from Unconscious Guilt   254

45: Being the Light *and* the Saviour of the World   259

46: The Power in Jesus' Name   265

47: Loving Beyond All Illusory Barriers   269

48: Bringing Darkness to the Light   275

49: The Rejoining of the Sonship   281

50: Revelation: The Key to Knowledge   287

51: Seeing the Reality within the Crucifixion   293

52: One Problem: Guilt. One Solution: Forgiveness.   300

Afterword   306

Author's Note About the Cover Illustration   309

Glossary   313

About the Author   317

Acknowledgements

THERE ARE MANY without whom this work could never have been brought before its readers. For this, and all involved, I wish to express heartfelt thanks and grateful acknowledgement. First and foremost is our Heavenly Father, the Creator Spirit, 'Papa'. Where would we be without Him? Truly Jesus spoke when he said of his relationship with Him, *Of myself I can do nothing.* He is the Source of All, in Whom we live and move and have our being. To You, beloved Papa, I am eternally grateful.

Then, it will be no surprise to the reader, comes Jesus, Papa's *Anointed Messenger.* He has befriended me, tutored me, Loved me completely, unconditionally, led me with infinite patience, and won my total trust, loyalty, following, devotion and Love. How wonderful will be the day when we are all brothers to each other as he has been to me, and in Truth, is to us all. On that day will the Kingdom of Heaven – 'the real world' – be well and truly operational on Earth.

I have no idea how to acknowledge the Holy Spirit. All I know is that my heart impels me to acknowledge Him. For He is the true, Whole (Holy) Self of us all, the Highest part of our mind; the Voice for God within us; the Voice that reminds us that we are all, along with Jesus, one in the Sonship of God; the Voice that will speak with us of the Truth of Eternity, if we are willing to be still and listen. *Ssshhh!*

Now, my beloved wife, Theresa. In 1967, I asked Jesus to bring to me a Companion of the Way. Within four months he fulfilled my request by bringing us together in the unlikeliest of circumstances; synchronicity performing at its best. Steadfast, long-suffering to a fault and stalwart are terms that come to mind to describe Theresa. But more than that, her support, patience and contribution in proofing and making suggestions for improving the manuscript and a thousand other ways as I worked on it, all have been invaluable, and in which I am *truly,* deeply blessed. Above all these precious qualities is the selfless but Self-full Love she emanates from her beautiful heart and radiant soul. Thank you, Darling, for being my beloved Companion of the Way.

To me, a kindergarten child in the world of computers, Tim is an unsung hero, who cannot go without mention here. Whenever a need for help with computers arose, since the mid-1990s, Tim has been there for us. And there has never been an issue that his indomitable approach to every challenge was not able to resolve, usually in two shakes of a lamb's tail. Thank you, Tim; please do not emigrate!

Last, but by no means least, is Denise Williams. It is completely evident that you are a consummate professional; diligent, competent, committed, comprehensive in your communications and to fulfilling your role as publisher to the last detail, yet with great empathy and sensitivity toward the perspective of the author. Altogether, Denise, since day one you have been, and remain, a pleasure and breath of fresh air to work with.

–Brian Longhurst

Introduction

Jesus counsels us, *Seek ye first the Kingdom* (of God, or Heaven) (Mt. 6:33). He also counsels us, *Seek and ye shall find* (Mt. 7:7), so it is inevitable that if one has been taking his advice and seeking the Kingdom *first*, one will – sooner rather than later – *find* the Kingdom.

My first book was entitled *"Seek ye First the Kingdom..."*, and subtitled *One man's journey with the living Jesus*. It tells of his manifesting to me in his glory in a basement lodging in 1967 and my decades-long journey with him ever since, during which I have placed myself within his care, guidance and protection, and have (mostly!) been following his lead.

This has brought incalculable benefits in the form of miracles, astonishing synchronicities, blessings, wise counsel, teaching and explanations of esoteric, mystical, eternal reality, which he described as *the Principles of Life of the Father* (PLFs), much of which is at variance with orthodox religious doctrines and dogmas about God, Jesus and Heaven, or eternity. All this was within a context of unconditional Love, infinite patience, gentleness, caring, lightness of heart and joyous, treasured humour. He told me he had come to lead me back to God, and that he was (is) my Guide to eternity. He won my absolute, undying trust and devoted Love for him from the beginning and ever since, revealing many proofs of the authenticity of his all-empowerment-by-perfect-Love. In Truth he is – or would gladly be if/when we are willing to trust him enough to *follow* his leading – the Guide of us *all*, his brothers in the Sonship of God. In

A Course in Miracles Jesus describes 'the Sonship of God' as the One Son of God – Christ – dreaming a momentary dream of separation from his Father and his Self and appearing in fragmented form as many separate bodies with separate identities and minds. His purpose is to lovingly, gently, caringly restore us all back to the unutterable bliss of Oneness, with him, that is the fully *Wakened* eternal Truth of our Being as the indivisible part of God that we are.

One could consider "*Seek ye First the Kingdom…*" as helping to open the door to acceptance of the reality and accessibility of the eternity that is Heaven, and the Loving, benign care, guidance and protection that is freely available to us all, *here and now*, from There.

Finding the Kingdom Within takes us deeper into Its ever-present joy, peace and Love, sharing and showing the ease with which we can be returned to awareness – *remembrance* – of the Truth of our limitless, radiant Being: the God-Self within. This restoration, also known as *The Great Rescue Programme*, or *Great Awakening*, or final phase of the *Atonement* (pronounced 'At-*One*-ment'; see Glossary of Terms, page 313, for explanation), is unfolding, moving toward its liberating, limitless conclusion, and so our Oneness with It moves along too, because we are all integral, intrinsic parts of It. Hence this follow-on book, to help us keep in step and up with the progress.

In our dense, embodied, somnolent state of forgetfulness of our true, immortal, spiritual Being, most of us can only encounter and assimilate eternity – what Jesus calls the Kingdom of Heaven – in small bites, rather than all in one go. Hence the subtitle – *Awakening to Eternity*, 'awakening' being a *progressive* process.

When we seek – and begin to find – the Kingdom of Heaven within, just as Jesus told us in the long ago that we would, we discover that there is, in Truth, nothing mysterious about It at all; that It is entirely clear, cogent, coherent, consistent, reasonable, relevant, unequivocal, uncomplicated, reliable, benign, perfectly structured … How could it be other, since it is the creation of the Creator Spirit – God? Eternity, or Heaven, has *never* been hidden from us; it is in plain view, and freely accessible, to all. There are and can be no exceptions to this. We have merely been seeking it in the wrong place: *without*. The Kingdom is *within* us, but if we will not go within to find it, we will, literally, go without. It is, and has always been, our free choice. The great treasure of the Kingdom is that it is the Truth of all Being, and that if we *live* that Truth it truly *does* set us free.

The purpose of the journey, following/walking *with* Jesus is, unsurprisingly, to arrive at our destination, with him as our guide. How else will we find our way? Our destination is God; 'Papa'. He, our true and only Home, is not far away. He is as close as our next heartbeat; closer than that. He is within us. He is not 'out there' and will never be found out there. He is the Great Treasure that, whether we are *consciously* aware or not, we all are seeking, and only when we have remembered that He is within us all, and we go within to find Him there, will fulfilment, completion, joy – far, far beyond any treasures we may believe this world has to offer – be our experience, our awareness, our reality, our Truth. Forever.

* * *

Each chapter in this book originated as a stand-alone article. Yet, from a larger perspective, all are connected and interwoven, sharing ways *into* and experiences *of* the within which bring us to the place of meeting, of joining, with Jesus, with the Spirit of Truth and with the Creator Spirit – the *I Am* that in Truth we all *Are*. Each chapter has been written under the generic concept of being a *Message of Encouragement*. This world is in sore need of encouragement.

In 2013 I began receiving promptings and requests to present these *Messages of Encouragement* writings in book format, because, so proponents assured me, they are a fount of inspiration, insight, wisdom – and help.

Here, then, they are offered in carefully, comprehensively revised, updated, embellished form. Not because the events or inspiration that brought them about changed, but because, as our Awakening to reality advances, so does our insight into, our discernment *of*, our oneness *with* eternity grow and expand commensurately, until our destination is reached: full wakefulness to Oneness in the Heart-Mind of God, our ever-Loving Father Creator.

* * *

In December 1995 Jesus told me:

"... It is not possible for the Father's purposes to fail, and the Light shall be shone in the dark places until all the shadows of death and fear shall have fled away. Rejoice greatly at this, my beloveds, and sing the New Song, that my little ones may hear, and dance the dance of freedom."

I have come to realise in recent years that his reference to singing *the New Song* was his poetic way of telling me he had an *ongoing, unfolding* message for me (and indeed, all of us who so desire) to 'sing', deliver to – share with – all who are ready, willing, able to *receive* it. I had no idea how I could possibly do that, but he (and the Holy Spirit, the Spirit of Truth that dwells within the mind of us all), I discovered, inspires those who are willing to serve the Great Rescue Programme (about which the reader will find further references and explanations amongst the following pages and in the Glossary of Terms at the back of this book) with the words of the New Song, to 'sing', to share with those he brings to us for such sharing. Indeed, he told me in 1968:

"Do not go out looking for people to share your message; for you do not know their hearts and minds. Rather, I will bring them to you, for I know the hearts and minds of all, and will bring only those who are ready to hear, and will inspire you and give you the words to speak [or, 'sing'] to their hearts."

The words are, I discovered as events progressed, a collaborative venture agreed 'aforetime' (his way of saying before I incarnated as persona Brian) between Jesus/Holy Spirit and me.

All in this writing accords with Jesus' teaching in *A Course in Miracles*. Each chapter has brought me, via the above-mentioned inspiration, new, deeper insights on eternal reality and the *Principles of Life of the Father*. When we are inspired, words become *enlivened* within us, part of our livingness, transforming them from mere symbols to the *Living* Word, or Word of *Life* which then emanate from us as part of our emergent Being.

* * *

Since 1967 I have recorded Jesus' speaking – and from time to time other souls, also from the Realms of Light – to me during a devotional *Service of Mystical Communion with Christ* as well as on other occasions. These records I have collectively referred to as the *Diary of a Christ Communicant*, or simply, *Diary*. Since these provide helpful information for minds ready to accept something beyond the chaos of this illusory world of time and place, a *Diary* entry is appended at the end of each chapter.

I have been repeatedly astonished at the synchronicity that has occurred between the content of the *Message of Encouragement* article/chapter and the *Diary* entry accompanying it. Each entry is simply taken in date sequence from the *Diary* – recorded years or even decades previously – after the article has been written. This synchronicity has been, for me, and remains, wonderful testimony to the closeness of involvement, inspiration and leadership of Jesus, the Holy Spirit, and our other Loved ones in Spirit – available to us *all* once we choose willingness to surrender our life into Their care, guidance and protection.

Also, *preceding* each chapter is a brief extract from the *Diary* entries – 'Essential Diary'; a sentence or two, also selected in purely chronological sequence, and exhibiting striking resonance with the subsequent chapter. These, I assure you, dear reader, are synchronicities far beyond the wit of persona Brian.

To those of us inured to the idea that we must keep a tight control over the affairs of our life, such surrender may seem a fearful thing to do, for in this world, who can we trust? So I offer here extracts from a *Diary* entry in 1988, for the encouragement and peace of mind of us all:

Beloved Lord Jesus, I have glimpsed the living, Loving Spirit of the Father Creator, right here in my own being, and realised that He is with us, *within* us, constant in the power and joy and uplifting energy of His Loving, transforming ability. Speak to me more of this.

> My son, the Father it is Who *is* your life; truly is He within all ... His Children. This it is that will transform and uplift mankind. ... It is ... by *allowing* the Father within ... to take control of your life, and giving up your own leasehold on your life – that He can ... grow and fulfil your inner being ...

First we must 'surrender our leasehold' to Him?

> Beloved, trust is *all*. His Love for all His little ones is total giving. Only by absolute surrender, as you put it, can He accomplish the Glorifying of Himself in you, even as He did in me ... Put your trust in Him and do that which is given you to do each day. Thus shall the Spirit of Truth, for the Father Creator, accomplish His purpose in you.
>
> My command is to bring this good news to the children of the Father. This command is won through surrender of self to His Will. Only by this *Atonement* can we fully receive His Spirit within us; only by this *Atonement* shall the Kingdom of God-awareness manifest in the lives of His children.
>
> Have no fear, my son; your *desire* shall enable Him to accomplish it *for* you. Therefore, be peaceful, let go, enjoy all the activities of your lives together, earthly and heavenly. Let them be of a pure motivation and be not anxious always to 'please' Him; *He* will please *you* with His good gifts.

* * *

My conscious awareness and experience of Jesus began in 1967, as described in this extract from Chapter 2 of *"Seek ye First the Kingdom..."*:

> ... suddenly he was there, in the corner, manifested,

superimposed in the place where stood a beechwood chest of drawers with a mirror on top. He was in the midst of an aura of golden, living sunlight, which radiated out from him more than an arm's length in all directions. He was about three or four paces from me.

As I became aware of his presence he began to move toward me. It was not a walking movement. He seemed to be above the floor a few inches, and he glided. The movement was relatively slow, certainly unhurried, but as he drew nearer he began to speak. I *heard* him with my ears, I *experienced* his speaking with my soul, with my heart; every cell in my body and every fibre of my being experienced his speaking. There was no part of my being that did not hear him...

... By the time he had finished speaking he had reached less than an arm's length from where I was standing. His aura of golden, living sunlight had enveloped me, and the feeling of Love – of *agapé* – to my being was so intense, so powerful, so uplifting to my spirit that I felt as if my heart had grown to the size of a football and was going to burst out of my chest cavity. This feeling of all-pervasive, all-inclusive Love was complete, permeating not just my body but my entire aura in an orgasm of the soul, immeasurably more intense than any such physical experience. I was blinded by a waterfall of joyful, rapturous tears, and every part of me was alive, electrified, as never before.

His presence was visible in the midst of the light of his aura, which was at least as bright as the sun but did not hurt my eyes at all. With me now fully enveloped by his aura, he stopped. His eyes were radiating the all-knowing wisdom of the ages, and love; personal love as well as universal, unconditional Love. I knew he loved me personally, in a way and with a Love that is utterly beyond any love I had ever known, heard about or experienced in this world. He embraced me; not with his 'physical' arms but with every

> part of his being – with his total, unconditional, intimate, penetrating, all-encompassing, all-pervasive Love. I was a quivering jelly. Not from fear (how could fear exist in such an exquisitely beautiful, magnificent encounter?) but from being overwhelmed by the power of his Love ...

I am prompted to add here that looking into his eyes was like looking into eternity, for that is the *nature* of his Being.

* * *

God is frequently referred to herein as *Papa*, so a word of explanation as to how this arose is shared here, also from *"Seek ye First the Kingdom..."* (p.109):

> By early 1996, I had a growing sense of inward desire to know God in a more intimate sense than as *God, Father, Holy One, Creator Spirit,* or some such rather remote, formal term ... so I asked Him for a suitable name by which I could show the personal Love, honour and respect I have for Him. His *instant* response was, *"Papa"*. So, henceforward God the Father was for me, by His invitation, *Papa*.

* * *

It will be noticed that throughout this writing certain aspects of the content are repeated, perhaps using varying terms, but conveying the same intent. There is an important reason for this. Esoteric Truth, or reality, is so alien to the *exoterically*-focused mind that although the individual words may be recognised and understood, the context of their conjoining to express what initially may be perceived as alien, upside-down ideas can take much repetition before the deeper meaning is eventually assimilated into the mind, the very *being* of the reader.

The reality of eternity, Heaven, the Creator, even our own nature and purpose are often referred to as *the mysteries*. Five decades of walking with Jesus has revealed to me, of a certainty beyond all doubt, that there *are* no mysteries. God has kept nothing hidden from us. We *perceive* them as mysteries because we have placed a mist before our eyes, blinding ourself to what is plainly visible to us when we go within to see them with our *inner* vision.

Several words appear with a capitalised initial letter, such as *Love, Truth, Light, Know/Knowing/Knowledge*, and even *One*. This is to indicate these words have a meaning beyond the daily use to which they are put in this world. With Love, for example, this indicates divine, perfect, unconditional Love, not as in *I love bananas* ...

It is my deepest hope and profoundest prayer that all who are ready, and have been brought to this writing, this sharing, will find joy, peace, inspiration, enlightenment, upliftment, blessing, encouragement, and above all, Love, within these pages, to accompany them on their own journey back to the Truth, the eternal, rapturous reality of the Kingdom within.

–Brian Longhurst

1: Darkness or the Light: Our Free Choice

Rejoice and be glad; do not rebuke yourself for those things that
you have not previously understood. Do you think for one moment
that the Kingdom is founded on self-rebuke and recrimination?
I tell you it is founded on Love and forgiveness,
tolerance and acceptance.

–Jesus, April 26, 1992

So, WINTER SOLSTICE 2012 – the end of the Mayan calendar – has come and gone, and the dream of bodies and a world of woes did not end in calamity or cataclysm. This was the slant of the media (ego's servant) on this event. It would be, wouldn't it?, because ego is of the without – illusions of separation and destruction – the seeming opposite of Oneness and Creation. The without knows *nothing* of the within, because the within is about Love, Peace, Joy, wholeness. The within – Heaven, eternity, Papa – knows nothing of ending or destruction. But in our dream of separation from Him, our journey to 'a far country', we have faced ourselves with two choices.

One choice appears as *myriad* choices, every moment, every day, but is actually only one: the choice for separation from the Light; how could that result in anything *other* than darkness? How can there be anything other than confusion in darkness? All the while we focus on darkness, that will be our experience, because that was our choice, and we get what we ask for. When we choose the Light, Light becomes our experience. When we make that other choice – for the Light – darkness ceases to be our experience because Light is everything and darkness is nothing; simply the *absence* of Light. Yet still we can choose to make separation from the Light *seem* real, even though it is nothing, just by *believing* it.

Perceiving from the perspective of darkness, everything is confused, distorted, upside-down, back-to-front. So beginnings seem like endings, Love seems like fear, fear seems like love; darkness seems like light, Light seems like darkness, and therefore, fearful, from the viewpoint of darkness. The winter solstice 2012 was/is a new beginning, not an ending. The beginning, one might say, of the New Earth, as indicated in Jesus' message to Olga Park in January 1965: (Olga Park was my spiritual mentor in 1965.)

> *In the midst of the Earth ariseth my city*
> *after the fashion of the heavenly,*
> *Wherein the multitude of them that love me and keep*
> *my words*
> *Minister unceasingly to the sick and fainting spirits of men.*
> *The call goeth out continually, Come, O come ye*
> *to the waters*
> *Everyone that thirsteth. Buy milk and wine without money*
> *and without price,*
> *And nourish your souls, and rejoice in health and joy;*
> *For it is my Father's good pleasure to bestow upon you*
> *the freedom of the city.*
> *Here is freedom from sickness: whosoever will,*
> *let him be free.*
> *Here are riches of wisdom and power: whosoever will,*
> *let him be rich.*
> *Here is knowledge: whosoever will, let him know*
> *the secrets of God*
> *and the power and perfection of His laws.*
> *Here is fulfilment: whosoever will, let him enlarge*
> *his capacity and his influence.*
> *Here is Peace: whosoever will,*
> *let him meditate therein.*
> *Grace be with you.*

This arising, and the wondrous blessings of empowerment and fulfilment that it brings does not appear to our awareness, in linear-time terms, as an instantaneous event. This is not because it isn't such, but because it takes time for our upside-down perception to become adjusted to it. The city of which Jesus speaks here is, of course, the Kingdom of Heaven on Earth, referred to in Revelation 21 as *the new Jerusalem*[1] and in *A Course in Miracles* (*ACIM*) as the *real world*. It is not intended to be construed as 'just' a *city*, as understood in modern parlance, but the whole world, and specifically *all the fragmented Sonship of God.*

The Kingdom of Heaven, or 'real world' has always existed, spread out in the Earth, *in the midst*, but because it is real it is not discernible with bodily senses, which are devised *solely* to perceive illusions. It is only by *choosing* the Light, steadfastly, sincerely, from the heart, that our vision of *reality* begins to become restored to our awareness. We can never see reality by looking for it in darkness, with eyes made to distract us from true seeing by showing us nothing but unreality. The Light is *within* us. Eyes cannot see the within because it is Life and it is Love, eternal and inextinguishable. It is the Creator Spirit, our heavenly Father, Whose Life is *our* Life because He shared It with His Son forever at his creation, and we are (all) His Son; *One* in Truth, appearing, temporarily – and thus, illusorily – as many.

That means the inextinguishable Light within us is also *our* Light; the Light of the Son. At the idea of wondering what it would be like to be what and where we are *not*, the appearance of separation and limitation arose. This did not mean *extinguishing* the Light because that is not possible, but a *veiling* of our sight, our awareness of the Light that *we*, forever, *are*. The only way an attempt at veiling could *seem* to be effective was by devising a counterfeit form of sight – bodily eyes – that was able to perceive only unreality and believe such sight was real and that all it beheld was real. So a counterfeit light was made to substitute for the Light of the Son: the light of the sun.

> And the city [the Kingdom of Heaven] had no need of the sun, neither of the moon, to shine in it: for the glory of God did lighten it, and the Lamb [Papa's beloved Son] *is* the light thereof (Rev. 21:23).

Once we accept that appearances are nothing but self-deception, and ask for Help to restore our True vision, that Help is there. It was always there, freely available, but by *believing* it was not there, because we could not see it or be aware of it with our self-deceiving bodily senses, it *seemed* to not be there. And because free will was part of the package that came with the creation of the Son – otherwise he could not have been like his Father, and the Father could not create anything unlike Himself – the freely-available Help could not be *pressed* upon us. We *have* to ask for it, for that *authorises* it to be given. It is only given by our choice of willingness to *receive* it.

Further, *asking* for Help means we actively, *consciously* desire it and thus will be *willing* to avail ourself of it. It is this switch of focus – from belief that no help is, or could be, available, and we must save ourself by our own endeavour (which, of course, is impossible, for we don't have the faintest idea how) to a little willingness to believe Help is, and has always been, freely available – that begins the transforming of our sight from spiritual blindness to True vision. It is the *conscious* desire for Help that is important, for it is in our conscious mind that it is needed.

This is because our conscious mind is focused on the without, or unreality, and believes it is real, so the conscious mind, functioning under ego-domination, the ego belief system, is *highly* resistant to the Truth, the Light, Love, Peace and Joy that is Papa – and our true, whole, One Self – because we have allowed ourself to be convinced we are unworthy, sinners, deserving of punishment. So we shut ourself off from awareness of Papa, Who dwells *within* us, by focusing on where He cannot be: the *without*. He cannot be there because there is no such thing as the without. We made it up, and what is made up cannot be real.

So, the dream of a finite world – universe, even – of unreality, of time and place, of guilt, fear and death, littleness and limitation *has* to end because it is not the nature of Papa's Son to sleep. Who amongst us can imagine *Papa* sleeping? Why would He *need* to sleep? The idea is absurd. And as His Son is like Him in every respect, it is equally absurd that the Son, in his true, eternal reality, would sleep. The sleep and the dream *appear* real but in fact are nothing, since illusion is not real, and thus it is already over because in Truth it could never have *actually* happened.

As soon as *one* of the *seemingly*-fragmented parts of the Sonship remembered the Truth of his Being as the eternally Awake, all-empowered, all-Loving, innocent Son of the Creator, it became inevitable that the *whole* Sonship would awaken, the dream would be over and the entire Sonship restored to its true estate of Oneness *with* his Self and *in* his Father, Whom he never left and *could* never leave. His Father is the Source of Life, so to leave Him – were it to be possible – could only mean one thing: death. Happily, death is impossible; for it to be real it would have had to be created by the Creator.

He Knows *nothing* of death. How could He? He Knows only of reality because He is the creator of reality, which can only be forever, otherwise it could not be reality. And Being Life, He can create only in His eternal likeness: eternal Life. Our body cannot die because it was never alive. What does not exist in reality does not exist at all, so could never be endowed with Life. As Jesus says in *A Course in Miracles,* our body is but a little mound of clay (*ACIM* ch 19 IV. B.4:8, p.413), which we animate for a span; a moment of unreality which we call an incarnation. And the spirit that we are can never die because it was never born.

Within the context of linear time – the state of self-deception into which Papa's Son imaginarily entered in a 'mad moment' of wondering what it would be like to not be what or where he is – the time has now arrived when, instead of the dream world ending in calamity or cataclysm, it is undergoing a transformation from a nightmare to a happy dream, as the prelude to the Great Awakening. That is the only way the dream *could* end: by *Awakening* from 'death' to Life. What could be happier than that? It is not possible to end a dream of death with death, for that would make the unreal real.

The Spirit of Truth is the transformer from sleeping to wakefulness; from dreaming of forgetfulness, misery and death to remembrance of eternal, uninterruptible happiness – immeasurably beyond Earth-mind understanding or experience – and Life. He is the mechanism of miracles, of undoing errors; the link between our self-limiting, upside-down mind and our true Self: Christ, Who also dwells within us. Jesus says of himself in The Clarification of Terms section of *A Course in Miracles* that he remembered God and so became identified with Christ, the Thought [i.e., Creation, or Word, or Son] of God (*ACIM*, Clar. of Terms, p.87, 5. Jesus-Christ), and also that he is the manifestation of the Holy Spirit (*ACIM*, Clarification of Terms, p.89, 6. The Holy Spirit).

We need not undertake contortions of the mind trying to reconcile these seemingly contradictory statements, for all creations *of* God are One with, or *in*, Him, so are effectively of *One* Mind: the Mind of the Creator – wherein all Creation has Its abode – Whose Living Word is *One* Truth. So, as soon as he whom we know as Jesus remembered Who he was (thousands of linear years before he incarnated as Jesus/Yeshua at the start of the Piscean Age, or second measure of meal [Mt. 13:33]), all power in Heaven and Earth was restored to him (Mt. 28:18).

This meant he *Knew* that it was possible to *transform* the ego's cycles of building up illusory civilisations only to have them end in disaster, so a new cycle, or epoch, would have to start again from scratch, thus perpetuating the cyclic nature of time and place. And because he was restored to *all* empowerment, he, with the Spirit of Truth – of which he was the manifestation, or embodiment, for the furtherance and fulfilment of the Great Rescue Programme – was able to reinterpret the ego's perception of cycles of birth and death and undo them by transforming them into perpetual, unending, unchanging, eternal Life.

It is within this context that considering the Winter Solstice 2012 can most constructively be seen and understood. And that, of course, is the opposite, or reverse, of the ego, fear-based perspective of death, disaster and destruction. From such a perspective, at worst there is no recovery, only oblivion, or at best, there is a near-extinction event, return to cave-dwelling for the few surviving bodily, only to travel the wearying, rock-strewn, misery-inducing path of indeterminate further aeons-long cycles of birth and death; cycles within cycles, endlessly journeying to nowhere.

But to One who *Knows* all things, is empowered in all things, those things of time and place – being nothing but illusions of challenges/adversity – are seen for what they are: the 'wrapping paper' of opportunity. Jesus *Knew* this, and is using this Knowledge – because Knowledge is empowerment – to transform cataclysm into salvation, resurrection, upliftment, leavening, *Awakening* his brethren, with and in whom he is irreversibly one. We all, each and every one of us, without exception, have an indispensable function, along with Jesus, in this transforming. The entering of this new cycle, seen as commencing at the 20th of December, 2012, is greatly facilitating and empowering us for fulfilling our function.

How priceless an opportunity we have called into our presence! May we be ever more ready to respond to it and gladly leave darkness behind as we move forward into the Light, to bear much fruit for the Kingdom.

Diary of a Christ Communicant

A.M. September 8, 1991

Draw close to me, that I may put upon you the cloak of my Love and the crown of your glory, that the Light within you may burst forth into the dark corners of your life and of your fellows and show to you there is truly nothing to fear.

Little Ones: I would speak with you. Be not afraid. I am your friend. I reach out my arms toward you in Love, in caring, in compassion, in understanding.

I long for you to know me, to open your heart to my

gentleness and to receive my blessing, that your lives may be uplifted, and that joy may enter in and wash away your caring and your burden, and that you may have life, new and abundant.

I counsel you, in your heart draw close to me, that I may put upon you the cloak of my Love and the crown of your glory, that the Light within you may burst forth into the dark corners of your life and of your fellows and show to you there is truly nothing to fear.

For we now enter the final phase of the banquet feast, wherein the New Heaven shall manifest itself into the New Earth.

I counsel you also, my beloveds, let not your vision be double, for that which you see with the earthly eye is confusion, created by the disintegration of that which passes away; rather, focus with thy single eye upon that which is new, upon that which already is: *my reality*; that which shall not pass away; that which is here in the midst, more real, more tangible, more lasting, more fulfilling than all that the double-vision can encompass.

And all this is yours freely and gladly and joyfully. It is your inheritance from the Father, which it is your birthright to receive, for you are all His children.

I am the Way by which this joy, this wholeness, this fulfilment may be yours. I am your friend. Speak with me as such. Walk with me, take my hand in yours. I give it always for your reassurance, for your peace, for your strengthening, that we may be together, for I know that which is in your heart and that which is your desire, and would release the chains, to unveil that which is truly you.

Ponder these things, and speak with me, and in the stillness I will speak with you. Peace, be still. All is well.

---

1. *Jerusalem* means *City of Peace.*

2: Leavening the Mind: an Operation of Hiddenness

*... each soul on the path of incarnation is guided and helped
by loved ones in the Inner Plane, from whence each soul has
incarnated. It is all according to the Law and was so also
with our Lord Jesus.*

–*John of Patmos, 'the Teacher', May 3, 1992*

I RECENTLY RECEIVED AN EMAIL asking what is – to me, anyway – a highly pertinent question about the leavening of the second measure of meal. For those unfamiliar with Jesus' parable of the leaven, or yeast, it states: *The kingdom of heaven is like unto leaven, which a woman took, and hid in three measures of meal, till the whole was leavened* (Mt. 13:33). This has a deep esoteric meaning, and is discussed comprehensively in chapter 10 of *"Seek ye First the Kingdom..."* In brief, the three measures symbolise three by two-thousand-year eras and their role in the restoration to Oneness of the fragmented mind of Papa's Son.

The first measure is the two-thousand years between Abraham and Jesus (the 'Abraham measure'), the second measure is between the time of Jesus and the latter part of the twentieth century (the 'Jesus measure') and the third measure is from the latter part of the twentieth century forward for the next two-thousand years (the 'Kingdom measure', or fulfilment measure). The email and my response follow:

Hi Brian,

I am doing some catching up on your writings. You recently stated:

> ...The second measure of meal, the leavening of which is now accomplished, has given place to, been superseded by the third, *fulfilment* measure of meal; the Aquarian, or Kingdom Age, in which the whole Great Rescue Programme is leavened. This means the restoration of Papa's Son to the reality of Perfect Love, characterised *by*, at One *with*, Peace and Joy; the dispelling of conflict and misery. Now that we are actually in the fulfilment measure, it is much easier for us to avail ourself of its restoring energy, for the healing of our mind.

I understand most of what you have been saying about the leavening of the three measures of meal, and can see that the third measure is now leavening at a mind-blowing pace, but I cannot see how the second measure, 'the Jesus Measure' as you call it, can have leavened. The history of the last 2k years has been full of conflict of indescribable proportions, and has, in many ways, actually got worse in the last 100 years or so. So much of the conflict has been caused by religion – supposedly in the name of God and Jesus. Please help me to understand how claiming the second measure has completely leavened can be justified.

Blessings, Brian, I love your writing; it makes sense of this whole mess, and helps me understand A Course in Miracles *more,*

Jerry

Hi Jerry,

This is a very significant question, and I am glad you have asked. The answer is actually astonishingly simple, though by its nature, hidden from the sensory awareness of the self-limited, fragmented Sonship. Jesus told me back in the 1970s why this has been so, and the reason for keeping the timing of the onset of the third measure hidden from the cognition of Earth-mind discernment. He said that this was to keep it hidden, obscured, from 'the enemy' – the ego – so that it would not know what it was up against! Sounds like a very good ploy to me.

The leavening of all three measures is only *able* to take place within, because everything about the without – the material world of bodies and time and place, i.e., separation – is by its very (illusory) nature entropic, which means decaying, disintegrating, dying. In other words, destructive, conflicted, divisive; nothing to do with the Creator, and therefore, cannot Awaken or heal itself. Conversely, the within is the Kingdom of God, and its foundation is Love, which is creative, eternal, holistic, whole, inseparable, indivisible. Its essence is Life; creative, blessing, inclusive.

The *leavening* of the second measure has not been discernible to the without-consciousness because it is an operation of hiddenness to blind eyes and closed, unbelieving hearts. It has been taking place mostly in the non-material, or metaphysical, world, and certainly in the *within*, of the hearts and minds of those, during the last two thousand years, who had/have a heart-mind for Jesus and his Great Rescue Programme. This is why he said: *I go to prepare a place for you. And if I go and prepare a place for you, I will come again, and receive you unto myself; that where I am, there ye may be also* (Jn. 14:2-3).

He had to *seem* to go away from the world of dreams of bodies to prepare that place because there would have been too much resistance in the without. He didn't *actually* leave us because he lives *within* us, as we live within him, but to those who are unaware of this mystical reality, he *appeared* to have gone away. Later in that same chapter he says: *I will not leave you comfortless: I will come to you. Yet a little while, and the world seeth me no more; but ye [who believe] see me: because I live, ye shall live also. At that day ye shall know that I am in my Father, and ye in me, and I in you* (Jn. 14:18-20).

Most are not yet consciously aware he is in us and we in him, but it has been so throughout the *Jesus* measure, **leavening beyond the world's discernment.** Having a heart-mind for Jesus, and being willing to follow him is important – *essential*, actually – because he *Knows* the Truth, the whole Truth and nothing but the Truth. In fact he IS the Truth, as well as the Way and the Life. He is also entirely, totally, absolutely, unquestionably trustworthy. I am aware of no other who ticks all those boxes.

Even most of those with a heart-mind for Jesus were duped – as most of us have been, by the ego-contrived false doctrines about him promulgated by institutionalised religion – through their successive experiences of being embodied, during that two-thousand year measure, or epoch. However, *between* embodiments they have had *much* greater access to the Truth about him – and indeed, about themselves during that epoch. To this they were drawn *because of the desire of their hearts*. This is possible immeasurably more readily in the etheric realms, or 'Inner Plane', than in the dense conditions of the Earth physical, where misperceptions abound.

The etheric counterpart of Earth is comprised of many levels of awareness, from complete spiritual darkness, which many of us would associate with hell, through numerous *degrees* of enlightenment, or spiritual awareness, to what one might describe as the heights of Heaven. I tend to use the term 'the Realms of Light' to describe these exalted levels. There is a book entitled *Life in the World Unseen* by Anthony Borgia, which tells of these levels, described by Jesus thusly: *'In my Father's house are many mansions'* (Jn. 14:2).

When we lay aside our body, we go to whichever of these 'mansions' most closely reflects our state of mind at the time of our transition. If we have paid scant heed to the eternal nature of our reality, and become deeply distracted by the temporal concerns of embodiment, then we will find ourself in one of the lesser-enlightened realms. If we believe the mythologies about being sinners, unworthy of the Love of Papa, deserving of condemnation by Him to the fires of hell, and have not 'repented of our sins' in accordance with the false doctrines of salvation-by-sacrifice, our misbeliefs will likely take us to such a place of our own invention, or fabrication – all, of course, in our mind only, and nowhere else at all.

This is *because* we are the Son of God; all-empowered-of-mind to call into our presence what we *choose* to believe is true, and *make* it our 'reality', however mistaken those beliefs might be. Even if they are not reality in the Mind of God – the only reality because It is eternal and unchangeable. Further, It is entirely benign, Loving and non-judgemental. So, whatever we believe that is not of God *cannot* be real, but we have free will to *believe* it is real, and mistakenly make it so in our mind. Believing unreality is real can have only one effect: it keeps us separate from God in our own perception and experience.

So, those with a heart-mind for Jesus – in other words, the Truth – go forward into the Truth, the Light, one step at a time, as they are ready, willing and able to receive it and accept it unto themselves. This progress is much easier in the etheric realms, as stated above. It means much more is able to be assimilated there about the Truth of eternity and our place within it, and a lot more of the Truth about Jesus and his Great Rescue Programme with each 'successive' between-incarnations phase. This is the leavening, the raising up, healing, restoring of the mind of Papa's Son to Oneness.

Reincarnation requires our re-entry into forgetfulness at the conscious level of awareness. However, nothing is lost, and all we have remembered during our between-embodiments sojourns in the etheric realms is retained in our unconscious mind. Our innate Love for Papa draws us back to conscious awareness of Jesus and the Spirit of Truth being our Helpers in the process of remembrance, **if our commitment is steadfast enough**. Otherwise, we are just spinning our wheels during each aimless, purposeless incarnation, needlessly delaying our return to endless peace and joy, and accruing more and more karma in the process.

The Truth is within us regardless of outward appearances. Within is the only place it will be found; just as Jesus told us two thousand years ago. His coming to tell us the Truth was the beginning of the leavening of the second ('Jesus') measure, and his emphasis on it being *within* was vital because that is where the leavening takes place – in our heart-mind. This is a mystical process and has nothing to do with the without, the device of an upside-down mind to distract us from remembering the Truth within.

So, all through the Jesus measure of meal its leavening was

taking place, in secret, *within*, and the ego didn't know or believe it. And untold millions espoused their lives to Jesus and the Great Rescue Programme, all the while coming and going between embodiment and disembodiment and growing (leavening, rising-up) in commitment, understanding, empowerment and rejoining, reconnecting with Jesus and other brothers of like mind and desire for the Kingdom; in preparation for the fulfilment of Jesus' words, *'Thy Kingdom come, Thy will be done on Earth as it is in Heaven'* in the third, 'Kingdom', measure.

During the second – and on into the early decades of the third – measure, the ego's agenda for death and destruction has been continuing unabated in the without, totally unaware of the infallible, unstoppable, wondrous, glorious events inexorably growing, leavening in secret, hidden from the awareness of the illusory world. Happily, that which is in secret has now entered its fulfilment phase – the third, or Kingdom, measure. As Jesus says: *'... for there is nothing covered, that shall not be revealed; and hid, that shall not be known. What I tell you in darkness* [secret], *that speak ye in light* [the open]: *and what ye hear in the ear, that preach ye upon the housetops.'* (Mt. 10:26-27).

And now that the leavening of the second measure has been completed, that which has been proving (using the terminology of breadmaking) in secret is coming out into the open; from the within into the without. This is happening by the incarnating of millions of fragments of the Sonship who have espoused Truth – become leavened – and are manifesting it, helped by Jesus and the Holy Spirit, in the third, completion measure. That which has its foundation in the within can endure in the without in order to be a communication mechanism for sharing the Living Word – just like Jesus. Such only *need* endure there until its purpose has been completed. That completion is the Awakening to the reality of eternity.

The reality of eternity is Love, Peace, Joy unbounded: the return *to* Oneness of Papa's beloved Son *in* his heavenly Father. Then, the many mansions of the Father's house will be re-united to one, in which the illusion of time no longer occupies our mind. This is because Papa has created but one house: Heaven. All the many illusory mansions have been fabricated by the upside-down mind of His Son, who has dreamt of separation. The Father and His Son need but one house in which to dwell. That house is Perfect Oneness, where All are equal, with no differences, no separate levels of Being.

Diary of a Christ Communicant

A.M. July 2, 2010

The Kingdom of Heaven is within you, so if you desire it, choose it, focus upon it, live it, BE it. You then cannot help but radiate it, extend it, give it, share it with your brothers who appear to be around you.

There are two worlds: the illusory, ego world of conflict, guilt, fear, grievance, condemnation, hatred, death ... and the *real* world: Holy Spirit's world of gentleness, peace, Love, compassion, kindness, forgiveness, Truth, giving, transparency, inclusion...

It is worth remembering that what you choose, what you believe, is what you get. The Kingdom of Heaven is within you, so if you desire it, choose it, focus upon it, *live* it, BE it. You then cannot help but radiate it, extend it, give it, share it with your brothers who appear to be around you. Is this not better than projecting the ego's principality of judgement, accusation, doubt, affray and death?

You, all the game-playing fragments, have not committed 'sins', but simply made errors of perception. Since you have blindfolded yourselves and blocked your ears, this is hardly surprising, and no-one – least of all Papa – is blaming, judging or condemning you for this; you do it well enough to yourself. But errors can be corrected.

The true method of correction is not punishment, as the world perceives it should be, and it is *never* forced

15

upon anyone. It is lovingly, gently, caringly given – only with your agreement – designed to *help*, not to engender fear. Correction is by Me – your true *Self* – shining the Light of eternal Truth in your mind. This illuminates it, shining away the darkness you seem to have been in, so that you can see the Truth and then *live* it, and it will make you free.

Truth makes absolute sense, is simple, uncomplicated, and immediately clears away the confusion that has had you so bewildered about who you are and how to Be. Knowing the Truth restores you to your right mind; which is a *joyous* experience. It brings *peace* of mind, certainty of *Knowing* who you really are and who your brothers really are – about all of which you have merely been mistaken.

Heaven, eternity, is your true and only Home, and the amnesiac fragments of the Sonship have no conscious awareness of it. Thus are they *unprepared* for Home.

> *I say unto you, Love your enemies, bless them that curse you, do good to them that hate you, and pray for them which despitefully use you, and persecute you; That ye may be the children of your Father which is in heaven (Mt. 5:44-45).*

None of these admonitions by Jesus is possible unless you *truly* forgive your 'enemies', thus transforming them into beloved brothers. Then, and only then, it *spontaneously* happens, without any effort on your part, and you are miraculously released from grievous burdens of unforgiveness.

You can never die, but simply lay aside a worn-out overcoat, or masquerade costume, which was never your true home, but a communication mechanism for fulfilling your only purpose for appearing in time and place: to heal and reunify the broken Sonship.

3: The Ease of Overcoming the Ego World

Meat and drink shall the Living Word ever be for you, and all who seek, who desire right, who Love the Truth, who come as little children before their Father, in Love, unashamed of their childhood and innocence.

–Jesus, July 9, 1989

As I took my communing walk in the hills one morning, I said to Jesus, "Why did you take the route of incarnating through an earthly mother, the illusory, ego-*made* mechanism for manifesting in ego's illusory realm, when you could have simply *assumed* the appearance of a body, just as Arten and Pursah did for their appearances to Gary Renard?"[1]

He immediately spoke in response, with the obvious answer (aren't answers always so obvious once we have them, even though they are invisible to us until then?):

So I could overcome from *within* egoland, and could demonstrate to my brethren still under its yoke that it *is* possible.

He went on speaking but I asked if we could wait until I had returned to my desk, so that I could write the rest of his reply. Being the perfect gentleman, he of course agreed, and an hour or so later he continued:

Overcoming appears to be hard, and most in the dream world perceive it as *impossible* for them; that it is possible only for 'exalted', 'special', 'highly favoured' beings, without wondering how such perceived beings attained to this 'status'. This is, of course, not so, for if *one* can overcome, *all* can overcome, since we who appear in the dream as many are, as you well now know, in truth, *One*.

All appearances to the contrary are misperception, which I am empowered to correct for all my beloveds, so that we may be restored to Oneness in Papa, as each becomes ready and willing to freely receive the Atonement.

This empowerment is available to all because it is the birthright of all. And all who are *willing* to receive it *shall* receive it, even though they may have mistakenly believed they disinherited themselves from their Father Creator. It takes commitment; one-pointed commitment to the Truth about themselves, to the exclusion of the lies of guilt and sin and fear. Such commitment comes from perceiving at first what may be but a tiny fragment of Truth, and holding fast to it with the certainty that comes only from one's own within.

You, my beloved, came into the world with such a level of commitment, engendered by events chosen by you in a former time, though awareness of such was withheld from you until the moment was right, when you drew into your presence your beloved mentor; the keeper for you of the door that opens unto the Light of Eternity; she[(2)]who patiently awaited your presence, so that she could instruct you in the Way of inner quietness and attunement. It is this one-pointed commitment that has brought you to this place in your remembrance, your awakening, by your faithful following of my leading. And it has been my *joy* to lead you. You have sought first the Kingdom of Heaven and all else has indeed been given you.

All are free to choose such one-pointed commitment to

getting Home with minimal delay, though only few will so choose immediately. It matters not; have no concern over this, for all are well within my care. Nevertheless, my faithful friend, I have chosen you to sow a seed, a kernel of truth, that it may lie dormant within their hearts, until it germinates and grows at the season of their readiness. All will come to this according to the hour appointed aforetime for them, just as it came to me. Then comes the moment of *self*-assessment (for Papa tests no man) for the chosen task ahead, each according to the path thus far travelled. As with all, my path was of my own choosing, for in Heaven there is no compulsion.

I so longed to save my beloved brethren that I had to come and experience their condition and overcome it from the desire of my own within. This is why I went alone into the wilderness, for my final confrontation with the 'enemy' – ego – that I might be sure of my readiness to choose the Way of Eternity and not the path of expediency. Ego knew very well how great was my desire for the Kingdom to be restored to the awareness of the little ones of Earth-mind misperception.

I was faced with the choice of establishing an earthly kingdom of peace and righteousness there and then (so great was my desire to hasten the Kingdom for my beloveds, for so great was their distress). But I had seen, and knew, that this could not last, from the example of my brothers, David and Solomon, because it was not free choice for *all*, so had to run its course and come to the end of its time and place cycle, ending in further separation. The same would have inevitably happened again, regardless of the mechanisms that could have been set in place in attempting to counter such backsliding. I knew then, as you know now, that the Kingdom of Heaven is *within*, and that is the only place from which it can *truly*, lastingly, eternally come to the awareness of all; until we are, once more, One.

Whilst from within the illusion of time and place it was the greatest self-assessment available to me (because of my earnest desire for my brethren), yet because I had remembered my Identity as One in Papa, it was, in reality, no test at all; but I had to be certain with all the certainty of *experiencing* the opportunity to transform adversity into fulfilment, because I had come to *over*come, so that I could be the Way-shower for *all* in overcoming. So has it been for you, that the self-assessment[3] has been no test at all, because under my leadership you were lovingly and gently prepared – made ready – for it, and the timing was perfect, just as it must, and shall, always be for all.

Love is the only way there is; total, unconditional Love, and Knowledge of its certainty, regardless of any temporal appearances to the contrary. So, my beloved, take heart; take strength from the confidence that all is well, all fulfilment is assured. Because I have overcome, *all* shall overcome, and all truth and righteousness is *already* accomplished.

Ego has those of us who toil under its spell convinced that by making our life a one-pointed commitment to the Kingdom of Heaven we are giving up something, and in a realm where apparent scarcity already causes more than enough fear, anguish and mayhem, to voluntarily give up something more (whatever little we may appear to have in time and place) has us thinking it seems like a bad idea. Jesus reminds us in *A Course in Miracles* as follows, which can help to set us back on the path of right thinking:

The ego is trying to teach you how to gain the whole world and lose your own soul. The Holy Spirit teaches that you cannot lose your soul and there is no gain in the world, for of itself it profits nothing. To invest without profit is surely to impoverish yourself, and the overhead is high. Not only is there no profit in the investment, but the cost to you is enormous. For this investment costs you the world's reality by denying yours, and gives you nothing in return. You cannot sell your soul, but you can sell your awareness of it. **You cannot perceive your soul, but you will not know it while you perceive something else as more valuable.**

The Holy Spirit is your strength because He knows nothing but the spirit as you. He is perfectly aware that you do not know yourself, and perfectly aware of how to teach you to remember what you are. Because He loves you, He will gladly teach you what He loves, for He wills to share it. **Remembering you always, He cannot let you forget your worth.** For the Father never ceases to remind Him of His Son, and He never ceases to remind His Son of the Father. God is in your memory because of Him. You chose to forget your Father but you do not really want to do so, and therefore you can decide otherwise. As it was my decision, so is it yours (*ACIM* Chapter 12, p.227, VI. 1–2).

The Great Rescue Programme continues to unfold unceasingly and bring our moment of Awakening ever closer. Every occasion or event on which we choose to co-operate with this Process (such as in practising true forgiveness, expressing Love, understanding and compassion), thereby helping the Holy Spirit (Who is the link to our own higher, big, true, *Christ* Self while we seem to sojourn in time) to collapse time, we thus bring that moment forward. And we are positively, actively contributing to ever greater joy, peace, Love and happiness for ourself and our fellows in the process.

Diary of a Christ Communicant

A.M. July 2, 1989

Let your heart be filled with Love and giving. You go forward a step at a time by the guidance and Light of Heaven and by your one-pointed commitment to the Way.

Beloved Jesus, the whole beauty of God's Creation and your Great Rescue Programme for mankind fills me with awe and joy and upliftment. (*I see blue lights dancing in my inner vision.*) When contrary vibrations abound in the 'mammon of unrighteousness' and in the Earth-mind consciousness, help me to be one-pointed in my Earth-life activities, to act according to your teaching, and to open my heart to your Love, guiding and fellowship.

> My son, all is well, let not your heart be troubled; my Programme goes forward. Your faithful communing and attuning shall keep you on the path of progress. Let your heart be filled with Love and giving. You go forward a step at a time by the guidance and Light of Heaven, and by your one-pointed commitment to the Way. Anxiety casts a shadow and shades you from the Light of the peace and joy of the Kingdom. Therefore I say to you, be at peace, be still and *receive* my Love and blessing.

---

1. As described in Gary's book *The Disappearance of the Universe;* Renard, Gary R.; Revised Edition 2004, (Hay House, Inc.).
2. Olga Park.
3. We all have moments, events, occasions of self-assessment. These afford us opportunity to consider whether we are ready to progress to a higher, or greater level of stewardship.

4: Distraction by Detail

As those who sojourn to take refreshment with you go forward
upon their journey rejoicing, so send them with your blessing, for
this shall continue to provide for them vitality for their progress
upon the Way.

–Jesus, May 10, 1992

W E HAVE ALL HEARD THE EXPRESSION, 'The devil is in the detail',
and mostly, in this dream of time and place, this does appear
to be the case. By inventing an external 'devil' we can project the
blame for our misfortunes away from ourself onto 'Satan'. Thus,
our woes become an *effect*, apparently caused by an outside force,
over which we have little or no control. But there *is* no external
devil. Instead there *seems* to be a split-off part of our True, innocent,
whole, all-Knowing, all-Loving Christ Mind. That split-off part acts
in opposition to our True Being. Jesus refers to this made-up state of
mind as the ego. This upside-down state of mind is entirely malign
and is characterised in Robert Louis Stevenson's story, *The Strange
Case of Dr Jeckyll and Mr Hyde.*

Even within the confines of the time and place consciousness
such an idea can readily be seen as absurd; a concept that cannot
last, because it is an illusion, a pretence, and however much we may
succumb to a *Hyde* identity, we inwardly know it is not who we
really are. We can *suppress* that knowing, even to the point where,

at a conscious level, we seem to have *forgotten* our One, correct, eternal, True Identity. But deep down, in our subliminal memory, we *never* forget the Truth, even though, in our conscious mind, we do *appear* to have forgotten.

Since we are Love, which is Light and Life, what we are *pretending* to be, to have as our experience, can only be guilt, fear, darkness and death. Since that was *our* choice, not a choice foisted upon us, it can only be that we are the cause of our own misery. We have chosen this, but we have God-given free will, so we can choose *anew*. Yet, to our self-limited conscious mind, the illusion seems so convoluted it appears there can be no way out of the maze.

It can seem very difficult to escape from a maze, or labyrinth, or wilderness, and this is because we get distracted by the mass of *detail* in which we find ourself. And the more we become confused trying to sort out the detail and make sense of it, *the more detail keeps arising*, to confuse us even more. Further, since the detail is *specifically* devised to confuse and sidetrack us – all the while we believe we can escape from guilt, which is mostly hidden from our awareness in our unconscious mind – focusing on the detail in the belief that it is all there is, and therefore *must* provide the solution to our predicament, do we become *more* ensnared.

This does seem to be a devilishly fiendish game we have made up. Like the adage 'when you are in a hole, stop digging', when detail is the cause of the confusion, *stop focusing on the detail*; for by attempting to unscramble it we simply scramble it further, preventing us from being able to see that the way out is actually very easy, uncomplicated and freely available to us. When my brother was about four years old he managed to completely dismantle our grandparents' travel-alarm clock. When our mother found him, surrounded by a mass of parts, he sheepishly said, 'I haven't quite got it back together again yet.' Of course he could never have reassembled it into working order without help because he was a child.

We are, in our Earth-mind consciousness, children pretending to be grown up. Not making much of a job of it, are we? But it doesn't have to be this way. The devil (ego) may be in the detail, but Papa is in the *Principle*. The two – detail and principle – are opposites. When a child gets itself in a muddle, it at least has the sense – sooner or later – to turn to a grown-up to help it straighten things out. Jesus is a grown-up, i.e., fully *Awake and empowered*. He is *offering* his help. Most of the fragments of the illusorily-broken Sonship are ignoring his offer.

This is because they don't recognise him for what he *actually* is. He has been misrepresented by those who claim to speak for him, claim to be bringing his message of help, and the offer has been distorted by completely valueless, *conditional*, fear-inducing detail. Thus has a veil – the Laodicean[1] church – been interposed between us and the Principle, obscuring It from our sight. But Jesus came from the *Source* of Principle to bring a message, and *demonstrate* That from Which he had come, and that message is unconditional Love. Love cannot be Love if conditions are attached to it. It becomes counterfeit; a parody; a lie.

But Jesus has never lost sight of the Principle and *in Truth* neither have we, his *seemingly* fragmented brothers in the *One* Son of God that he and we all are. We became *momentarily* distracted by detail. Detail is the ego's domain. It suggests there is something wrong, something to do; that we must 'make things happen' and we are 'running out of time' to achieve our uncertain, ever-changing objectives, with elusive, finite resources. Papa and His creation function *only* according to perfect, eternal, unchanging Principle. His Son is His creation, therefore it is the only way we, also, can function *creatively*.

Detail is darkness and we can never find the Light we *are* by looking in darkness. Detail is deliberately complicated, ever changing; Principle is Light, is simple, straightforward, easy to follow and stay with because once we have seen It we have seen It forever, since It *never* changes. Yet all the while we seem to be in time and place, *detail* calls to us, demands our attention. It is not possible to pay *no* heed to detail while we perceive ourself as what we are not: a body. No doubt my brother was paying heed to the dismantled clock, but still he had no chance of reassembling it to functionality because he was too young to see the Principle, and distracted by the detail of many parts. So is it for all who perceive the myriad distractions of time and place as reality.

Help is required. I have a post-it note on my computer monitor that reads, *Today I will make no decisions by myself.* It is from *A Course in Miracles* (*ACIM* Chapter 30, p.625, I.2:2). How can a child decide, by himself, how to reassemble his life into a fluidly-functioning, flawless order of progressive purpose? He cannot because he does not know or understand the rules – the *Principles* – for making decisions that will serve not just himself but *all* his brothers. This is where ego leads us astray, by deceiving us into believing we are separate from our brothers; that our choices do not affect them. But we are *not* separate, thus decisions, whether for self *or* for Self are decisions for all.

So, the best decision we can make is to ask for Help in our decision-making. From One Who *Knows*, and Who we can trust as ourself, because He *is* our Self. He Knows and is trustworthy *because* He *Knows* Who He Is. Conversely, we – in our ego-confused, Earth-mind consciousness, deceived by appearances, perceived by eyes devised to show us only illusions, never the Truth, because Truth is eternal and unchanging – have been distracted by detail, causing us to *forget* our true Identity. Therefore, asking for Help in remembering and applying the *Principles of Life of the Father* (PLFs) is the only way forward.

It is like Jesus says in *A Course in Miracles*, that we must bring our illusions to the Truth, not the Truth to our illusions. It does not work if we try to ask for help sorting out the details. Many years ago I was getting entangled in some detail that was knotting my mind, so I tried to bring Jesus into this mess. I asked him for his input; no doubt so I could be 'right' in my perception. Nothing. Not a word. Some minutes went by and still there was no response. Then, when enough time had elapsed for some semblance of equilibrium to return to my mind, he simply said, 'I speak only in principle'.

He was not going to allow me to drag him down into my

tortuous mental briar patch. If he did it for one he would have to do it for all and he would then be of no Help to any of us. That doesn't mean millions don't *think* they have dragged him into their misperceptions. There are nearly forty thousand schismatic, so-called *Christian* denominations, all, no doubt, claiming *theirs* is right, thus implying all the others are wrong. They each have their rules, to which their followers must adhere. But rules are man-made, causing us to be distracted from the PLFs. *'Love God and love your neighbour as yourself'* (Mk. 12:30, 31) are PLFs.

So, how do we deal with detail in a world full of seemingly endless, entangled detail, without getting swamped by it, causing us to lose sight of the PLFs? The answer is, we don't. Not the detail that would divert us from the Way back Home to the eternity of Heaven. Other detail – such as which shirt to wear, or which path to take on our communing walk in the hills – is hardly going to divert us from the direction of our journey back to Oneness in God. For the details, or decisions, that *will* affect our spiritual Awakening, such as how to respond to a brother, we ask our Self to guide us, and He will always counsel that our response have Love at its core.

Jesus told me in 1978, "A single step does not determine the direction of your journey; for you have placed your life in my care, and you will, therefore, always be redirected back onto your chosen course, so that your purpose in the world is not lost. This redirection will be by the unfolding of events rather than by the spoken word. Be watchful, therefore, for events, and if in doubt, do nothing; guidance will be given *in response to your asking* and your steadfast commitment to the Way."

This demonstrates the vital importance of surrendering the ego-leasehold on our life back into his (or Holy Spirit-Self's) care, guidance and protection. For without our authorising him thusly he cannot help us because we have free will to head off into the wilderness of outer darkness.

Many are fearful of asking because they either believe they are incapable (for which read *unworthy*) of hearing Jesus or the Spirit of Truth, or that He will not speak with them (because, wait for it ... they believe they are unworthy). Or maybe He is too busy to bother with our trivial issues (unworthiness disguised). But this is not some exalted, separate, high and mighty (in the religionist sense) being, who might deign to smile upon us if we have been 'good'. This is our own, true *Self*; the Being that we *are*, Who dwells within us every moment, indivisibly; *Who Loves us unconditionally and never judges us.*

Jesus has some very sound, practical advice for us in such matters, from Chapter 30, section I, page 625 of *A Course in Miracles*, headed 'Rules for Decision':

> Decisions are continuous. You do not always know when you are making them. But with a little practice with those you recognize, a set begins to form which sees you through the rest. *It is not wise to let yourself become preoccupied with every step you take.* The proper set, adopted consciously each time you wake, will put you well ahead. And if you [ego-led little self] find resistance strong and dedication weak, you are not ready. **Do not fight yourself.** But think about the kind of day you want, and tell yourself there is a way in which this very day can happen just like that. Then try again to have the day you want.
>
> The outlook starts with this:
>
> *Today I will make no decisions by myself.*
>
> This means that you are choosing not to be the judge of what to do. But it must also mean you will not judge the situations where you will be called upon to make response. **For if you judge them, you have set the rules for how you should react to them**. And then another answer cannot but produce [further] confusion and uncertainty and fear.

There is much further helpful guidance in this section, which is too long for inclusion here, save for the final sentences: ... *Your judgment has been lifted from the world by your decision for a happy day. And as you have received, so must you give.* I commend its full consideration for greater Help on our journey Home. By steadfastly following his counsel we are unconsciously, intuitively, *automatically* attuning ourself with our Whole (and thus, Holy) Self within, until it becomes our normal, retrained, healed, happy, *right* mind.

There are three further, enormously uplifting aspects to this approach to decision-making, or handling details in our daily lives jointly with our Higher, all-Loving, all-*Knowing* Self. (1) It will increasingly give us the peace of mind that our decisions are right, not just for ourself, but for all; (2) it increasingly dispels ego's script from our thinking, and (3) it frees our mind to commune with Papa. Communing with Papa is singing *the Song of Prayer* (which is the Song of *One*ness, Gratitude, Love, Innocence, Rejoicing, Adoration, Joy ...) with Him. This is our *true*, natural, eternal state. To practise this is to collapse time, restoring us to wholeness inestimably quicker.

The alternative is indeterminate further circuits of the carousel; continuing indefinitely in uncertainty, limitation, *dis*ease, misery and 'death'. In our communing we experience Love beyond human imagining; inner peace of which this world knows nothing; joy unbounded; certainty beyond all doubt of our all-*Knowing*, all-empowerment, wholeness, innocence, completion, perfection and freedom. Everything. And the more we commune the more everything becomes ours uninterruptedly and uninterruptibly.

Once we choose, remember, *Know*, the **Principles** *of Life of the Father*, then the details take care of themselves. Then we find that Love, Peace and Joy bless and comfort us during our journey back to Oneness.

Diary of a Christ Communicant

A.M. July 9, 2010

> **Your accurate discernment of reality is important for you to acknowledge to yourself. For this denotes that your vision is being restored to clarity. That is worthy of celebration.**

Beloved Holy Spirit-Self, I bless You for your wonderful Help in simplifying my understanding of Being. *Knowing* You are with me – *within* me – every moment, indivisibly, is so completely, comprehensively reassuring. Truly, You are *the Comforter*, when ego's script is written to destroy our acceptance of our Self and *literally*, leave us for 'dead'.

> Since that is the opposite of reality, your discernment is accurate; it is not mistaken, and this is important for you to acknowledge to yourself. For this denotes that your vision is being restored to clarity. That is worthy of celebration, not of dwelling in and judging the misperception that has held the *apparently* fragmented, separated Sonship – the joy and completion of Papa – in its grip.

The great thing about recognising Truth is that the illusion that obscured it can be released.

> Correction: The great thing about recognising Truth is that the illusion that obscured it <u>has been</u> released.

That has to be worth a few *Alleluia!* choruses.

> Start conducting, Maestro.

---

1. The Laodicean church: see Rev. 3:14

5: Mind-to-Mind Communing

*Have no concern for the imperfections of life. They are as nothing
in the sight of He Who makes all things new. All moves forward
by desire. You know your desire is as ever and the pattern is
unchanged by conditions of time and place, for it is such which are
being transformed from above.*

–*John of Patmos*, 'the Teacher', May 24, 1992

QUANTUM IMPROVEMENTS have been made in communications
facilities and systems in the last generation or so, with email,
internet, social networking, Skype, mobile phones, smart phones
… No doubt there will emerge further mechanisms in the coming
years. All these help to make our dream existence in time and place
'better', more convenient. But if we allow them to distract us from,
or substitute for, the only *true* mechanism of communicating, then
we will not be fulfilling our only true purpose for making a body
(yet again).

Such technological advances in electronic wizardry can serve
us well in the re-joining of the Sonship by enabling reconnection
of kindred souls. We all have close relationships with others
with whom we have been in loving association for numerous
incarnations. And even though each of us enters a state of absolute
forgetfulness with each new body we make, that forgetfulness is
only at the *conscious* level. Consciousness is the level of our mind
which engages in the illusory world of time and place, responding

or reacting to the events that seem to be occurring around us, but which we are simply projecting out there from a part of our mind that believes in separation, to 'prove' separation is real.

Our conscious mind is also capable of responding to the *super*conscious, or God-aware part of our mind – through which Revelation comes direct from Him – and to the *sub*conscious part of our mind, through which, so says Jesus, miracles come. But because we have free will, we can choose to *not* respond to impulses from our superconscious or subconscious mind. Most of the embodied fragments of the Sonship remain in the choice for forgetfulness, and thus, in a state of unawareness of their superconscious *and* subconscious mind. This perpetuates the illusion of separation.

Some of those with whom we are in a multi-incarnation association will be embodied simultaneously with us and some, disembodied. Those who are disembodied can help us from spirit during our incarnate state of mind, but for them to do that to *optimal* effect we must consciously acknowledge their presence with us in order to engage their Loving assistance. They can still help us, even without our conscious awareness/acceptance of their Loving presence; but our *lack* of acceptance – engendered by fear – severely limits this because they honour our free will choice for separation.

An open, receptive heart-mind therefore serves us well.

Some of those embodied simultaneously with us might be geographically nearby and some on another continent. Modern communications technology is massively assisting the reconnecting of the fragmented Sonship, albeit, initially only at the conscious level. What happens thereafter remains our free choice. We can maintain that contact at only the superficial, mundane level of awareness, or we can extend, or develop this into the holy (Loving, heart-centred, guilt- and judgement-free) relationship that *all* relationships between brothers are destined to become, again. How can sooner not be preferable to later?

If we commit our life and all our endeavours into the care of the Spirit of Truth, our Holy Self, Who is the mind-to-mind, heart-to-heart, soul-to-soul, life-to-life connection between us all,

He will *effect* the reconnecting of those who belong together but might be separated bodily by geography. He is perfectly capable of enabling such reconnections using electronic technology, or simply by 'chance' encounters in the street, on a plane ... anywhere, *by any means*. He *Knows* all minds because He Knows that in Truth there is but *One* Mind and we are all equal, complete parts of that One Mind – because the Whole(ness) is in (all) the part(s) – so He can restore Loving, holy relationships between brothers, or bring relationships broken in one incarnation back into contact for healing opportunities in another.

Either way, we have but one purpose for taking a body: to re-join the fragmented Sonship from all levels of consciousness to Oneness. Oneness is the reality of us all, but can only be *experienced* at the highest level of Being. It matters not a scrap that we may *appear* to not be functioning at that level. That is an illusion, so is neither real nor true; nor can it ever be. It is our *desire* that connects us with reality, our true, perfect, unchanging, eternal, all-Loving *One* Self. This is true of us all, however much outward appearances may indicate otherwise. In July 1997 Jesus told me:

> My son, your heart's desire is not something that is *becoming*; a faltering, chance, haphazard development. It is a strong, well-established creation, as I have already said, perfectly forged in the fire of Spirit, <u>in pure harmony with eternal reality</u>. It is unfolding before you in your earthly life awareness as you go forward upon the path, led by me, your guide to Eternity, motivated from within by that strong desire ... [Restoration to awareness of those] with whom you are in close association [is inevitable] *because* of like desires.

This is true for us *all* because it is a Principle of Life of the Father. There are, and can be, *no* exceptions. Most of us are in denial of this, lost in the illusion of littleness, limitation, unworthiness ... unaware of the glory of our eternal reality. So it may *seem* like we do not have such a desire – for Oneness in the Kingdom – but this word, above, from Jesus, clarifies this point unequivocally.

When we encounter one with whom there is antipathy we can allow that state to continue – ego's preference – or we can choose, with our Holy Self, to heal that brokenness through true forgiveness. There are many such broken relationships that are beyond the reach of healing on a *face-to-face* basis, but none is beyond the reach of healing via the mechanism of our Holy Self. There is but *One* Holy Self, which is who *we* are and also who our brother is; thus are we One, even with our 'worst enemy'. In such extreme (yet immensely widespread) situations, true forgiveness will ALWAYS effect the healing.

It takes only *one* to heal a broken relationship, by forgiving his estranged brother for what he has, *in Truth*, never done – because what he *appeared* to have done was only in time and place. What, therefore, appeared to be done only in illusion *never happened in reality*. Holding onto a grievance, maintaining an attitude of unforgiveness for what never actually happened, can only be by an insane mind that is intent on remaining forgetful of his true Being, committed to loneliness, misery, illness and 'death'. If we believe all such is inevitable truly have we forgotten who we really are.

But Papa has not forgotten Who His beloved Son is, and neither has Jesus. And because we are indivisibly One in Truth, we can never *be* guilty, separate, lonely, miserable or 'die' *in Truth*, even if we *believe* we can. Such beliefs are mistaken, and though we can make them *appear* real in the dream – the illusion of time and place – we cannot undermine the Will of God for Him and His One Son to BE One in eternity. So, one forgiving his brother heals them *both* – even if the other remains *outwardly* unforgiving – because the forgiver breaks the karmic entanglement that had kept both locked together in hell.

The healing is the choice for rejoining at the level of mind, not necessitating the involvement of bodies – which can never be joined because they are a symbol of separation – even if the brother is not consciously aware, in time, of that joining. That makes no difference because the rejoining of illusorily separated minds is within the domain of the Holy Spirit, Who is entirely *outside* time, Being the Spirit of Truth, Which is purely of eternity.

The brother cannot maintain his now *solitary* stance of unforgiveness indefinitely, even if it continues one-sidedly for years. As the old saying goes, *It takes two to tango*. A tug of war also takes two opposing sides, and when one side has let go the rope, the war is over (however much the other wishes it to continue). This is because only split minds can believe in war, and that only within the confines of *dreaming* of war. Bodies get used in warfare but they are not real, and are entirely neutral, merely blindly obeying what minds instruct them to do. There is no war, only peace, in Heaven.

When one mind chooses to re-join with the other, the Law of God says they are re-joined. The one who so chose, through forgiveness, will begin to *experience* that as his reality, which manifests as Peace, Joy, Love – to *all*. The former angst in him has been dispelled, and goodwill and blessing taken its place. There does not need to be contact at the bodily level of awareness. We are not a body. The contact can freely continue, uninterrupted, at the level of rejoined mind. The now-righted mind can send Love and blessings to his brother via their unbreakable link: Holy Spirit Self, Which joins them irreversibly.

This is mind-to-mind communing. The *conscious* attitude of unforgiveness, or grievance – which *appears* to continue to be held by the forgiven brother – now has no power because the cycle of *un*forgiveness requires input of the negative, destructive energy of conflict by *both* parties to give it power (and then, only at the illusory level; the battleground of time and place). Just as when one side has let go the rope, the tug of war is over, however much the other side may wish it to continue. Mind-to-mind communing takes place *above* the battleground, where the Spirit of Truth is the conveyor of Love and blessing.

Here, the ego is undone forever and a once unholy, broken, fear-, judgement-, and hate-ridden relationship is restored to wholeness, holiness, Oneness. Here, the brother who forgave is *also* forgiven, by his own *choice* for forgiveness, which has released him from the yoke, the *prison* of unforgiveness. Now *both* once-separated minds are free of the defences, the barricades that blocked the Revelation and miracle impulses in our superconscious and subconscious mind from emerging into our awareness. Mind-to-mind communion connects us via the common (i.e., shared) union of our Holy Spirit Self.

The ego has no awareness or understanding of this at all, and may continue waging its now one-sided, disempowered, purposeless war of judgement and grievance down on the battleground of Earth-mind consciousness. But this is of none-effect because mind-to-mind communing is *above* the battlefield, where no conflict exists, nor *can* exist. All conflict is misperceived because it is fear-engendered, and fear is unreal. When we forgive and bless our brother we cast out fear, which is destructive, and engage our God-given, all-empowering creative mind. Here is what Jesus has to say about this:

> All aspects of fear are untrue because they do not exist at the *creative* level, and therefore do not exist at all. **To whatever extent you are willing to submit your beliefs to this test, to that extent are your perceptions corrected.** In sorting out the false from the true, the miracle proceeds along these lines:
> *Perfect love casts out fear.*
> *If fear exists,*
> *Then there is not perfect love.*
> > But:
> *Only perfect love exists.*
> *If there is fear,*
> *It produces a state that does not exist.*
>
> **Believe this and you will be free.** Only God can establish this solution, and this faith *is* His gift (*ACIM* Chapter 1, p.14, VI.5).

Then he continues, in the next section:

> Your distorted perceptions produce a dense cover over miracle impulses [including healing through forgiveness], making it hard for them to reach your own awareness. The confusion of miracle impulses with physical impulses is a major perceptual distortion. Physical impulses are misdirected miracle impulses. **All *real pleasure* comes from doing God's Will. This is because *not* doing it is a denial of Self.** Denial of Self results in illusions, while correction of the error brings release from it. <u>Do not deceive yourself into believing that you can relate in peace to God *or to your brothers* with anything external</u>.
>
> **Child of God, you were created to create the good, the beautiful and the holy.** *Do not forget this.* The Love of God, *for a little while*, must still be expressed through one body to another, because vision is still so dim. You can use your body best to help you enlarge your perception so you can achieve *real* vision, of which the physical eye is incapable. *Learning to do this is the body's only true usefulness* (ACIM Chapter 1, p. 15, VII.1, 2).

Advances in technology can serve us well in the re-joining of the Sonship, but if we allow them to substitute for the one, *true* communication mechanism that will restore us all to Oneness in Peace, Joy and Love, we allow ourself to continue being sidetracked by the ego into forgetfulness of our One, Whole, Holy Self. Mind-to-mind communing with our brother means we are preparing, practising Mind-to-Mind communion with Papa (what other form of communion can we have with Him?) because we share the One, Universal Mind with Him and with our brothers. Thus is it inevitable that we all become restored to remembrance, awareness of our Oneness in His Mind.

Diary of a Christ Communicant

A.M. July 12, 2010

**Knowing the Truth cannot but cause you to *live* it,
because it brings inner peace, and by living it are you
made free.**

We can *believe* anything, but we can only *Know* the Truth. When we choose to believe the Truth it will *demonstrate* its reality, so that we can then *Know*, and no false doctrine can dissuade us from the Truth. When we *experience* the Truth it automatically engenders inner peace, and that peace is our affirmation that we then *Know*. Not *Knowing* can only mean doubting, and doubting is uncertainty, which is absence of trust.

We can set aside doubt by placing our trust in the Spirit of Truth, in Whose care we are safe, and therefore can be at peace, even when we don't yet consciously *Know*. Trusting is prerequisite to *Knowing*. If we do not trust, or have faith, we are blocking peace and *Knowing* from our experience.

The Spirit of Truth will lead us into peace by demonstrating His *trustworthiness* if we have a little *willingness* to trust Him. The same applies with Jesus.

> This is true. I will lead you into peace by demonstrating that true forgiveness transforms the loneliness and fear of separation into wholeness. This is an entirely practical, participant process in which you heal yourself through bringing the illusion of separated identity to your one, true, *Christ* Identity.
>
> *Knowing* the Truth cannot *but* cause you to *live* it, because it brings inner peace, and by living it are you made free.

6: True Forgiveness

*Have I not said, "Be thou faithful"? So shall thy faith make thee
whole – One in the Father, even as I and my Father are One.*

–Jesus, June 21, 1992

I N MATTHEW, CHAPTER 9, a man afflicted with paralysis is brought
to Jesus for healing. Jesus is recorded as saying to him, 'Your sins
are forgiven you.' The fundamentalist religionists who overheard
this perceived it as being a blasphemy, on the basis that, according
to their understanding, forgiveness is in the sole domain of God.
But Jesus did not say '*I* forgive you your sins.' It is characteristic of
most of us, whose mind labours under ego's yoke, to hear what ego
wants us to hear. They were looking for ways to condemn him, and
this was an opportunity, however slim.

'Forgiven' is the *past* participle of the verb to *forgive*. Past refers
to history; what has already happened. Therefore, he was simply
using the opportunity to provide a reminder for all of us who
are ready, willing and able to receive the message, that not only
the paralytic, but *all of us* have been forgiven from day one (the
instant of the illusory separation). This accords entirely with the
central thrust of his message to us in *A Course in Miracles*. There is
a dichotomy between the doctrine that only God is able to forgive

('sins' or any other error or omission) and other Christian teachings.

Christianity concurs with each of us (perceived as separate from God) being forgiven our 'trespasses' by God as *we forgive* those we perceive as 'trespassing' against us. Thus, if we are unforgiving, we are unable to *receive* forgiveness. Not because Papa is unwilling to forgive us – He has *already* forgiven us, and never changes His Mind – but because unwillingness to forgive blocks our channels of *receptivity* to awareness of the forgiveness that is *already* ours. How many of us – 'believers' or no – are willing to forgive our brother his 'trespasses against us' *seventy times seven*, as famously counselled by Jesus?

We only need to practise forgiveness all the while we believe there is something to forgive. When we have forgiven a perceived 'trespass', or 'sin' – actually, *error* – we are released from the burden of that 'sin' we have laid upon ourself, and that has kept us imprisoned in body after body on the carousel of birth and death. Whether perceived in ourself *or* a brother, it makes no difference, for *in reality* we are one. It is easier to see *'errors'* in our brothers than in ourself, because we have projected our own *imagined* sins, or errors – and therefore, guilt – onto our brothers in an attempt to rid ourself of the unbearable burden. Thus do we choose to not see them in ourself.

No-one can say the ego is not devious. One could go so far as to say *doubly-devious*, to cause maximum confusion in our upside-down, misperceiving mind. For on the one hand, by persuading us to project the perceived sins and guilt onto our brother, we can be misled into believing that we are free of the burden. That may convince our *conscious* mind. But lurking beneath that is our *un*conscious mind, which still harbours the horrors of our *imagined* sin (tearing a part of God – us – away from Him, thereby 'attacking' Him by rendering Him 'incomplete'). That means they are still with us, yet we are mostly unaware of them.

But *because* they are still with us, haunting us *unconsciously*, we call judgement, punishment into our presence *unconsciously*, for though we cannot admit it consciously – that would be far too painful – deep down we believe we *deserve* punishment. Unconscious self-punishment comes in many forms … 'accidents', illness, addictions; the latter to numb our mind and provide us with a way of hurting/killing ourself (quickly or slowly; it makes no difference) yet remain in denial of this. These unconsciously called-upon punishments *seem* unrelated to our guilt, due to seeming time-lapses between cause and effect; thus we miss the connection.

So, projection does not rid us of guilt, the progenitor of fear, which blocks our awareness of Love's presence within us. It simply hides the guilt from our awareness – causing us to believe we have rid ourself of it – yet remains within us, working its destructive works upon us. We do this to ourself unconsciously, as it is too confusing, frightening, terrible to contemplate – because we believe that which we see as unforgivable *warrants* punishment. Meanwhile we have lulled our conscious mind into the half-hearted belief that we are not guilty, so we feel justified in accepting – or at least, telling ourself – that we are not.

How hellish is the conflict within us, between our conscious and unconscious mind. Our conscious mind feverishly tries to persuade us we are not guilty, so we have no need to root it out and dispel it by forgiving *ourself*. And if we *are* guilty, God is going to punish us anyway, so let us keep on with the pretence that we are innocent; after all, it's everybody *else* that is guilty, so we have no need to forgive ourself. And if we *are* guilty, who are we to forgive ourself, since forgiveness – or otherwise – is in the sole domain of God? No wonder the religionists, yoked to ego's script, didn't want Jesus to spill the beans.

And if we see no need to forgive ourself, then we are not open to *receive* the forgiveness that is rightfully ours because Papa created His Son in His own likeness – perfect, pure and innocent. This means that in our perception we do not *have* true forgiveness, so we cannot give it to our brother, since we cannot give what we believe we do not have. Ego, ever being the doubly-devious, duplicitous devil, devised the deception of *false* forgiveness to confuse us into believing we *have* forgiven a 'trespass'; but false forgiveness *affirms* the sin, thus giving reality, in our confused perception, to the unreal.

Full marks for any who have managed to follow this endeavour to straighten-out these convolutions so far. To further assist is an extract from Vignette 5 in Part Two of *"Seek ye First the Kingdom..."*:

5: The Free Gift of Forgiveness

This event took place during a Communion Service in 1998 ...

... I felt Papa above and around me. He held me in the stillness and said, "My son, draw closer to Me. Open yourself to receive My Love *more.*"...

At the Kingdom prayer, as I spoke the words to Papa '... forgive us our debts [or 'trespasses'], as we forgive our debtors ...' He jumped in instantly, and emphatically said, *"I forgive you!"* He was holding in His right hand what looked like a bolt of lightning, about sixty centimetres (two feet) long. It was jagged, rather reminiscent of stylised illustrations of such. It was pure, living gold, radiant and bright as the sun. He swooped His hand down with it and placed it in my spine. I felt the restorative power with which it filled me.

I realised that forgiveness – and the wholeness into which it releases us – is ours because He has *given* it to us, and He longs for us to *receive* it ... Until we 'come to ourselves' and turn around one hundred and eighty degrees from facing the darkness, and face toward the Light, which is Papa, how can the free gift of forgiveness (and with it the restoration to wholeness and Life) that He constantly proffers be ours at such time as we are willing to gladly receive and *accept* it unto ourself?

I said to Him, "Beloved Papa, ... I thank You for Your revelation today, and joyfully open myself, the door of my life, to receive Your Love more. Thank You for giving me Your forgiveness. It is, I now know, the real experience, and *does* transform our lives from within. I feel freed from the burdens of unforgiveness that have been ebbing and flowing around and within me."

He replied:

"… this is My free gift to all who desire, earnestly, to receive it and hold fast in faith, trust, obedience[1] and commitment to My Word. It is not possible for you to forgive[2] others, only to *desire* to forgive others. By so desiring, I give you the gift of forgiveness [i.e., we open ourself to *receiving* what He has *always* proffered, because in eternal reality the gift is only given when it is *received*] and then you truly *have* forgiveness. It flows out from you, through you. In Truth, it is not yours to give. All things come of Me and are My free gift to all who will receive freely. Thus can these good gifts not be abused or manipulated by distorted desires."

He then went on to say:

"Eternal life is My free gift also to all who desire to receive it. Let your desire be pure in all things, My son. I empowered My beloved Firstborn [i.e., Jesus, the first fragment to remember, and thus be restored to, his true Being] for forgiveness of 'sins' on Earth because it is My gift to give to whomsoever I choose [i.e., whosoever is *ready to receive it*]. This was befitting of his status and his mission, so that as many as I gave to him should recognise him as My Anointed Messenger. To you I say, pray for your fellows as many and as often as you are able. So shall the incense rise up to Me as a pleasant aroma and enable the outpouring of My Love and wholeness to be received, to enter in whereunto I send it.

"Peace be with you; all is well."

This communion was seven years before I came to *A Course in Miracles* and the above quote about false forgiveness. When Papa says that it is not possible for me [i.e., any of us] to forgive others, only to *desire* to forgive, but that He had empowered Jesus in this, I interpret this as meaning that all the while the fragmented Sonship perceives sin as real, we are unable, of our limited, persona self, to *truly* forgive, but when we *desire* to forgive, we begin on the path back to wakefulness, remembrance of our true Being as His one, innocent Son, Christ. *Then*, like Jesus, we come to realise that there is no *actual* sin, only a dream of sin, so *true* forgiveness becomes possible for us because, as Jesus states in *A Course in Miracles,* page 401 (second edition) of the 'Workbook for Students':

> "[True] Forgiveness recognizes what you *thought* your brother did to you has not occurred. It does not pardon sins and [thus] make them real ['false' forgiveness]. It sees there *was* no sin. And in that view are all your sins forgiven. What is sin, except a false idea about God's Son? Forgiveness merely sees its falsity, and therefore lets it go. What then is free to take its place is now the Will of God."

Forgiving ourself – for what, *in Truth* we have never done – is, then, both the most important and the hardest thing any of us can accomplish. 'Most important' because it releases us from the burden of unforgiveness we have placed upon ourself, freeing us to *receive* the forgiveness that has always actually been ours, but has been veiled from our sight by ego's deception about our true Being. Equally 'most important' because until we receive and accept unto ourself (or are *willing* so to do) the forgiveness that has always been our free gift from Papa, we are not able to *truly* forgive our brother.

'Hardest' because whatever we believe in our *conscious* mind, in our *unconscious* mind we believe we are guilty and thus not worthy of forgiveness; only punishment. Self-forgiveness is very, very hard because unforgiveness of self is obscured, hidden from our conscious mind. It is impossible without the Help of Holy Spirit-Self and/or Jesus and our own *unequivocal willingness* and commitment to co-operate. And in the absence of our committed willingness, indeterminate further circuits of the not-so-merry-go-round are inescapable, because They cannot help us without our agreement, which is our *authority* for Them to Help.

Willingness to *accept* Papa's forgiveness of our self (self-forgiveness) enables us to experience the release of guilt, fear, anger, grievance, judgement, hurt, resentment … into the inner peace we *feel*, which tells us when we have *truly* forgiven our brother. That inner peace is far, far beyond the understanding of the world. Only when we have forgiven ourself and our brother is the cycle of unforgiveness that has held us in its thrall since the beginning of time released. When we accept forgiveness unto ourself, forgiving our brother becomes a doddle, because we then are able to see that it only *appeared* hard while we were subject to the blinding and deception of the ego caused by our *un*forgiveness. It *seemed* to be a vicious cycle, but forgiveness breaks that pernicious cycle, setting us free of its illusory iron grip. Then we really begin to experience miracles because forgiveness brings us into a state of miracle-mindedness, or miracle-readiness.

So, how do we reconcile the *seeming* conflict between God being the Source of All – including our forgiveness – and the need to forgive ourself? Simply by saying "Beloved Papa, thank You for giving me Your forgiveness. I gladly receive it and accept it unto myself so that I now *Know*, of a certainty beyond all doubt, that I *have* forgiveness, and am thus able to freely give it to my brother."

Diary of a Christ Communicant

A.M. July 20, 2010

> **Eternity is now, and does not change because it is of God, the Creator Spirit, and is therefore perfect.**
> **Perfection cannot change or it would not be perfect.**
> **Equally, God cannot change or He would not be perfect.**

Time and place seem completely real to our bodily senses, which are devised for perceiving phenomena at that vibration, so are our witnesses to illusion, and *only* to illusion. They cannot, therefore, bear witness to reality. However, our mind, which is *not* a bodily sense, nor *of* the body, is capable of awareness of reality, which is not of time and place. This is described as abstract because it is not represented by any time and place, or concrete, manifestation.

Love is the primary example of this because all can agree to its reality even though it does not exist in manifest, objective, concrete form. Time and place can be observed to be temporal, meaning always changing, passing in and out of manifestation over time.

As the mind is capable of apprehending the apparently

abstract idea of Love being real, so is it capable of apprehending the abstract idea of eternity being real, even though the bodily senses are unable to perceive it. This demonstrates that mind and body (including brain) are not one and the same. The mind continues to exist and function after the body (and brain) has ceased to function and exist.

The mind is capable of understanding the idea that eternity is *now*, and does not change because it is of God, the Creator Spirit, and is therefore perfect. Perfection cannot change or it would not be perfect. Equally, God cannot change or He would not be perfect. Therefore He cannot create or be involved in that which is temporal because it appears to be constantly changing – coming into and out of perception, or being 'born' and 'dying'.

If the unchangeable eternity is real, that which appears to be changeable, or of a temporal (which by definition is counter to eternity) state cannot be real; for opposites, which contradict each other, cannot both be real. Therefore, either what *appears* to be real to bodily senses – which themselves are temporal – is real, or eternity is real. For, undeniably, temporal and eternal cannot both be.

Since the mind is not dependent on the body for its existence – anymore than is Love – and the body is unarguably temporal, one can ask oneself, 'Am I mind or body?' Mind is capable of functioning through, or with a body, but a body clearly is unable to function without mind. Therefore, while you appear to be with a body, I commend to you the purposeful use of it with your right mind.

---

1. This means obedience to our own, inner Self, shining the Light of eternal Truth into our mind.

2. This refers to 'false forgiveness'. As stated on page 638 (second edition) in the Text of *A Course in Miracles*: "It pardons 'sinners' sometimes, but remains aware that they have sinned. And so they do not merit the forgiveness that it gives. This is the false forgiveness which the world

employs to keep the sense of sin alive."

False forgiveness, then, is where the 'sin' is *acknowledged* and then 'forgiven'. However, the flaw in this misperception is that by *acknowledging* the sin, we give it reality. This is a ploy of ego mind, which wants us to remain bogged-down in a false world of sin.

7: Responding to Opportunities

. . . let rejoicing fill your innermost heart and soul. For though the conditions of Earth-mind consciousness are not yet One with the Kingdom, all moves forward and the manifestation from the Inner Plane into the Outer Plane of Earth-life awareness proceeds apace.

–Jesus, June 28, 1992

I AM BEING PROMPTED to share our recent experience. Theresa and I have had a brother and his wife staying for a few days. He is bipolar and, sadly, perceives the world against him, out to do him down, rip him off. For many years he worked in the world of finance. No doubt large sums passed his way over the years, and money can be very beguiling. Throughout the millennia many have succumbed to its draw as an idol. It can be like the carrot and stick, leading us down some rocky side-roads, yet ever evading our grasp.

It is a poor substitute for Papa, Who is always reliable and never evades us when we turn to Him. Yet there is nothing wrong with money; it is our *attitude* toward it that is where the potential for distraction from the Highway Home – and thus, the danger – lies. In recent years I have been asking for my Love for this brother to become unfettered from petty, worldly, ego misperceptions and judgements, and that I might become an instrument of assistance in his releasing from his self-imprisonment in misery. So this visit was an opportunity I did not wish to let pass without some forward progress.

But I also did not wish to let persona Brian and any ego monkey-wrenches get in the way of the Holy Spirit's releasing-to-freedom intentions. So I told Him I was giving all into His care and that I would simply seek to *respond* to opportunities provided by Him for healing/releasing, rather than trying to devise them myself. This made me feel completely comfortable and at peace, instead of anxiously examining every moment to see how it could be manipulated to my 'contrived, saving agenda'.

As it happened, no outstanding opportunities for sharing profound wisdom from *A Course in Miracles* arose (which I had secretly hoped might be the case). Instead, there was carefree, loving, spontaneous, easy, relaxed intercourse between us the whole visit, with no awkward moments. When it came time for them to depart we hugged warmly, easily and I could feel how the Love, compassion and blessing for him in my heart had grown, and equally how he felt the same toward me. This was immeasurably more rewarding than engaging in intellectual debate about what is 'right'.

This precious time together palpably brought home to me that *only* Love – *without* condition – can restore us, Papa's beloved Son, to Oneness, wholeness. Contorting our mind with intellectualising and polemic about which belief or doctrine is the solution to mankind's problems is much more likely to lead to more division and conflicted perception, rather than union. Vision is an integral aspect of our Being. It is the free gift of God, *already* ours, complete and perfect, so entails no thinking. Allowing our vision to simply BE enables our *awareness* of Papa, revealing Himself to His Son, *without effort*.

That revelation can only be Love, perfect and total, because that is all Papa IS. Nothing else. Love encompasses ALL; It is *everything*. This is all He has to give us, and is therefore all we have to give to our brothers. He hides nothing from us when we open ourself to Him. Then, we have placed ourself back where we belong: within

His Love and Light. Darkness, doubt, fear, despair, loneliness are instantly shone away by the Light that is His Love. Then, all the details in our illusory embodiment in time and place simply come into equilibrium, comfortably and easily. This is what – and *only* what – restores us to Oneness, by clearing the way to enable unconditional forgiveness.

Time has nothing to do with this process, and is irrelevant to its accomplishment. If we allow time into the equation it sets off anxiety, thereby blocking, veiling our vision from the *eternal*, unchangeable reality of our Being in Him. In our attunement with the *timelessness* of eternity our unencumbered vision shows us that we both *have* and *are* Love, so we cannot help but share, give, extend Love to all our brothers. This is what Jesus does, without exertion, and he is our example, our template for Being. When this is our sole desire, as it is for him, then is our objective – Oneness – accomplished.

A Course in Miracles can help us incalculably in the process of remembering this, but cannot be an intellectual substitute for it. Talking the talk is a hollow, ineffectual diversion from walking the walk, hand-in-hand with Jesus. Taking his hand reconnects us to him, opening us back to Love, because he *is* Love. When we open to Love the cataracts fall from our eyes and we are restored to our true estate of all-*Knowing*; that we are One, in the Heart-Mind of God, with no striving, anxiety, judgement, grievance or conflict.

This awareness was the beautiful gift that became mine (again) by my willingness to leave all to the Spirit of Truth during this God-given opportunity of a few days of togetherness with my brother, with no ego-dominated agenda getting in the way.

Diary of a Christ Communicant

A.M. July 29, 2010

Because you have placed yourself within the care, guidance and protection of the Spirit of Truth, Which is the same as your brother, Jesus, you are within that care and guidance. This cannot fail you because you have placed yourself there, so you can trust in It.

You are doing exactly what you are supposed to be *doing* and you are exactly where you are supposed to *be*. Do not allow questioning thoughts or doubting thoughts to find any resting place in your mind. Know instead that because you have placed yourself within the care, guidance and protection of the Spirit of Truth, Which is the same as your brother, Jesus, you *are* within that care and guidance. This cannot fail you *because* you have placed yourself there, so you can *trust* in It.

When such idle thoughts enter, do not resist them. Stand aside as an *observer* of them, for they are not yours; they do not belong to you. If it is your desire, above all, to do, Be and align yourself with Papa's Will, that is what you are Being and functioning within. So do not wrestle with such intruders. There is nothing of them in you, and nothing of you that serves them, so engage them not and they will meet no resistance, and thus depart to the nothingness from which they came.

Throughout, remain steadfastly focused on what you *Know* is Truth. This is the rock that anchors you and prevents you from being swept away.

8: Reflections on Our Eternal Reality

All who come to the Table shall be given, and none shall be refused.
Let this be your message, from your heart, that darkness, which
enshrouds souls in despair, may be lifted, to reveal to each one the
Light of his or her own within, where shines the Love and Light of
the Father Creator.

–Jesus, July 5, 1992

I WOKE A FEW MORNINGS AGO to find myself spontaneously communing with Papa, so got notebook and pen and wrote the words that flowed into, or through, my mind. It was ostensibly as if I was speaking the words to Him, but at the same time it was He Who was giving, placing the words for me to express, to provide further clarity and affirmation. I share those words here in the hope they will help extend clarity further through the confused, illusorily-fragmented mind of the Sonship:

Papa, You are in me every moment, in a part of my mind of which I am not consciously aware; to which I am not yet fully restored to wakefulness. Yet I can rejoice and give thanks for the certainty beyond all doubt that You *are* in me, with me, immovably, always, eternally; Loving me totally, unconditionally; *Knowing* that as Your beloved Son I am forever pure, innocent, everlasting Love – just as You created me.

It seems absurd, ludicrous that I could choose uncertainty about everything, including my own Identity, and try to hide from You in so many masquerade costumes; that I could/should go to such lengths – even fabricating idols, such as fear-based religion, to 'prove' to myself that the unrealities of separation, guilt and fear are real, arising from my own 'sinfulness', for which You are set on punishing me, and that sacrifice is the path to salvation – to deceive myself into forgetting to laugh.

Now, thanks to the Spirit of Truth – Your gift to me – and my beloved brother, Jesus, I can laugh again because I now accept and *Know* that none of this is real.

For a moment I had placed a veil between us, causing me to believe You are 'up there' and I am 'down here', beneath Your reach. Now I am remembering that You are right here, with me, in me, even as I am in You, this very moment, sharing Your Joy and laughter; that this is the *only* moment, forever unchanging. Now there is no past to feel guilty or fearful about, and there can be no future either, to cause me doubt, anxiety or uncertainty.

Now I *Know* that the veil never was anything but a figment of my confused imagination, which I thought was hiding me from You, the Light – the very *Source* – of Life, because I believed I was guilty. Now I am choosing, learning, remembering to see right past that spurious veil. It had been inveigling me to project onto it dark shadows of death, obscuring my vision so that I was no longer aware of Your Presence, Your Love, Your Grace.

Now I am choosing my only awareness to be remembrance of Being – with all my brothers and every living thing – One in You and You in me; simply Being ... *Being* LOVE, *Being* LIGHT, *Being* PEACE, *Being* JOY, *Being* LIFE Itself. In my dream of being a little, confused mind in a weak, limited, vulnerable, mortal body I cannot experience, have awareness of *Being* and *having* all these heavenly attributes because I made up this persona-self, and that which is made-up is not real, cannot be real, *cannot Know reality.*

So I must awaken from the dream of unreality to the Truth of my eternal Self: the Christ, Your One, beloved Son, just as Jesus has wakened. For only reality can be aware of reality, so persona Brian needs the Help of reality in the form of Your Voice – the Spirit of Truth, to be with me and comfort me as I dream of sojourning in a far, famine-stricken country – and Jesus, to hold my hand, so that I may be strengthened and upheld when I feel the dream threatening to engulf me and blind me with erroneous thinking and misperception.

By Their Help can I be certain that even when I momentarily *appear* to be choosing illusion I am – in the undivided part of my mind that never slumbers – *really* choosing Oneness in You. And by holding Jesus' hand, which he *always* freely proffers, I can *Know* that I am not alone; that I am travelling in the right direction – toward the Light, even though I am not always, yet, *aware* of the Light – because I trust implicitly that he not only *Knows* the way but *is* the Way.

And I Know that You have forgiven me; therefore I *have* forgiveness, and can *readily* pardon myself. For what I thought was real was only a dream, so I have not 'sinned', but merely strayed a moment, in my mind, from You. I thought I could rid myself of perceived guilt by projecting it onto my imaginary brother – making him guilty in my place – but now I *Know* I can *easily* forgive him, so we can be lovingly re-joined, as One, in You.

For I now remember that all I perceive in a brother is but a reflection of my own *self*-perception. Even if I do not perceive him as guilty in my *conscious* awareness, if I do not feel Your Love for him in my heart, I now *Know* that I am projecting guilt and fear onto him from my *unconscious* mind. This can only be released by forgiving him; for as I forgive him, so am *I* forgiven, that we both may have Your

Peace in our experience and freely enter the Kingdom of Your Love, together, as One.

So, I now repudiate guilt, fear, scarcity, loss, loneliness, illness, death ... *all* that is not of You.

Beloved Papa, I welcome You into my abode, my heart, rejoicing that as host to You, I can no longer be hostage to ego. And I give joyous, heart-surging thanks for Your Grace in welcoming me Home, to celebrate the glory of our reunion.

Thanks also to all for the priceless gift of allowing me to share this treasured moment of communion; for true communion is *common* union in which we all can freely, lovingly share.

Diary of a Christ Communicant

A.M. July 31, 2010

> **The ego tempts with judgements, accusations, nega-
> tivity. *Allow* this; observe it but do not own it, do not
> engage with it and in due course these intrusions di-
> minish and fade away. Celebrate and rejoice, for these
> are all signs of your growing commitment to, and desire
> for, your true will.**

The ego opposes the Spirit of Truth. The ego does not let go, and
does not want to 'allow', for allowing means *not* opposing.

Even as you go forward to the Light, having committed to
following the lead of My kindly Light, ego can yet sneak
in at every opportunity, having been lurking in the dark
recesses of every split mind. From there the ego tempts
with judgements, accusations, grievances, negativity.

Allow this; observe it but do not own it, do not engage
with it and in due course these intrusions diminish and
fade away. Celebrate and rejoice, for these are all signs of
your growing commitment to, and desire for, your *true*
will. Well now do you *Know* that your will is One with
Papa's Will, which is Love, Peace, Joy, Wholeness, Truth.

9: The Great Leavening

Now is the time of great fulfilment, great rejoicing, great wonder-working. And this is possible only by willingness to work one's desire in harmony with the perfect timing of the Father's Way. Herein is discipline. Herein is faith. Herein is Love. Herein is all sufficiency for all.

–Jesus, July 12, 1992

D URING RECENT FELLOWSHIP the subject of Jesus' parable of the ten virgins (Mt. 25) arose. It is, in allegoric form, highly pertinent to these 'end times'. This parable tells of five wise and five foolish virgins attending a wedding. The wise took vessels of extra oil with them to keep their lamps lit while they waited for the bridegroom; the foolish did not. Jesus says the bridegroom 'tarried' (delayed his return from the wedding ceremony and banquet celebrations) and meanwhile the virgins 'slumbered and slept' (incarnated and reincarnated during the second measure of meal epoch).

Then, *at midnight* (the end of the second measure of meal epoch, and thus the beginning of the New Day, the third measure of meal, the Aquarian, or Kingdom, Age) *a cry was made, 'The bridegroom cometh, go ye out to meet him.'* (Mt. 25:6).

This, being a parable, is full of symbol and metaphor, using a cultural event of the Middle East in those times, and most of us in the West today are unaware of the order of events of such an occasion. *Barnes' Notes on the New Testament* are helpful here. Below are some extracts from those Notes, and as inspired so to do, I have added comments in brackets amongst them.

> The *lamps* used on such occasions [weddings] were rather *torches* or *flambeaux*. They were made by winding rags around pieces of iron or earthenware, sometimes hollowed so as to contain oil, and fastened to handles of wood. These torches were dipped in oil, and gave a large light. Marriage ceremonies in the East were conducted with great pomp and solemnity.
>
> The ceremony of marriage was performed commonly in the open air, on the banks of a stream [symbolising *the Waters of Life*]. Both the bridegroom and bride were attended by friends; they were escorted in a *palanquin*, carried by four or more persons. After the ceremony of marriage there followed a feast of seven days if the bride was a virgin, or three days if she was a widow. This feast was celebrated in her father's house.

Here one could readily observe that this symbolises the Father's House, or Heaven. Heaven – although *believed in* by many – was not consciously *Known* or experienced by almost all of humanity in the Earth-life consciousness during this two-thousand-year celebratory period: the second measure of meal. But It *was* known about by those who espoused their lives to the 'bridegroom' – Jesus – in the Realms of Light in the etheric counterpart of the 'physical' Earth. Such souls have been coming and going between those heavenly realms and the earthly life by multiple incarnations during that era.

For most of us, even if we were awake to the realities of this parable during our intervals in spirit between incarnations, we have had little or no conscious awareness of that reality during our repeated returns to Earth-life embodiment, since incarnating entails amnesia. And because the institutionalised church has not understood these esoteric Truths, it has been singularly unable to provide any light of spiritual discernment about it here, on Earth. Barnes goes on to say:

> At the end of that time [the two-thousand-year Piscean Age, or second, *'Jesus'*, measure of meal] the bridegroom conducted the bride, with great pomp and splendour, to his own home …

Revelation 21:2 describes it thusly: *And I John saw the holy city, new Jerusalem, coming down from God out of heaven* [the Father's House], *prepared as a bride adorned for her husband*. This indicates that the Plan, Jesus' great desire for us all, is to bring the Kingdom of Heaven *to Earth* – the *consummation* of the marriage of Heaven (Eternal awareness) with Earth (time-and-place consciousness).

> … This was done in the evening, or at night …

This gives meaning to Jesus' references to his coming as a thief in the night *'and thou shalt not know what hour I will come'* (Rev. 3:3) – especially in the context of his statement that the bridegroom 'tarried'.

Orthodox interpretations of his emphasis on the great need to watch for his (the bridegroom's) coming have inferred that the event holds a terrible, judgemental, retributional portent for those who are caught unawares by his return. But this was not Jesus' intent at all. What he was saying was, his coming is an esoteric, mystical, metaphysical process, not a physical, bodily event, and to have cognisance of it, focus, attunement of the mind, at the spiritual level of awareness is essential to our experience of it.

He was also emphasising that it is a JOYFUL event, as indicated by this quote from Lk. 12:37, 38: *Blessed are those servants, whom the lord when he cometh shall find watching: verily I say unto you, that he shall gird himself, and make them to sit down to meat, and will come forth and serve them. And if he shall come in the second watch* [second measure of meal], *or come in the third watch* [third measure of meal], *and find them so, blessed are those servants.*

> … Many friends and relations attended them [bride and groom]; and besides those who went with them from the house of the bride [the Father's House; Heaven], there

> was another company that came out from the house of the
> bridegroom [Earth] to meet them, and welcome them ...

This indicates a great <u>joining</u> of souls from the Realms of Light
with those of like mind, desire and commitment who are incarnate
during this event, or process.

> ... These were probably female friends and relatives of the
> bridegroom, who went out to welcome him and his new
> companion [bride] to their home. These are the virgins
> mentioned in this parable. Not knowing precisely the
> time when the procession would come, they probably
> went out early, and waited by the way till they should see
> indications of its approach.

So, this explains that a wedding and its attendant celebrations was
a prolonged, *joyous* occasion. First came the formalities of the actual
wedding ceremony, then the banquet feast, in the Father's House,
<u>to which *all* are invited</u>, and the doors to the banquet are kept
open throughout the seven-days' – for which read two thousand
years' – festivities in the Father's House, *Heaven*. We all sojourn in
spirit between incarnations, and have been freely invited to attend
that banquet. Many millions of us *have* attended, even though we
do not bring the details through to our *conscious* memory at each
reincarnation. *Now is the time of remembering.*

Then, at the end of the banquet, the bridegroom conveys
the bride to his own home: the NEW Earth, or 'real world'; *raised
up*, 'leavened', transformed, awakened to remembrance of the
Kingdom awareness. This symbolises what is happening now. It
is clear from Jesus' story that the foolish virgins are those of us
who have not kept/desired to keep the lamp of their spiritual
awareness lit during this two-thousand-year era, but rather, have
remained focused only at the illusory, distracting, Earth-life level
of consciousness.

The parable then says, in verse 10, 'and the door was shut'.
This means that souls outside the door would be prevented from
entering in and being part of the consummation (rejoining, or

completion of the Sonship as One) procedures. It is hard for us to imagine how any, *other than the bride and groom*, could be present at the consummation procedures, an intensely private activity in any such marital situation! But in this parable/allegory, *all who will* are the bride. There are billions of us, and neither the numbers nor the gender of the participants has any relevance in this because it is a *spiritual*, not a bodily, event.

Of Jesus' manifesting to me in his glory in 1967, I wrote in chapter 2 of *"Seek ye First the Kingdom..."*:

> ... His aura of golden, living sunlight had enveloped me and the feeling of love – of *Agapé* – to my being was so intense, so powerful, so uplifting to my spirit that I felt as if my heart had grown to the size of a football and was going to burst out of my chest cavity. The feeling of love, not just throughout my body but through my entire aura was <u>an orgasm of the soul but intensified immeasurably more than any such physical experience</u> ...

This was incomparably more rapturous than any sexual experience and was so *because* it was a spiritual event. How greatly have we limited ourself by reducing our ecstasy to momentary, *bodily* intercourse orgasm! At such a self-diminished level of encounter, how easily it can – and so often does – become debased to merely wanton gratification; an ego-device to keep us imprisoned in a body.

As for the door being shut, thus preventing ingress for any who had not kept the lamp of their spiritual awareness lit, this indicates that such awareness *of*, or entry *into* the place, the NEW Earth or *Kingdom of Heaven on Earth*, or *real world*, is <u>a state of awareness</u>, dependent upon desire, commitment, one-pointedness. That *desire* is the oil that keeps the lamp of our mind illuminated. And so the shutting of the door is by those *outside*, <u>not by the bridegroom or the bride</u>, who would/will *always* welcome those who truly seek and earnestly desire the Kingdom of Heaven on Earth.

The parable states: *They that were foolish took their lamps, and took no oil with them: But the wise took oil in their vessels with their lamps* (Mt. 25:3, 4). The oil refers to awareness – or at least, desire for remembrance – of the marriage ceremony and celebration banquet in the Father's House (Heaven) during the second measure of meal, to which all were invited. The lamps would have had some oil, to start the period of watching and waiting for the bridegroom, signifying soul awareness during the early stages of an incarnation. But the distractions of time and place would soon use up that supply, and without reserve vessels of oil (desire, motivation, commitment) the spiritual illumination of our mind soon grows dim.

Then, inevitably, those who did not bring a vessel of oil (desire for eternal, spiritual Truth) with them into earthly embodiment shut the door to their own soul-awareness-and-experience, or consummation of the Kingdom of Heaven on Earth, or 'real world', keeping *themselves* 'without'. This was/is their own choice, their own decision and is not to be construed as a judgemental God or Jesus excluding *any* from the Kingdom.

The marriage ceremony and celebratory banquet have now been completed (during the Piscean Age, or second, *Jesus*, measure of meal). The bridegroom is now accompanying the bride (coming down – i.e., reincarnating, as Crystal, or *Christ-all*, children – from Heaven [Rev. 21:2]) toward the marital home: the Kingdom of Heaven *on Earth*; the consummating/completing of the rejoining, or raising-up of the fragmented Earth-mind-conscious Sonship, with the all-Loving, all-Knowing, all-empowered Christ. On July 6, 1997 Jesus said to me:

> … My Plan is all encompassing; every opportunity is catered for, according to the power of the Spirit of Truth. No event in my earthly life was 'chance' fulfilment of prophecy. So also is the fulfilment of your birth vision *because you have committed your life into my care*. Let no-one say to you there is no joy in such commitment of life, for I am the Lord of the Purple Ray – the perfect blend of Earth life [red] and fulfilment with eternal Truth and reality [blue].

The joy of Heaven is thus yours *in the Earth life* and by no other means is this possible. *So is it with all who come to me.*

The fulfilment, completion or consummating of our Earth-life purpose is the transforming of our lowly, crawling, misperception-of-self into the soaring, radiant One-Life that we all are, by the all-empowered-by-God Jesus, in his fully-realised Identity in Christ – Papa's One Son. The rapturous, nuptial consummation is taking place *now*, in the bridegroom's home, the NEW Earth, or *'real world'*, in our very midst, for 'all who will' to participate, during the third measure of meal, the Kingdom, or Aquarian, Age: the next two millennia.

This is what awaits us all, *right now*. Doubt, that great dismantler of faith and hope, is all that holds *any* of us back. Faith, trust, obedience (to our inner calling and desire for spiritual Truth and reality) and commitment (FTOC) are the Keys to the Kingdom, which is at hand, even at the doors. Only our own self-misperception stands between us and this, our glorious, eternal reality.

Diary of a Christ Communicant

A.M. August 2, 2010

**Now do all the 'sons of men' progress into the comple-
tion, fulfilment, Kingdom measure; leavening, raising
all up to the inner awareness, remembrance of their
true Being as the Son of God,
One with Jesus.**

Jesus referred to himself as 'the son of man' because he was, along with the rest of us – symbolically speaking – 'a son of Abraham'(which has nothing to do with ethnicity). Abraham, though he was beginning to awaken to God-awareness, was still confused about his relationship *to*, his Sonship *of*, God. This is exemplified by his perception that God wanted him to sacrifice his only son (Isaac) by his wife, Sarah (Gen. 22).

Jesus *Knew* that he, himself, was Papa's Son, along with all the fragments; but for the benefit of those around him he was identifying with all in 'the son of *man*' consciousness. This enabled him to win their trust *in* him, rather than fear *of* him, which is the tendency of ego-dominated man. Then, having established the leavening activity of the second measure of meal, he could begin the process of raising his brothers to Son-of-God awareness. This is now, at the beginning of the leavening of the third measure, 'proving' [Using the terminology of bread making].

Referring to himself as the son of man also was to demonstrate his solidarity with his brothers; it was not false modesty. To claim his Son-of-God stature then would have confused them into a greater degree of misperception of the duality consciousness ... God, and His only Son, Jesus, 'up there' – exalted, beyond reach – and the rest, wretched, unworthy, sinners, 'down here'.

It is of no consequence that this duality consciousness appears *outwardly* to have persisted throughout the second measure of meal. For now do all the 'sons of men' progress into the completion, fulfilment, Kingdom measure; leavening, raising all up to the *inner* awareness, remembrance of their true Being as the One Son of God, One with Jesus.

10: Shining Away the Veil

Pray for the Kingdom for all mankind, and bless souls in darkness,
for their healing, holiness, enlightenment, upliftment and
going forward.

–*Jesus*, August 9, 1992

SOME WHILE AGO I wrote about the esoteric meaning behind the symbols of the *Most Holy Place*, the *Holy Place* and the veil that divides them in the Jerusalem temple built by Solomon about three thousand years ago, and their significance to the events unfolding before us in these times. In summary, the inmost part of the temple has two chambers; the *Most Holy Place* symbolises the Presence of God and the *Holy Place* symbolises His Son, (now referred to as the Christ). The chambers abut, separated from each other by a thick, woven veil, symbolising the perceived separation by the Son from his Father.

I had had a mystical experience in which the Light that is God shone so brightly from the *Most Holy Place*, or *Holy of Holies*, that it penetrated through the veil, shining away the hellish images of separation that the illusorily-fragmented, -separated Son was projecting onto the veil – giving it a semblance of reality – from the Holy Place. This experience had a profound effect on me, and I had been recalling it last thing at night, going into the Holy Place and attuning to the experience of Papa's Light shining away the false images I/we have been projecting onto the veil – a symbol of time and place; the without.

This has engendered a great, palpable sense of Papa's Presence, so close, so Loving, leaving me with the certainty of *Knowing* that He is forever, inescapably, unavoidably *with* us. Yet, for all that, was the sense that the veil was still there between us, even though the false images had been shone away. This left me feeling somewhat disheartened; that I was, somehow, maintaining that degree of separateness from Him *in spite* of being aware of His Light shining through the veil, but not shining it *away* .

In September 1998 He had said to me, as He held me in the stillness: "My son, draw closer to Me. Open yourself to receive My Love *more.*" Years later, as I recalled to mind this image of His Light shining through the veil of my conflicted mind, I said to Him, "Papa, I *am* drawing closer to You, opening myself to You, that I may receive Your Love *more.*" He immediately responded:

"Beloved, to *receive* My Love more you must *give* Love more; to *receive* blessing more you must *give* blessing more. To *receive* My good gifts more freely you must *give* them more freely. For as you now *Know*, giving and receiving are one, and to give is but to receive. You are now stronger, more grown, more restored in your remembrance of Truth. Therefore, you are better placed, better able to give more purposefully, more powerfully of that which has been freely given to you. Bless, even as you are blessed; Love, even as you are Loved; forgive, even as you are forgiven.

"All is well; all can *only* be well, Beloved."

As I took this in and straight away began focusing on blessing, Loving and forgiving, ego-projections within the Holy Place (my own within) ceased, and in their place the Light now shone also from where I was observing this experience – within the Holy Place – which now was full of Light instead of ego shadows of darkness. Now I was *aware* of the Light that is the Son also, as perfectly bright as the Father, in Whose likeness he is equally created. We, the One Son, have *always* been that Light. But by pretending to be what we are not, we have veiled the Light that we *are* from our sight; *but never from Papa's*.

This pretence has us projecting images of darkness – guilt, fear, conflict, judgement, grievance, unforgiveness, *disease*, 'death' … – onto our made-up veil, or screen: the world of time and place, including our imaginary brothers and our illusorily-belittled self. Yet all the while, uninterruptedly, we *are* the Light – just as Jesus told us two thousand years ago (Mt. 5:14) – shining, extending Life, Love, Peace, Joy from our own within to all creation. To become *aware* of this, our true Being, all we need is to *focus* on the Light, rather than the (spiritual) darkness – time and place – we have so long duped ourself into believing is reality.

As we all now *Know*, there is no such thing as darkness; it is merely the *imagined* absence of reality: Light. Darkness is nothing – no-thing. We have been focusing on no-thing since time began. To focus on the Light, which is one and the same as Love, Life, Truth – all of which are accompanied by Peace, Joy, abundance … *everything* that is of Papa, in fact – our true Being, we simply follow Papa's counsel:

> 'To *receive* My Love more you must *give* Love more; to *re-ceive* blessing more you must *give* blessing more. To *receive* My good gifts more freely you must *give* them more freely.'

We do this remembering that giving and receiving are one and the same, and that therefore, without giving we *cannot* receive.

Now, as the leavening of the third measure of meal progresses, we are remembering who we really are, and becoming *aware* of the perfect effulgence of our true, eternal, undimmable Light shining, equal to Papa's (because He can only create in equality), from within the Holy Place – our own within – onto the veil: time and place. The Light of eternal Truth can but shine away the illusory veil, because it only appears 'real' to our imagination within the upside-down game of make-believe. In the Light it ceases to have any 'reality', any meaning, any presence, any existence. Thus, with the veil gone, do Father and Son become rejoined as One again.

Papa's Light from within the Holy of Holies had not shone-*away* the veil – even though His Light had become discernible to me *through* it – because to Him there *was* no veil. Ever. It was still there to *my* perception because I (a symbol/representative of the fragmented, confused Sonship) had believed, and thus, *perceived* it as still being there. The process of changing my focus from the veil still being in place – on the mistaken presumption that *Papa* had put it there – to focusing on blessing, Loving and forgiving, brought my vision, my remembrance, back into alignment with the Truth of Who and What I *Am*/we all really *Are*: Papa's perfect, eternal, immortal Son; *exactly* like his Father.

Papa is singing the Song of Love to us, His beloved Son, every moment, unceasingly. We are unable to hear Him unless we sing our Song of Love to Him, from our heart, in return. This is because singing the Song of Love to Him opens the *receptor* channels in our heart, enabling His singing to *reach* us. We can practise this Song by singing it to ourself *and to our brothers*. Without effort such practise automatically extends it to Papa, Who hears and replies, with His ineffable Love and blessing. The words are the *Living Word* – the Word of Life – and beget Life ever more abundantly for all. They revolve around the theme, 'I Love You; I bless You; I rejoice in You with exceedingly great joy; All that I Am I freely give/extend to, share with, You.'

Diary of a Christ Communicant

A.M. August 7, 2010

Your thoughts are your 'reality' because you believe them. Such is the power of the mind of Papa's Son. Because you believed ego's thoughts were your thoughts, they became your reality.

Your thoughts are your 'reality' because you *believe* them. Such is the power of the mind of Papa's Son. Because you *believed* ego's thoughts were your thoughts, they became your reality. Since ego's thoughts are the seeming opposite, or reversal, of Papa's Thoughts – which are, I hardly need remind you, creative, Love, Peace, Joy, blessing, Oneness ... – they are negative, destructive, divisive, judgemental ... This obscures the Light, Truth, Love, Wholeness, Oneness ... that is your true Being, from your awareness.

Yet if you choose not to own ego's thoughts, but simply observe, allow and do not *resist* them – and rather, focus on the Light – then will they gradually diminish in your awareness and cease to occupy your attention; cease to have any existence for you. To *resist* no-thing is to make something out of nothing; folly indeed.

You can give seeming pain and suffering to Papa and thank Him for removing it – just as Jesus did – by choosing to believe, and remember, your innocence. Thus did he experience neither pain nor suffering at crucifixion. You could say to yourself, "Wholeness is mine right now, in this holy instant. I *claim* it, receive it, accept it unto myself and give thanks for it. I *Know* these negative thoughts of guilt, judgement, unworthiness, anger, pain, suffering are not mine, Papa, because I am just as You created me, and therefore only perfect Love, Peace, Joy, Wholeness and unity can be my reality."

11: The Open Door to the Most Holy Place

My son, this is a day for change – water into wine, war into peace, death into life. Let this desire in your heart go out at any time with blessing in my name and my purpose for the transforming and uplifting of any and all who will receive.

–Jesus, November 8, 1992

To our Earth-mind perception much that we experience in time and place is seen as chance, random events. And when things occur that are undeniably more than that, it is dismissed as 'coincidence'. Yet, we can choose to observe these events *not* as chance but as design, synchronicity, the outworking of a plan that is far bigger than our sensory perception and intellectual analysis allows. Part of the reason for this lack of ability to discern the connectedness of events is the trick we have played on ourself called linear time.

When connected events are 'separated' by a linear time interval that can be weeks, months, years, even lifetimes, the connection is often missed by our self-limiting perception. In the separating of the Son into myriad fragments, each has awareness of but a *part* of the complete picture and sees it as the *whole* picture. Yet if we are committed to the healing and restoration of the illusorily fragmented mind of Papa's Son, and place ourself for this healing in the absolute care, guidance and protection of the Holy Spirit for our Awakening, connected events separated by extended periods of linear time become rejoined in our mind.

This then becomes experienced as part – an important, crucial part – of the healing process, because He works His works, usually beyond our conscious awareness, joining back together the parts of the picture until we are able to see, understand and experience the whole, just as Jesus does. It is then that time becomes seen as irrelevant, and thus do we move more into the awareness and experience that *eternity* is the only reality. Just as Jesus does.

There *is* no separation between Father and Son in reality (eternity) but the 'prodigal' Son went, in his mind, into 'a far country' (time and place) and the union between Them *appeared* to become divided, as represented by the veil, (described in chapter 10). Onto that veil (the world) the Son projected from his now-confused, upside-down, split-off-from-Truth mind, shadows of darkness – guilt, fear, conflict, judgement, grievance, unforgiveness, *dis*ease, 'death'…

In June 1995 a young man appeared to me from spirit and said, *I want you to enter the Holy of Holies* (see chapter 10 of *"Seek ye First the Kingdom…"* for details). The words of the young man, who was bringing me a message from 'on High', were indicating that this is what Papa wants for us. From His perspective – the only *true* perspective – there *is* no veil, no barrier, no restriction, to our entry.

We, Papa's beloved Son, are invited in. Papa is hardly going to invite His Son to enter in and then place a barrier to his/our entry. That would be illogical, perverse, unreasonable, capricious; such terms apply only to the thinking of the ego. I then was reminded of the wondrous occasion – back in the 1990s – best described by this extract, also from chapter 10 of *"Seek ye First the Kingdom…"*:

I was walking with Jesus along a gently winding, gravelled pathway through what appeared to be at first open countryside, with woodland [all unordered, random, symbolising this world], and then gradually, as we progressed on our journey together, becoming landscaped areas with lawns and shrubs [all beautifully, yet naturally, ordered, symbolising the *real world*; the Kingdom of Heaven on Earth]… He was walking on my right, no more than a hand's breadth in front. This signified to me that he was at the same time leading and walking *with* me, beside me …

… We were engaged in warm, companionable, easy conversation, just as do two close, loving, trusting friends of long-standing acquaintance, but I had a sense that there was a definite purpose about our journey, with a specific destination to be reached, somewhere ahead …

After a few minutes we rounded one of the gentle bends in the path and I could see before us, across a more expansive, undulating lawned area, a building. It was all white – pure, alabaster white – cube-shaped, about four or five metres high. It was constructed from stone blocks, perfectly cut and fitted and had neither windows nor doors. The stone blocks were *alive* and radiating living light.

We progressed toward this structure, and as we got about fifteen or twenty paces from it the Master began to rise from the ground, moving more rapidly ahead of me toward the building until up against the wall facing us. During this progress he had begun to morph from his human form until, by the time he reached the wall, he had transformed into an opening in the wall. He *became* the opening, the entrance, where previously there was none. The opening, which <u>was</u> Jesus, morphed, finished as a door frame; there was no door, just the frame. It was about two metres square and made from solid, living, radiant gold … His movement toward the building was not walking but *gliding* through the air above the ground, morphing as he progressed, so that the entire move from beside me to when he became the entranceway was a seamless process. At the same time the very movement was, without a word being spoken, an *invitation* for me to enter into the building though the Golden Portal that he had become. ("I know thy works: behold, *I have set before thee an open door, and no man can shut it*: for thou hast a little strength, and hast kept my word, and hast not denied my name." [Rev. 3:8]).

With awe and curiosity I moved toward the Living Portal until I was standing within it, able to see inside …

This structure, it hardly need be said, was a representation of the Most Holy Place, and the last sentence above clearly indicates that, in response to the invitation to enter, I moved to the point of standing within – not outside – the living entranceway. *There was no veil blocking access* because Jesus had, on behalf of all of us – the entire Sonship – dispelled that veil and set in its place an open door that no man can shut.

It appeared to be a single room; all the walls were white, as on the outside. However, it was not the structure that caught my attention but the occupant. It was Papa. His appearance was just as I had seen Him when He told me the Keys to the Kingdom lie not in answers but in faith, trust, obedience and commitment (May 5, 1996) … He stood about two or three paces into the room from the entranceway. His countenance was filled with unutterable, ineffable joy, and His smile radiated that joy and Love toward me. His joy was so great that He could not speak. Instead, with body movements He welcomed me, bade me enter, by a slight bowing, a gesture of the arms and taking a small step backwards. I felt that His joy was as the joy of the father in Jesus' parable of the prodigal son, who watched every day for his son and when he saw him returning 'a great way off', ran to meet him and 'fell on his neck and kissed him …'.

I entered, as He had invited …

The whole point – that will serve us immeasurably well to keep uppermost in our mind during our journey Home from this 'far country' – is that there *is* no veil, no screen onto which dark images are, or can be, projected; no obstacles, deterrents or hindrances to reaching our Destination, other than those we have made up, and which *seem* to exist only in our misperceiving mind. Being misperceptions, they *have* no reality. I had, somehow, ludicrously, been confused by seeing that veil, thinking that surely, Papa would remove it and *then* I could enter the Most Holy Place, the Holy of Holies.

But how could He remove what was not there? Not even *we* have to remove it. All we need is to *remember it is not there* and it will cease to have any presence to our awareness. And as we enter in we will remember that we are but One, and that Papa's Son never left his Home in his Father. Then will there be much rejoicing. We need not wait. It is NOW. The Holy Place is our heart. Let us, with Jesus' help, shine away the veil – open the door – that seems to separate us from the Most Holy Place – Papa's Heart – and enter in, there to be greeted, welcomed by the Holy One.

Diary of a Christ Communicant

A.M. September 20, 2010

> **'Dying' is of bodies, which are not real because they are not eternal; thus can they neither live nor die, because they are nothing. So the dream continues beyond 'death', because the very act of 'dying' demonstrates dreaming, rather than waking to reality.**

Some believe that when we 'die' we go to Heaven (or hell!). But we can only 'go' to Heaven by *waking up* to the fact that we are *already* there. So, let us consider what happens when we 'die'.

Effectively, nothing, since 'dying' is part of the dream of unreality. 'Dying' is of bodies, which are not real because they are not eternal; thus can they neither live *nor* 'die', because they are nothing. So the dream continues beyond 'death', because the very act of 'dying' demonstrates dreaming, rather than waking to reality. But waking to reality is the realisation, the remembrance, that there *is* no hereafter; there is only NOW, *forever*.

Grieving when a loved one 'dies' is prolonging the dream because it is holding a *grievance* against the dream. And because the dream, and all its aspects, including 'dying', is unreal – and therefore, nothing – so does grieving make nothing real, thus *perpetuating* unreality; the dream of separation.

So, the waking process can be greatly helped by recognising the unreality of 'dying' by continuing in loving mind-to-mind communion with the 'deceased' person. This, it hardly need be said, is because relationships are mind-to-mind, since mind is real and eternal; bodies are not. Oneness is a mind thing, not a body thing.

Just as each soul creates his own 'reality' while with a body, so does this continue after laying aside his body at the event mistakenly called 'dying'. The 'reality' for the 'afterlife' is constructed here, now, daily, week after week, year after year. That construction is worthy, is it not, of care and consideration?

12: Karmic Tug of War

*My son, it is the Light of God's Love, given to me for the
redemption of His little ones, that reveals the path before you. It
is a new path for Earth-mind man, never before trodden in the
valley of the shadow of death, for it is the New Way, by which the
children of Earth return to their heavenly Father.*

–Jesus, September 6, 1992

BECAUSE WE CHOSE TO MAKE-UP the veil of apparent separation
from Papa, we can equally *un*-make it, simply by deciding it is
no longer our choice. We do this by choosing, instead, to remember
and experience that we are the Light, just as Papa created us, His
Son. When we accept that we both *are* and *have* the Light we can
allow the Light of eternal Love, Life and Truth to shine *unveiled* –
just like Jesus – for our brothers. This we can do by forgiving any
and all conflict – however *seemingly* major or minor – we thought
existed between us, and blessing all with the Love, Peace and Joy
that we desire for ourself.

For that Love, Peace and Joy cannot be ours *alone*. Alone means
separate from others. That does not mean alone or separate *bodily*.
Aloneness or separation – from Papa, Jesus and all our brothers in
the Sonship – exists only as an illusion, a false idea, in our *mind*,
and it is there, and only there, that we can choose to rejoin with
ALL. That may seem hard, even 'impossible', but it is actually
very easy because that is our natural, eternal, unchanging and

unchangeable estate. Separation is *unnatural* and is difficult and painful to maintain. Since neither Papa nor Jesus (now) are bodies, clearly union is not about bodies.

We all have loved-ones who have laid aside their bodies, yet of whom we have fond and loving memories. Memories are in the mind, but seem to be of the *past*, yet we can bring to mind those loved-ones also in the *present*, if we so desire, for they *are* with us in the present. To say 'they are dead and gone' is meaningless; an ego idea to prolong the sense of loneliness, abandonment and separation. In 1968 Jesus told me, "*I am attuned to all mankind all the time; there is never a moment when I am not with you all. All that is needed to complete the contact is for you to attune with me and we are together, at any time.*"

The underlined sentence applies to us all, with and for all, for there is no difference between us and Jesus, other than in our perception. It is a *mis*perception, which we can correct by choosing to perceive truly. This is entirely possible and simple, for such is the power of the mind of Papa's Son. Most of us are not yet ready to be '*attuned* to all mankind all the time' – there is still some leavening to occur! But only *we* are stopping ourself from accepting that mind-to-mind communing – in the present, the here and now – is entirely practicable. Many experience this already. We call them 'sensitives'.

Such are not special; they simply *accept* the gift that is freely available to us all. There is no danger to this if we place ourself under Christ care, guidance and protection, allowing Him to fulfil our heart's desire for Loving communion and wholeness – i.e., Oneness – *for* us. If we believe we can accomplish this without Him we are likely to be disappointed at best and exposing ourselves to unenlightened souls in the lower-astral planes at worst. And since the reunion – i.e., restoration to Oneness – of the mind of the fragmented Sonship is the purpose of the Great Rescue Programme, there is no time like the present for us to practise; for eternity is *now*, not when we are 'dead'!

By choosing to forgive, Love and bless our self and our brothers we are co-operating with our Holy Spirit-Self in removing – shining away – the veil of littleness and limitation we have *imagined* we placed over our vision, our mind, restricting it to perception of illusions: bodies, including 'our own', that come and are gone in a fleeting moment. By choosing anew, we start the journey without distance back to *awareness, remembrance* of where we belong, where we already are, have always been and could never not be – in the Heart of Papa; the Source of All Love, with Which we are equally One, and equally empowered. Can continuing to pretend otherwise be other than a futile ploy of ego to avert the inevitable?

When a brother is deep in the illusion of fear and attack/defence, trying to talk him out of it will not, *cannot*, work if he is not *ready* to see/choose the Light in place of the illusion he perceives. When he is able to see *past* illusion, then is he close to remembering that inner Peace – the goal of us all – comes only through the open door of defencelessness, not the barrier to Its Way that is defence/attack. When we accept our function of forgiving, Loving, blessing we are automatically, spontaneously released from any karmic entanglement we may have perceived bound us in enmity to our brother. Then are we *both* free.

If we are in a 'karmic tug of war' with our brother and *we* let go the rope – by forgiving him and ourself for what, in *reality*, neither of us has ever done – we have immediately released both ourself *and* our brother from the conflict. This is so even if he *appears* not to immediately let go his end of the rope. This is of no consequence because when *we* let it go, the rope ceases to have any reality for *us*, so we are no longer bound to him in what formerly appeared to be a karmic entanglement. Our continuing to Love and bless that brother provides the power, *releases* the power – for such is the power of the mind of Papa's Son – to enable the Holy Spirit to work His works for delivering release and freedom to the mind of that brother.

Not only must we *let go* the rope; we must *disentangle* ourself from it. The rope symbolises the dream of *time*, for only in time are we not at-One with our brother. Our purpose is to join with the dreamer, *never with the dream*, and by Loving and blessing him in and for remembrance of Who he *really* is – outside time – we help release him from the dream of time. And by so doing are we, ourself, released. If we concern ourself with time – '*when* will the healing/rejoining happen?' – we leave the door open to anxiety. Omitting time from our considerations of the healing, Atonement process dispels such blocks to our experience of inner peace.

Forgiveness, Loving and blessing are our only functions in healing broken relationships. All the rest is the Holy Spirit's job, *performed outside time*. How could He include illusion (time) in reality (eternity, wholeness, Oneness) and have it remain reality? It matters not whether our brother remembers the Oneness of our relationship this year, or next, or before he lays aside his illusory body – or we, ours. For Oneness is an aspect of eternity, not of time and place, though we *can* experience it *in* time and place. But all the while we make time a feature in our desire for healing we are trying to bring Truth to illusion, rather than bringing our illusions to the Truth.

Jesus brings this into a broader perspective thusly:

> God turns to you to ask the world be saved, for by your own salvation [i.e., Awakening] is it healed. And no one walks upon the earth but must depend on your decision, that he learn death has no power over him, because he shares your freedom as he shares your will. It *is* your will to heal him, and because you have decided with him, he is healed. And now is God forgiven, <u>for you chose to look upon your brother as a friend</u> (*ACIM*, Chapter 30, p. 630, II. 5).

We may wonder what Papa has done to warrant forgiveness. This can only seem so in recognition that His Son is an indivisible part, or aspect of Him, so in that sense, forgiveness of His Son (by His Son) means the Father also is forgiven. However, it suffices us to know (and rejoice!) that by forgiving, Loving and blessing our brother we are released from the self-made, illusory impediments to seeing him as our friend. Thus is our purpose fulfilled as the

Light *and* the saviour of the world. Anything less than this keeps us separate from our brother, our true Self and Papa, thus continuing to bind us to the carousel of birth and death.

Diary of a Christ Communicant

A.M. August 14, 2010

Reality is NOW, and that which is not as IT is cannot be Now. It is, illusorily speaking, 'in the past', hoping, wishing for things to be better 'in the future', and therefore continually playing it out, like watching a film that was made in the past projected onto a screen.

According to Jesus in *A Course in Miracles*, the Son of God – Christ, Which is not 'just' Jesus, the man, because Papa's Son is pure, eternal Spirit, just like his Father – had a 'mad, momentary thought' of wondering what it would be like to experience things not being what they are. What they *are* is Heaven, eternity, perfect Love, Peace, Joy; wanting for nothing because at his creation by his Father, Papa gave, shared, extended to him all that his Father *Is*.

In the moment of wishing to experience other, what we call the Big Bang occurred and the separation of the Son from his Father in eternity *seemed* to begin. The Singularity appeared to end and fragmentation, separation, duality began to be the experience of the Son. The unending ecstasy of Oneness in Heaven seemed to disappear from his awareness as his momentary thought appeared to come about. This could present itself only as the seeming opposite, or reversal, of Reality, otherwise it would not be different.

Linear time, instead of the eternal moment of Now, appeared; changelessness was lost to awareness in exchange for change and instability; certainty became doubt; Love, fear. As stated in NTI[1]:

'If this is the experience you have asked to receive, why do you suffer from it? Because you have *asked* to suffer by asking not to experience Heaven.'

But this not only *did* not happen in *reality*; it *could* not happen in reality. The momentary thought was over the same instant it happened. So why are we *still* experiencing it?

Because Reality is NOW, and that which is not as IT is *cannot* be Now. It is, illusorily speaking, 'in the past', hoping, wishing for things to be better 'in the future', and therefore continually playing it out, like watching a film that was made in the past projected onto a screen. But that which is past can never be better in the future because neither past nor future exist in Reality. The events being projected look as if they are happening as they are being projected, but were only ever a dream, a script, acted out; never real.

---

1. NTI: *The Holy Spirit's Interpretation of the New Testament*, ©2008, Regina Dawn Akers, (O Books, UK, Publisher).p.313: 2 Corinthians, chapter 5.

13: Entering-in to the Real World

*My son, we go forward by the outpouring of Love and compassion
and healing upon all the Father's little ones – all who will receive.
Freely have you received of this blessing; freely give to all who will
receive it.*

–*Jesus,* September 27, 1992

SHARED HERE IS A QUESTION raised from a recent *Message of
Encouragement* on page 61 of Chapter 9 of this book, with the
reply I was prompted to give:

Hi Brian,

Your *Message of Encouragement* about the parable of the ten virgins
[Mt. 25] sure cast some light on what's going on in the GRP [Great
Rescue Programme]. Boy, Jesus really knew the big picture, even
'back then', 2,000 years ago. However, I have some concerns still,
and this leaves me hanging, uncertain of the final outcome.

The parable says 'and the door was shut', and your explanation
of what that *actually* means is a real eye-opener for me! But I
couldn't tell what this means for those 'foolish virgins' who had
shut themselves out from the consummation of the marriage of
Heaven with Earth. The Church has Jesus speaking of judgement
and those found wanting being condemned and cast into hell …
That suggests billions burning; not exactly in harmony with the

Jesus who said he had not come to judge the world, but to save the world!

So, what is your take on this? Do we ALL get saved and restored to Oneness, or is this to be only the *wise* virgins? In other words, are billions of fragments to be left out of the Kingdom? That doesn't sound much like an *unconditionally*-Loving God.

Thanks, Brian, in anticipation, and for your insights into these arcane matters.

Peace, Alex

Hi Alex,

Yes, Jesus surely *did Know* the big picture back then. In fact he knew it many thousands of years before that. How else could he have organised, initiated and preside over, the Great Rescue Programme?

I realised I had not covered this crucial question you have so observantly raised, but the *Message of Encouragement* was already two thousand words and I know many are busy and don't have time to read long messages (though of course, we all 'make time' for what interests us). The news is all good in regard to your question. Would we expect anything less from our ALL-Loving Papa and His all-Loving anointed messenger? Let me explain:

The consummation, or completion of the marriage of Heaven and Earth, is, in linear-time terms, a two-thousand-year period: the third measure of meal, or *Kingdom* (Aquarian) Age. Jesus is a pragmatist, and *Knew* that he had to function – could *only* function – within the inviolable Law, or Principle of Life of the Father, of the free will given by Papa to His beloved Son (all of us) at his creation. He therefore also *Knew*, within the context of the dream of being what we are not, it would take time for his brethren to accept the Truth, when they had believed a lie since the dawn of time.

One might refer to this, the third measure of meal, as the Honeymoon; two thousand years could hardly be mistaken for a one-night stand!

It is crucial to the meaningful interpretation of this parable, that we understand that the bride is the entire, *seemingly* fragmented

Sonship. This means that, even though the five foolish virgins were left without – and had in effect shut the door against their own entry – Jesus, the bridegroom, and the aspect, or portion, of the bride that had entered with the groom have no desire or intent to leave the other aspect of the Sonship (symbolised by the foolish virgins) without, or 'in outer darkness'.

The fulfilment, or leavening, of the third measure of meal, being the two-thousand-year Aquarian Age, gives the fragmented Sonship plenty of 'time' to waken to remembrance of Oneness and *join the nuptials*. These nuptials are ecstasy beyond all Earth-mind comprehension, or Earth-body experience.

During this two thousand years – of which we are now advancing well in the early stages – those 'foolish virgins' who shut themselves out, or chose not to join the honeymoon, will undergo numerous embodiment events (reincarnations), which, of course, also entails the period of reflection in the etheric counterpart of Earth *between* embodiments. During those cycles of birth and death they will be presented with multitudinous opportunities to hear the Truth of who we all *really* are, and when the moment is right for each individual fragment, their Awakening will happen; it is inevitable because in reality it has *already* happened.

If linear time were to appear to progress as it has been perceived to have progressed in the illusory past, many might observe that two thousand years will not be anywhere near long enough to awaken the fragments who have hardened their hearts and closed their minds to the mystical reality (perfect, unconditional Love) of eternity. But as the leavening progresses, and signs, wonders and miracles accelerate and abound in number and frequency, even the hardest of hearts, most plugged of ears and veiled of sight will find it increasingly difficult to ignore events unfolding before them.

Then will the door open for them *by their own desire to enter in*, just as it closed – or, more meaningfully, *seemed* to close, because in reality there *is* no door – by their own choice *not* to enter. Let none of us be mistaken: our only judgement and condemnation is of and by ourselves, *never* by Papa, Who knows nothing of our game of pretend; only of Reality.

This, Jesus describes in *A Course in Miracles* as the collapsing of time, effected by miracles – particularly the miracle of Atonement. Miracles can be performed by all who, attuning their minds and lives to Jesus and/or the Holy Spirit, become *miracle-minded*, and thus, *miracle-ready*. Miracles are already taking place every moment of every day, but the constructs, or servants, of ego – mainstream broadcast and printed media, guilt-, fear- and judgement-based religions, the mammon of unrighteousness (see Lk. 16), halls of intellectual learning, etc. – try very hard to ignore all such, and will continue so to do for as long as possible.

But this is like trying to hold back the tide. That which is the Will of God – Truth – cannot be hidden indefinitely, and *will* out. As I was told on August 25, 1991:

> Little ones: In these times the confusion is greatest as the old order crumbles and Earth-mind man reels to and fro. The energies are concentrated at all levels and intensified as the programme focuses upon the 'final assault' on antiChrist. Fear not, it is not a 'full frontal' assault as in warfare of Earth, but an infiltration of energy as cracks appear in the system – and believe me, there are plenty of those. The energy shall thus gain entry and transform from *within*. It is like cancer in reverse. The system shall not be aware of its defences being 'breached' and shall continue as traditionally. But changes will begin to happen from within, and great surprise and wonderment shall come upon the inhabitants of the citadel.[1]
>
> New awareness shall be the order of the day. This is real, tangible, transforming activity. Be aware of the *new* energy – take no notice of the *old*; it shall be astonishing, but let not your equilibrium be disturbed by it ...

In the reality of eternity, the illusion of separation is not simply *already* over; it never even happened, so we can safely concur with repeated assurances given me from the Realms of Light, that 'the Great Rescue Programme is both infallible and unstoppable'. And it encompasses us all, without exception. How could there be exceptions, when that would mean completion was not complete? Can Papa and His Son be incomplete?

Diary of a Christ Communicant

A.M. August 19, 2010

When you return judgement and attack with forgiveness and blessings of Peace and Love, so is the downward, destructive spiral broken, and ascent toward the Light is engendered in its place, until all the shadows of grievance and judgement are shone away by the Light.

It is easy to observe that in time and place history repeats itself.

This is because the misperceiving mind of humanity keeps reflecting back to itself that which it keeps projecting out. All the while it keeps projecting out thoughts of guilt, judgement, grievance and conflict, so will it keep reflecting back from the screen, which comprises bodies and the world/universe at large. The saying 'What goes around comes around' is *literally* true.

When thoughts of forgiveness, Love, Peace, Joy and blessing are extended to your brothers, that, of a certainty beyond all doubt, is what will, inevitably, be reflected back to you, amplified each time it comes around. This is because blessings of forgiveness, Love, Peace and Joy can but *increase* with the giving. This is the nature of Creation, for It is of Papa, the Creator Spirit, Who is forever increasing through the Creation process.

When you realign yourself with Him you become *aware* of your true Self, the Christ, who is created – by extension, by increase – in the likeness of the Father Creator. If you return judgement, grievance, condemnation and attack like for like, so is the condition continued, spiralling toward oblivion. Such is the power of the mind of the Son of God to make illusions seem real.

Yet, when you return judgement and attack with forgiveness and blessings of Peace and Love, steadfastly refusing to continue the downward, destructive spiral, so is it broken, and an upward ascent toward the Light of eternal reality – Heaven, your true and only Home – is engendered in its place, growing and increasing at each and every blessing, until all the shadows of grievance and judgement are shone away by the Light.

It does not matter how long the effects of ending the cycle *seem* to take outwardly, for the *actual* end is always immediate, *according to the desire*. Time is an illusion, so is irrelevant; a deception, best ignored because giving it your attention makes it your reality. Rather, remember that *only infinite patience produces immediate effects* [*ACIM* Chapter 5, p.88, VI.12:1].

When the moment is right, according to the all-*Knowing*, all-empowered, all-beneficent Holy Self, that which you have expressed to end the cycle will be reflected back to you from your brother. Broken relationships will be healed, restored to wholeness, Oneness in Christ, the Son of the Father Creator.

---

1. This refers to the 'citadel' of ego-minded thinking and its recalcitrant ways in the Earth.

14: Identity Discernment

*Turn within and hold fast, my son, to that which you have
received, that which you Know, that which is new, that which is
alive, that which grows; the new order of enlightened Being and
living, for it is restoring, Life-giving, uplifting and renewing to the
souls of all who will receive of it.*

–*Jesus,* October 18, 1992

THIS CHAPTER IS ALSO PROMPTED by a perceptive enquiry about where illusion ends and reality begins, and the reply that arose from within me:

Dear Brian,

Please help my understanding. In your book [*"Seek ye First the Kingdom..."*], and often in your *Messages of Encouragement*, you speak of seeing Jesus and others from the Realms of Light. In fact, in a couple of places in your book you even describe Papa as if He were in human form, a 'fatherly figure'. It is clear from your descriptions that your discernment of them is as bodies, even though Jesus tells us in *A Course in Miracles* that we are not a body. This must be particularly true at all levels of perception of those who have laid aside their Earth body. So, are not your encounters somehow mistaken? Don't get me wrong; I love hearing of your experiences and find them inspiring, wishing I could have awareness of my loved ones in spirit, but this ambiguity seems to be holding me back, with part of me wanting to believe, but another part finding it contradictory, and blocking my acceptance.

Bless you, Brian, and thank you for your help,

Anita

Dear Anita,

This is, perhaps, a question many may ponder, so thank you for providing the opportunity to explain.

Indeed, Jesus is right (it will come as no surprise to hear!), we are not a body, and when we are fully Awake to the reality of our eternal Being, bodies will – if we are willing to take his word for it – definitely cease to be part of the awareness of Papa's Son. So, perceiving ourself, Jesus and any or all our brothers in the illusorily-fragmented Sonship as bodies is, assuredly, a misperception. However, this is an *interim* perception as we journey toward wakefulness, and will not last. It will, inevitably, change – *is* changing – as our remembrance of the Truth grows with the *leavening* of the third measure of meal.

Papa's Son has believed a lie for so long that to an upside-down, split mind it *seems* like the Truth. So, perceiving bodies is the only way we can have awareness of a brother – including Jesus – at this stage in the leavening process. The separation into myriad fragments, perceived as bodies, symbolises our self-deception. As the deception fades from our belief, so does – or will – the misperception become replaced with *true vision*, via the interim stage of true *perception* . True vision is of the soul and is nothing to do with our ocular faculty, which is capable of perception only between limited, illusory frequencies of vibration.

Our brethren who have laid aside their body vibrate at a higher-than-physical frequency, so the limited, ocular faculty of embodied souls is unable to see them. What, then, is one seeing when one experiences awareness of disembodied souls, and with what faculty does one have such awareness? When we lay aside our Earth-life body, and for an indeterminate period thereafter, depending on our degree of wakefulness, we retain that sense of persona-self, not yet having fully remembered who we really are –

our unified, true Identity as Papa's One and only Son.

This appears as a less dense, etheric-substance equivalent of our physical body, and is discernible to our *soul* awareness. Although we all have the potential for this soul-sight, it lies dormant in most embodied souls due to fear causing unbelief, and the unbelief veils our sight. It is not just in *appearance* that a persona is discernible. Each of us radiates, emits, a signature auric colour and an aroma, or personal scent, though sight is the most common factor in recognising a disembodied soul.

The difference between Jesus and most other disembodied but not yet fully spiritually Awake souls is that he is in *complete control* of how he presents himself to us, and that will always accord with the degree of readiness of him to whom he is presenting himself, and the circumstances of the presentation. Most others, not yet having moved fully beyond perceiving themselves as a persona/body, retain an etheric counterpart of their Earth-life body, and it is with our soul-sense that we have awareness of such. This obviates any uncertainty regarding identity.

Jesus knows this, so he simply takes advantage of that and shows himself in like manner, though he is equally able to show himself in a much more exalted state than that – as described in chapter two of *"Seek ye First the Kingdom..."* – because he is *beyond* limitation. He shows himself to us in bodily representation because we, as yet, are *not* beyond limitation.

Desiring the Oneness of the Sonship will lead to the dispelling of the illusion of bodies by restoring the fragmented Son (us) from perception of the without – time and place, which passes away – as 'temporal reality', to remembrance and awareness of eternal reality within. This is a state of mind, which has no physicality but is purely abstract, in which nothing 'out there' means anything because in the Oneness the without is *Known* not to exist.

This may seem impossible, meaningless to a broken, fragmented, split mind that sees everything upside down, distorted. But when we think and see as Jesus thinks and sees, and thus become like him, (1 Jn. 3:2) then will the brokenness be healed and restored to Oneness. There will be, can only be, one true perspective, and that is the *recognition* of eternal reality, in which the Son is like His Father: One, whole, complete, forever. The fragmented mind perceives only ever-changing, ever-decaying differences; the healed, re-unified mind sees only the unchangeable, everlasting *perfection* of sameness. Oneness cannot be Oneness without sameness!

Differences are made up; destined to disappear in the Light of Truth *because* they are not true. The Light that we are, which is Love (like Father, like Son) shines away the fleeting, shadowy perceptions – which are merely projections of what we are *not* – and unveils the eternal reality of Oneness, in which it will be seen, again, that there are not, and never were, bodies. This can happen only within a mind *willing* to be healed, restored to wholeness – and thus, holiness – from its fragmented state. This cannot happen without first desire and then a willingness to believe.

That willingness enables it to be easily accomplished *for* us by our Holy Spirit-Self because willingness sets aside, dispels the ego's *resistance* that masquerades as our own mind, causing us to fear the Truth. It also, vitally, authorises Him to act on our behalf. This will happen when we, individually, are *ready*, for this is not an exercise of the intellect (an ego device to keep us confused, doubting, questioning), nor is it a physical, chemical or biological process; it is a mystical one. The realm of the mystical can only be fully entered through the portal of faith and trust; a willingness to believe that only eternity *can* be real, and thus the temporal *must* be unreal.

It is our *unbelief* that denies us freedom of entry into this realm, which belongs to eternity – our true and only Home – not to time and place. It is a free gift, available to us *all* always, every moment, every instant; but attainable only when we can accept that instant as holy, unable to be misused by expediency motive. Spiritual humility is the key to this aperture; accessible to us by our willingness to surrender our Earth-mind, ego leasehold on life back to its rightful freeholder, which is Christ, our true Being, and accept His leading us in absolute trust. This is entirely safe because

He is entirely trust*worthy*.

Jesus said he would remain with us until the end of the world (Mt. 28:20). In our as yet unhealed state of mind we could not have awareness of him unless he represented himself in a way, a form that we can recognise as him. *He* is not limited by *our* limitations of perception – thanks be to Papa – but we limit ourself, for the moment, by being able only to perceive him, all our other brothers (embodied or disembodied, it makes no difference) and ourself as individual personas.

That does not mean that is what we *are*, and when our Awakening is complete we will *Know*, and be integral aspects of, the entire Sonship as One, whole, undivided, perfect Being; Papa's beloved Son, exactly like his Father.

Diary of a Christ Communicant

A.M. August 30, 2010

**The illusion of time and place seems to be reality to
the children of Earth-mind consciousness because they
value it. When they arrive at the position where nothing
of time and place holds any value for them, they are
Awake to the glory and grandeur of What they
really are.**

The illusion of time and place seems to be reality to the children of Earth-mind consciousness because they value it. When they arrive at the position where nothing of time and place holds any value for them, they are Awake to the glory and grandeur of What they really are. They are the Light because they all are Papa's Son. Papa is the Source of Light and He created His Son in His own likeness.

As well you Know, this Light, *the* Light, is infinite; eternal. It is nothing to do with nuclear fusion in solar bodies, all of which are finite; temporal; without. The Light that you all are shines, inextinguishably, *within*, where lies reality. It cannot shine in the without because It is real and the without is unreal. For It to shine in the without would make the Light unreal, or part of the illusion; bringing Truth to illusion, which you Know is impossible.

Seek, therefore, *within* for the Light that you are, for only there is It to be found. Just as Jesus told you two thousand years ago. Now is the moment, the leavening of the third measure of meal, by which ALL is leavened so that all might believe it, and believing, shall *see* It. Then shall it become reality for all the self-limiting fragments, that all become as One again.

15: On Grace

Measure not the success of your progress in worldly goods or terms, my son, but rather in the treasure you are storing up in eternal value. For it is here that you are called to serve. Your needs for the Earth-life path shall be provided as you have requirement.

–Jesus, October 25, 1992

E ACH WEEK I ASK THE SPIRIT OF TRUTH for inspiration on a subject for a *Message of Encouragement.* And so, I have been prompted to write on the matter of Grace. Yet part of me rather shrinks from this, for I feel it is a word that describes a state or quality of Papa for which I *intuitively* have a feeling of understanding, and yet struggle for words to describe it. Nevertheless, I have written before on subjects that I felt unable to cover without His inspiring Help, only to find ideas emerging through my keyboard of which I had no previous understanding. So, I resolve to proceed, in trust, with this.

Here are my starting thoughts, in no particular order, but how they come to me as I focus upon it:

Grace means no sacrifice is asked or required by Papa because His Son has *not* 'sinned'. The question of sacrifice simply does not arise, because he, being created exactly like his Father, is no more capable of sin than is his Father Creator. Rather, he is merely *mistaken* because he has interpreted a foolish *dream* as reality, and made up the idea that dreaming of errors that are entirely alien to his true Being are sins, known to God, Who will punish His Son because He hates sin. How can He, Who is but Love, hate? This is impossible. How can He, Who is the Source of Grace, require sacrifice? Believing this can only be madness.

Grace must be that from which forgiveness is born, for by forgiveness are we restored to *awareness* of the grace that is ours. It *must* be ours because, being the Father's, it would be meaningless if He *withheld* it from His Son. Grace is a quality, or aspect of Papa that is ours also because He gave us *everything* at our creation. Grace and forgiveness are adjuncts to each other. Grace encompasses acceptance and inclusion, knowing nothing of judgement or condemnation, of separation or guilt, of sin or death, for grace is the pathway by which we are awakened, from a dream of death, to Life.

Grace *appears* to be absent from, unavailable to, a mind that believes it is separate, lost, lonely, guilty, conflicted, yet it is forever with us regardless of our state of mind or apparent circumstance. It is ours for the asking and *by* asking is *instantly* given – restored – to a heart-mind willing to receive and accept remembrance of it. But we must express it, extend it, share it in order to be aware of it and *Know* it is ours. We are free to engage grace when our brother *seems* to attack us, for grace restores us to true perception, enabling us to see he was merely mistaken, and had neither sinned nor attacked. For, being like his Father, he is capable of neither.

Language, being of time and place, is devised for describing unreality. Therefore it is, perhaps, easier to describe what grace is not rather than what it is, for in grace there is no cruelty, grievance, judgement, conflict, condemnation, punishment, retribution ... Papa's Love and Grace endure forever, for if Love did not endure forever, grace could not be grace, and Papa never changes His Mind, so He is NEVER going to judge or punish His Son, or require sacrifice of him – including, of course, Jesus. Grace is an attribute that unforgiveness keeps from our experience, but is restored to our awareness *by* forgiveness.

Since Jesus is so much more able to describe and convey

meaning to the qualities that are of our Father than by one who still journeys toward true, perfect vision, let us include here some of his wisdom on the matter in these extracts from the *ACIM* Workbook for Students, Lesson 168 on page 321, and Lesson 169 on page 323:

Your grace is given me. I claim it now. [Lesson 168]

God speaks to us. Shall we not speak to Him? He is not distant. He makes no attempt to hide from us. We try to hide from Him, and suffer from deception. He remains entirely accessible [even while we dream we are in hell]. *He loves His Son. There is no certainty but this, yet this suffices* [is not *that* grace?]…

… His grace His answer is to all despair, for in it lies remembrance of His Love … His grace is yours <u>by your acknowledgment</u> …

Today we ask of God the gift He has most carefully preserved within our hearts, waiting to be acknowledged. This the gift by which God leans to us and lifts us up, taking salvation's final step Himself … He comes Himself, and takes us in His Arms and sweeps away the cobwebs of our sleep. *His gift of grace is more than just an answer.* It restores all memories the sleeping mind forgot; all certainty of what Love's meaning is.

God loves His Son. Request Him now to give the means by which this world will disappear, and vision first will come, with knowledge but an instant later. For <u>in grace you see a light that covers all the world in love, and watch fear disappear from every face as hearts rise up and claim the light as theirs</u>. What now remains that Heaven be delayed an instant longer? What is still undone when your forgiveness rests on everything?

It is a new and holy day today, for we receive what has been given us… We acknowledge our mistakes [as distinct from sins], but He to Whom all error is unknown is yet the

One Who answers our mistakes by giving us the means to lay them down, and rise to Him in gratitude and love.

... To Him we pray today, returning but the word He gave to us through His Own Voice, His Word, His Love:
Your grace is given me. I claim it now. Father, I come to You. And You will come to me who ask. I am the Son You love.

By grace I live. By grace I am released. [Lesson 169]

Grace is an aspect of the Love of God ... It is the world's most lofty aspiration, for it leads beyond the world entirely ... Grace becomes inevitable instantly in those who have prepared a table where it can be gently laid and willingly received; an altar clean and holy for the gift [cleansed by laying aside judgement in favour of forgiveness].

Grace is acceptance of the Love of God within a world of seeming hate and fear. By grace alone the hate and fear are gone, for grace presents a state so opposite to everything the world contains, that those whose minds are lighted by the gift of grace can not believe the world of fear is real...

... And now we ask for grace, the final gift salvation can bestow ...

> By grace I live. By grace I am released.
> By grace I give. By grace I will release.

Do not these words of Jesus indicate the importance he attaches to grace? If it is important to him, how could it be unimportant to us? Love and endless blessings be with us all, for the remembrance, acceptance and extending of grace.

Diary of a Christ Communicant

A.M. September 3, 2010

Peace is available only from within the Now. Peace cannot exist in time because time is unreal and Peace, as a quality of Love, is real. *Now* and *time* are mutually exclusive, as are peace and fear. Time is the consciousness of fear.

Truth is NOW; illusions are of linear time. Living in awareness of *Now*, allowing, accepting, surrendering ego-controlled resistance enables Truth to become, again, *our* eternal Truth, and the Holy Instant becomes *our* reality because we have attuned our mind to its frequency instead of time and place.

Time is the ultimate illusion, or unreality, and is the symbol of belief in separation from Truth, from the eternal *Now*. Peace is available only from within the Now. Peace cannot exist in time because time is unreal and Peace, as a quality of Love, is real. Now and time are mutually exclusive, as are peace and fear. Time is the consciousness of fear. It is possible to think, speak and write about the holy instant and inner peace indefinitely, but they can only become reality by *desiring* them above all things, committing to them absolutely, and surrendering all else into the trustworthiness of the Spirit of Truth.

The world is a *manifestation* of time. It is 'place', and goes inextricably with time.

In the holy instant of *experiencing* eternal reality, Truth and Self become One. This is the Being of One-Self that is the 'real-isation' of *Who* one really Is, which is the all-inclusive Oneness that is God. Truth is not just *of* eternity; it *is* eternity, which is Now. Jesus said he was the Truth (and the Way and the Life) along with all who yet perceive themselves as separate from Truth, but *are* of eternity because all are Papa's Son, just *like* Him.

Truth and Knowing are hand-in-glove. Jesus said that abiding by his teaching the Truth is Known, and by living it the imprisoned are made free [Jn. 8:31,32]. By choosing, being willing, to *Know* the Truth, the sight is unveiled, revealing the freedom that has always been there for all to see. This *Knowing* is the Truth, for that is all there *is* to Know. It does not require learning, researching, testing, proving, acquiring; for it is already within all, not 'out there'. It simply requires the *choice*, above all, to remember it.

16: Opening to Greater Awareness of Brotherhood

As you go forward from this place so shall your singleness of vision increase and draw the earthly sight into Oneness with it so that the two gradually become one vision. As this happens so shall your understanding and awareness of the realities of the Father's creation increase.

–Jesus, November 1, 1992

THERE ARE, ON THE INTERNET, untold numbers of sites claiming 'Conversations with Jesus' (and, in some cases, Buddha). Some of these sites are spoofs, some malicious, some inauthentic but I can attest to the bona fide nature of others. I recall reading some a few years ago on a website entitled *Blue Dog Bob* (now untraceable by my Google search), administered by one named Mike.

In one particular reported conversation, Jesus told Mike that we, who perceive ourselves as embodied, are receiving devoted care, guidance and protection unceasingly from three billion helpers in the etheric envelope of Earth. From my own experiences of contact with the etheric realms, there are, also, still unenlightened – or only *dimly* lit – populated mansions in Papa's House. How can it be otherwise when each year millions lay aside their body while still in a spiritually unilluminated state of mind?

Either way, within the context of the dream of separation from Papa, there are vast numbers of our brothers-in-the-Sonship in a disembodied state. There are two valid reasons for us to acknowledge this: Firstly, gratitude to, and closer co-operation with, those devoted to caring for, guiding and protecting us, not 'just' in terms of our spiritual awakening; their very palpable, practical help keeping us safe from misfortune (e.g. 'accident', assault, burglary – being in the wrong place at the wrong time); inspiring us with beneficial ideas about mindfulness and lifestyle, clues for improving our nutrition, and more.

Who would not want to take greater advantage of all this if they knew just how *easy* it is to access it? Simply ASK, *being willing to believe*; open oneself to it, allow it, accept it; relinquish, *repudiate* the ego perception that we are alone, without help, destined to suffer and die. That perception can only keep us enslaved to, imprisoned on, the carousel of birth and death; preventing us from being restored to the *limitlessness* of our Power and the eternalness of our true, radiant Being.

The second, and equally important, reason is that none of us can be restored to eternal Joy in Papa unless and until *all* the fragments of the illusorily-broken Sonship are returned to wholeness – i.e., Oneness. It is only by the *rejoining* to conscious Oneness, of *all* the fragments that the Sonship – of which we are each an intrinsic part – is healed, i.e., brought back to wholeness. Papa has but *One*, eternal, perfect, all-*Knowing*, all-empowered Son, not myriad, disparate, warring, bewildered, mortal sons.

When all those disparate, warring, mortal, fragmented sons are rejoined, the Sonship will be healed, whole, One – the Christ – again. There are, and can be, no exceptions, none excluded, because in eternity, Heaven, there is only *in*clusion. How, otherwise could Heaven be complete? The healing of the Sonship – embodied *and* disembodied – is happening right Now.

It would serve us all and thus, the Great Rescue Programme (GRP), well to be more aware of our brothers in spirit – including, of course, Jesus. This would enable us more readily to co-operate with them in the healing – ours and theirs. Jesus is said to 'preside' over the GRP but he is not outworking it on his own! In fact, we who perceive ourselves as embodied are all – right along with our disembodied brothers – *integral* aspects *of* and contributors *to* the GRP; even those of us who have never heard of it, do not understand it and know nothing of it; even those in blind denial or rejection of it.

In a few, short years – the twinkling of an eye – we will each find ourselves disembodied. What will we do, what will be our desire *then*? Will we not desire to help our still-embodied loved ones in the awakening, the leavening, the resurrecting and rejoining of minds? How unserviceable will we find it when they ignore us, thinking, believing we are 'dead and gone' and therefore, beyond their reach for loving commun(icat)ion?

How much more, will we say to ourselves, could we help them, from our now less self-restricted, more illumined, state in spirit, if only they were more conscious of our loving presence, the help we can give, and reassure them of how much more perfectly, fantastically well the GRP is progressing than the dream world of bodies is aware? We will be all too clear that holding onto the belief of being embodied in a self-blinding-and-deafening – *deadening*, actually – state of consciousness, or, more accurately, *un*consciousness, is entirely unnatural, unnecessary and unserviceable in our Awakening to eternal reality.

There are those who would say, 'If we can't see our loved ones in spirit how can we know we are in touch with *them*, and not some malign, lower-astral entity?' This is a crucial question, and has a very simple, important and comforting answer: we *unreservedly* commit to placing ourself in the care, guidance and protection of Jesus and all those appointed by him and functioning within Christ empowerment and authority while we perceive ourself as in an embodied state. He knows all in spirit who are right for beneficial intercourse with us.

'And why do we need others if we have Jesus as our Guide to Eternity?' This is not just about need but about *Love* and the reconnecting, the rejoining, the *healing*, of the fragmented Sonship; *all* of it. We may not, yet, have much faith in ourself but we can readily have total, absolute faith and trust in him, and thus, in those connecting with us, when we entrust ourself to him. That will help us immeasurably in restoring, growing, strengthening our faith in ourself. And any who appear in our awareness from spirit with whom we are less than comfortable or peaceful, we ask if they come in the name and by the power and authority of Jesus Christ of Nazareth. If they do not, they will likely vamoose at the mention of his name. And if they don't, we are authorised by our faith in him to command them to leave and not to return until they *do* come in his name.

In my journey with Jesus since the 1960s, I have been inestimably blessed by the gift of opportunities to help many distressed souls in the etheric realms. This was possible because I had (and still have) a Loving and compassionate attitude toward souls in distress, and a *willingness* to accept communion with the spirit realms. Jesus has a Loving and compassionate attitude toward *all* of us and he can and is helping, guiding and protecting us all, in ways of which most of us have no awareness or understanding.

It is our inescapable destiny to become not only '*like* unto the Son of man' (Rev. 1:13, 14:14) (Jesus) but One *with* him in his Son of *God* stature because that is not just *his* but equally *our* true, eternal Being and thus, our inescapable destiny also. We may see ourself as being unable to help our brothers very much here in the physical world, let alone in the etheric world. This is where the news enables us to exult, for we do not have to *do* anything to help them. Instead, all that is asked of us – and that is highly serviceable to our *own* spiritual Awakening – is to *desire* to help our brothers in distress, embodied or otherwise.

If we have a conscious, sincere, committed desire to help, to be of service to Papa's Son, in any or all of his illusory fragments, embodied or not, then that desire is a *creative*, empowered-for-good energy, and is broadcast – consciously and/or unconsciously – out into the universe. Such broadcast is always greatly enabled – supercharged – by *blessing* those to whom we direct our desire for being of help. This broadcast is received by those in the Realms of Light who, out of selfless (but Self-*full*) Love are caring for, guiding and protecting us – right along with Jesus – during our seemingly embodied state. They will then organise, on our behalf, opportunities for our Love and blessing energy to be of help to our distressed brothers.

Those who have laid aside their Earth body (but not, yet, their Earth mind) can be helped by our *Praying* for them, *Committing* them into the care, guidance and protection of Jesus/Holy Spirit, and *Blessing* them (PCB-ing). We do not need to know them or even be aware of their circumstances. All *that* is taken care of by those in the Realms of Light who are empowered to help wherever help is needed. Why then, one may enquire, do those in the Light need *our* input for the help of those in darkness?

Because those in darkness have no *awareness* of the Light. They cannot receive what they are unaware is proffered, and those in the Light cannot force help on those who have not asked for it. Those in darkness have not asked for it because they do not know – or do not believe – help is always freely *available* to them. The Light Beings can use our freely-given PCB energies because they are engendered from our Earth-life vibration and are thus more palpable to those in spiritual darkness – etheric *or* physical. In short, *we* provide the help *resource*, the Light Beings direct and administer it where it is needed.

All this is contributing *purposefully* to the coming together and healing in Loving brotherhood of the broken Sonship *in its entirety*. For the Son of God is not a body but eternal Spirit, creatively activated by Mind. In its seemingly split, fragmented state, the mind of Papa's Son believes itself to be 'mortal'. Therefore it takes a form that can 'die'. The part that believes it is 'alive' (in a body) *and* the part that believes it has 'died' need help to remember who, what and where they *really* are.

Since they are, in Truth, all our beloved brothers, will we deny them the help we can all so easily and freely give, when we *Know* it is but ourself we really help?

Diary of a Christ Communicant

A.M. September 12, 2010

History repeats itself because it has not been *forgiven*
by the fractured mind that keeps re-viewing it, trying to
change it, trying to make it better. But what is *nothing*
cannot *be* **made better; it can but be** *forgiven*, **along**
with the mind that made it up.

If we put our faith in what is changeable – time and place – what
we will experience is change: birth and death and all that seems to
occur in-between. If we put our faith in the perfect, unchangeable
reality that is God, Heaven, Eternity, *that* is what we will experience.

It is but a releasing, a relinquishing, a letting go of the
dream, because the dream is the past; a terrible nightmare
of separation, in which Papa's Son experienced that which
is not – and never can be – as that which is.

Yet it is past, over, gone. Papa is Calling His Son
Home and the only way he can hear His Call is to gladly,
voluntarily, relinquish his attachment to the past. It does
not *seem* to be the past because the separated mind is *re-
visiting, re-living* what has already gone. History repeats
itself because it has not been *forgiven* by the fractured mind
that keeps re-viewing it, trying to change it, trying to make
it better. But what is *nothing* cannot *be* made better; it can
but be *forgiven*, along with the mind that made it up.

Thus is that mind *released* from the past and free to
return to the Present, the Holy Instant, the Eternal Now.

17: Forgetting-not to Laugh

Even as I have been restored to Oneness with the Father, so all my little brothers and sisters who earnestly desire the Kingdom and follow me shall be One with me, and by this shall also become One with our Father.

–*Jesus,* November 22, 1992

I N RECENT WEEKS, words from chapter 27 of the *A Course in Miracles* text have loomed large in my mind. Here, Jesus speaks of the tiny, mad idea of separation that crept into the mind of Papa's Son, and at which *he forgot to laugh.* The seeming effects that idea incurred do appear so serious that laughing at them can be perceived as inappropriate to a world that believes pain, suffering and death to be real. I have long accepted that to ignore such inner prompting is to miss a growth opportunity, so I decided that it could only be serviceable to consider laughter in more depth.

At around that time Theresa and I began to experience the symptoms of a debilitating cold and cough. By the evening of day two it didn't feel like much fun, and as I lay in bed it looked as if it would be a sleep-disrupted night. As I am addicted to quality sleep, this was not a happy prospect. Then I remembered Jesus' words about forgetting to laugh, so I said to him, 'Okay, Beloved, I choose not to go down that path, so I am reaching for your hand, *Knowing* you are here with me always, just as you promised, so let us laugh *together* at the comical absurdity of the human condition.'

Instantly, he was there beside me on the bed. Actually, that does not convey the experience well. It is more accurate to say that instantly I was *aware* of his presence beside me on the bed. He had been there all the while – inspiring me to think again, change my mind, my perspective – and as I *accepted* that inspiration and began focusing upon him and his constant, uplifting, Light-hearted presence, so did I become *aware* of it. His very presence – or, again, more accurately, *awareness* of it, since he is with us *all*, every moment – is easily adequate to instantly lift one's spirits to the heights.

His mood was joy. It is *always* joy. *He has remembered to laugh.* Nothing of the illusion of separation affects that. If it did, he would not be who, what and where he is. When we have remembered this also, we will be like him, One with him, where he is: eternity; Heaven. His joy instantly filled the room. It assuredly filled the whole house ... the whole street. In Truth, it fills the whole world, though most of the slumbering, dreaming world has no awareness of it. His joy immediately filled me, raised me to *his* vibration and I was aware that he knew what had been going through my mind.

Since he has his abode (along with Papa; [Jn. 14:23]) in us, in our mind – and we will be consciously aware of this if we Love him and keep his word, and rejoice in him – it is obvious, *inevitable* that he would know what is going through our mind. This is so even if we *don't* Love him, keep his word and rejoice in him. He joins with the dreamer (i.e., each of us who perceives the dream of time and place as reality) – because we are his beloved brothers in the Sonship – but *never* with the dream, even though he knows the dream because he has dreamt it; he has seen *through* it and wakened *from* it.

Immediately I was One with him and observing, with him, the sheer folly and unserviceableness of believing we are vulnerable to sickness (not to speak of limitation, littleness, frailty, mortality) and thus, make sickness our 'reality'. We lay on the bed and laughed and laughed and laughed, as One, at the whole, tiny, mad idea. This, it should be emphasised, was not *mocking* laughter, for that would have been to make the illusion real. Rather, it was *joyful* laughter because from his perspective – the perspective of eternal Truth and reality, and which perspective he gladly will share with us if we are *willing* to join our mind with his – it is seen, *Known*, to be nothing but a foolish dream, and therefore, *nothing at all*.

To mock nothing would be folly indeed. But *because* it is nothing we can all wake from it at any and every moment of our choosing, simply by discerning, remembering that that is all it is, so it not only *has* no reality (however real it seems while we choose to continue believing it is real), but *can* have no reality. As soon as we make that choice, the Awakening process begins.

The adage that laughter is the best medicine has value indeed, and great healing properties. Yet while laughter has but one level of reality – Joy – the slumbering, fragmented Sonship has made up other levels of laughter that are not Joy-engendered. As already mentioned, we have made up mocking laughter. There is laughter at a coarse joke; hollow laughter at the misfortune of ourself or another; embarrassed laughter … Joy, true Joy – the Joy of Heaven – is in none of those. They may produce *momentary* relief from guilt, fear, self-deception, but have no lasting healing properties.

The Joy of Heaven, which can but induce laughter, is healing, and medics know that uplifting, joy-filled laughter releases healing endorphins. This doesn't necessarily mean healing of bodily ailments will become inevitable, or even speeded up, but Joyful laughter reduces, or even eliminates, our resistance to letting go of the illusion of *dis*ease. It also helps us focus on a state of mind where the 'apparent' illness is seen as of less, or no, consequence, thus enabling it to be diminished in our awareness, our experience. All this changes our perception of reality from illness to wholeness, thus dispelling the illness perception.

The level at which we choose laughter causes a resonance within us at that level. If we choose mocking as the level that causes us to laugh there will be no upliftment of our mind and soul to a level of spiritual Joy, so there will be no health-inducing endorphins released to enhance our sense of well-being. Indeed, the more we find mocking or derision to be a source of amusement, the lower our level of spiritual Atonement. And thus, our sense of inner peace and well-being can only be inclined to sink. The same principle applies with coarseness, or embarrassment ... We can *Know* this must be so if we consider the impossibility of mocking, coarseness or embarrassment in Heaven. How could there be need of any of those things There?

Conversely, the Joy of Heaven – the *true* state of spiritual upliftment – *spontaneously* induces laughter at a vibration engendering a sense of well-being that can only be ... you got it: heavenly. This laughter does not have to manifest itself at an audible level. Indeed, there may be circumstances in which such an outward expression could be inappropriate. Joy, and its attendant laughter are of the *heart*-mind and can be experienced at the highest, unencumbered, unhindered level with little or no outward signs discernible, save, perhaps for a smile and a twinkle of the eyes.

But *inwardly* is the radiance that is Joy, and Joy *is* heavenly. Since then I have joined with Jesus on numerous occasions – including my communing walks in the hills – for Joy-filled laughter, transforming, in an instant, mundane, ego-led, distracting-from-reality thoughts into open-ended moments of upliftment to the inner awareness of the Kingdom of Heaven on Earth. Just as he desires for us all. Joy, Peace and Love are inseparable, intrinsic aspects of eternal, heavenly reality.

Diary of a Christ Communicant

A.M. September 24, 2010

Gathering information about unreality – time and place; the temporal – is nothing to do with Knowledge. Knowledge is, and can only be, of reality, which is eternity; Heaven. That is *within* and requires no gathering; only *acceptance* of what is already there.

All who believe in separation are fearful of judgement because, at some level, conscious and/or unconscious, they believe they are guilty. If we perceive Jesus as wrathful, judgemental, we are mistaken. He is the Lord of perfect, *unconditional* Love. Love does not accuse, judge, condemn, seek retribution or punish. *Ever.*

It is needful to release the illusory 'iron band' of limitation, restriction to time and place consciousness, to a so-called 'physical' realm of perception. To perceive differences, barriers, gaps between Papa's Son is to effect limitation, imprisonment in bodies.

'Love believeth all things' [1 Cor. 13:7]. It is the ego-adopted *unbelief*, doubting, scepticism – even cynicism – of the fragmented, self-deluded Sonship that seems to keep him imprisoned in the chaos of guilt, fear, mortality; all due to an unwillingness to believe in and accept his true Being. This, even though Jesus clearly, magnificently, *perfectly* demonstrated and taught that belief brings release from *all* limitation – including, of course, 'death'. Limitation is ego's burdensome, uncomfortable yoke that must be *voluntarily* abandoned in favour of Jesus' freely offered yoke, which is easy (comfortable), and whose 'burden' is Light [Mt. 11:30].

Choosing such a switch of allegiance transforms fragmented minds from darkness, ignorance, forgetfulness, powerlessness to Light, wisdom, remembrance of Oneness, Knowledge, all-empowerment, all of which comes direct from the *Source* of All. Endlessly gathering information about unreality – time and place; the temporal – is nothing to do with Knowledge. Knowledge is, and can only be, of reality, which is eternity; Heaven. That is *within* and requires no gathering; only *acceptance* of what is already there, freely, unconditionally. Only continuing belief in unreality prevents belief in reality. Who can believe in unreality *and* reality?

18: Restoration to Oneness Through Forgiveness

My beloveds, this is a time for bringing close to the hearts and lives of all my little ones of Earth the great Love of Heaven, and of Him Who is the Source of all that Love. You glimpse that this Love and giving are unconditional and there is no spirit of judgement or condemnation in it.

–Jesus, December 20, 1992

PAPA'S SON APPEARS TO BE in time and place – the *without* – because he believes he has separated himself from his Father. He cannot be *a little bit* separate. He is separate – in his experience – or *not*. And by the belief in separation he has also shut himself off from awareness of his Self. This is inevitable because his Self is One in his Father in the *within*, and it is not possible to believe oneself to be without *and* within; it has to be one *or* the other. The illusion of separation – including from the One Self – is not something that seemed to occur just in the illusory *past*.

He still *believes* himself as separate, so separation, or division, still *seems* to be happening, in every way. This manifests itself in the appearance in the without of more bodies every minute of every hour of every day. And each is produced by separation, or division at the cellular level from the moment of conception; in fact, even *before* conception, because gametes themselves symbolise, denote separation, incompleteness. Separation manifests itself also in such constructs as religion, which keeps dividing into ever more sects, or denominations, as the separation consciousness causes schisms; warring over their separate misperceptions of Truth.

The seemingly-fragmented Son – we, all of us – cannot be restored to Oneness all the while he believes, and thus perceives, himself separated, broken, divided. Since Oneness is our true, natural estate and means uninterruptible Peace, Joy and Love, and belief in separation means experiencing constant change, uncertainty, guilt, fear, division … there can be only one meaningful, serviceable purpose for being here: to *heal* the brokenness. The brokenness is apparent only in the mind that *believes* it to be true, and thus gives it specious 'reality', so it is here that the healing must be effected.

This means the minds of the fragments, who perceive themselves each as separate, unique bodies, with individual minds and identities. Only the *mind* needs healing, restoring to wholeness/ holiness, since it is a *split-off part* of the Son's mind that believes itself separate; that has made bodies, which, being temporal, are not real. The *Spirit* of the Son is indivisibly, eternally, perfectly, unchangeably *One*, so needs no healing.

The only way the split-off-from-Truth mind can be healed, restored to Oneness is by communion (common [*shared*] union) – i.e., rejoining – between the *seemingly* separated parts. The only true communion is between minds, or mind-to-mind. The most serviceable prerequisite to communing is forgiving, loving and blessing *ourself*. This opens our door, our channel of commun(icat)ion with our Self, which we have kept shut by unconsciously believing we are guilty. Forgiveness enables us to see past the (unconscious) *presumed* guilt within ourself, so that we can access our own, *innocent*, inner Being.

All the while we believe we are guilty, we are keeping that door shut, out of fear. If we cannot commune with that part of the Sonship that is our true Self, how can we commune with our brothers, including Jesus? He is the best brother with whom we might start our mind-to-mind communing because he is *already* in our mind and empowered to help us remember the Truth of our eternal Oneness within. He is walking with each and every one of us, every moment, whether we are aware of his presence or not.

We might ask ourself how we envision the relationship, the intercourse between dearest friends. Would it not be with terms such as comfortableness, ease, relaxation, joy, peace, humour, light-heartedness; and, of course, abiding Love? This – and immeasurably more – is exactly how it is between Jesus and us; *each and every one of us*. There are, and can be, no exceptions because he is brother to us *all*, and we *all*, therefore, to him. Not being aware of that does not make it *not* so. He *longs* for us to become aware of it, and will help our awareness, if we so desire and are *willing* to accept his help.

He can, will and *is* restoring the mind of us all to awareness, remembrance of our Oneness with his healed, whole *Christ*-Identified Mind. Once we are willing to accept this: that he is the Way by which we remember the Truth of our Being, and that we are all One in that brotherhood, founded in perfect Love, we can extend this mind-to-mind communing to any – and in principle, *all* – of our brothers, embodied *or* disembodied. Since in reality we are all of One Mind, it can but be our forgetfulness, our misplaced guilt, fear, *unbelief* that would block it from our awareness, prevent it from becoming our *experience*.

This healing is possible even with those with whom we find ourself in a karmic entanglement. Such conditions *often* extend back through 'previous' incarnations; all the more reason for desiring to heal them *now*, and save ourself and our brother(s) indeterminate *further* embodiments. The apparent degree of brokenness – major or minor – is of no consequence, because brokenness is but an illusion; something we made up to establish so-called individual, separate persona identities. Seeing, *accepting* ourself again as undivided, One whole (holy) Self – Christ – immediately ends our belief in the dream. And what we no longer believe in ceases to have reality for us. This applies to guilt, fear, disease, scarcity, pain, suffering, 'death' and all other illusory forms of separation.

All our perceptions of separateness are defence mechanisms against the Truth of our eternal, indivisible Oneness. This is why attempting mind-to-mind communion at the ego-mind level cannot, will not, work, for separation is devised to prevent, to *break*, commun(icat)ion. But neither we nor the brother with whom we are in a tug of karmic war are *actually* separate; that is merely a game we are playing. We are both, equally, *One* Self, and it is at the level of Self that we can commune lovingly, peaceably, joyfully. All the while we believe we *are*, and wish to *remain*, separate from that brother, communion *cannot* work.

Thus is forgiveness prerequisite to the healing of brokenness. And it only takes one – i.e., *One* – to forgive for the breach to be healed. Forgiveness dispels the illusion of separateness, restoring us to remembrance of Oneness. If this does not manifest *outwardly* it makes no difference to the healing, for such a perception is only at the temporal, illusory level, and inner, *mind* healing is at the *Self*-aware level. We do not attempt to commune with the ego-mind of our brother, which will, temporarily, remain unaware of any such communing. All *that* we commit to and *leave with* the Spirit of Truth.

Only by committing it to Him – and ignoring outward appearances (as with all ego matters if we want release from its thrall), focusing solely, steadfastly, resolutely on the whole, *higher* mind of our brother, sending Love, blessing, forgiveness (and *asking* forgiveness from his Self) – will communing work, and heal the breaches in the Sonship, brother to brother. Thus do we play *our part* in the process, and that is *all* that is asked of us. Then, when the Holy Spirit has performed *His* part, *His* healing work in and through us, the healing will be *complete* and it will become of no importance to us whether or when, or not, it *manifests* at the outer, horizontal level of relationship.

For only eternity is real, and having *sincerely* done the forgiveness and healing work, in conjunction with, and at the level of Self/Holy Spirit Mind, the healing is accomplished. It is of no consequence if we are not consciously aware of this because our conscious mind has not, yet, been unified with Higher Mind awareness. I *Know* this of a certainty beyond all doubt because I have been joyfully communing mind-to-Mind with the whole, holy mind of Jesus since the 1960s and in recent years have *experienced* healing communion (i.e., rejoining) at the Self/Holy Spirit level with brothers with whom there is (still, at this time of writing) *apparent*, outward brokenness of relationship.

Only by focusing *on* and steadfastly committing *to* the healing of our mind, and invoking the willing, Loving help of Jesus/Holy Spirit – and thus, ignoring its outwardly-*seeming* brokenness – can we become wholly, uninterruptedly, aware of its reality for us, in our own within, and therefore the within of All, because we are, in Truth, One.

Diary of a Christ Communicant

A.M. September 30, 2010

Perfect Love and Light are what Papa's Son really is, but the choice for experience of good and evil – duality – has separated the Love and Light into its fractions, which are sullied, distorted, dimmed by the belief in, and thus the appearance of, darkness, or *absence* of Love/Light.

If we are separate from God we must manifest, or portray, traits that *oppose*, or are the reversal of, or have none of the qualities of God. For if we express an attribute commensurate with any of God's, then we must be at One with Him – at least in respect of *that* quality. For example if we perform an act – or simply have an attitude – of kindness toward a brother, we are at One with God within that context ('And the King shall answer and say unto them, Verily I say unto you, Inasmuch as ye have done *it* unto one of the least of these my brethren, ye have done *it* unto me.' [Mt. 25:40]) because God is perfect Love, and kindness is an aspect of Love.

Perfect Love can be likened to Light. Light, in its completeness, is comprised of all the colours of the spectrum that make it Light; what is described in worldly terms as *white* light. So, blue, for example, is an *aspect* of white light, in the same way that kindness is an aspect of perfect Love. An act of kindness ('blue') may be a quality of light, but that does not make it whole, or complete, or *perfect* Light/Love.

Love and Light are indivisible aspects of the Creator. Perfect Love and Light are what Papa's Son really is, but the choice for experience of good and evil – duality – has separated the Love and Light into its fractions, which are sullied, distorted, dimmed by the belief in, and thus the appearance of, darkness, or absence of Love/Light. Yet the Light is eternal, unchangeable, indestructible; *cannot* be separated, and is thus forever whole, complete, perfect.

The choice for fragmentation, for separateness, can only *seem* to present choices of colour but that is only when perceived through the illusory 'prism' of separation. Choosing to move back through the prism of separation to Oneness is a choice for the undivided wholeness of perfect Light and Love.

19: How to Save the World

The transforming and renewing power of the Creator Spirit can only manifest in and through souls whose commitment, dedication and one-pointed desire for the Kingdom and all it represents has gradually created a channel through which such can manifest.

–Jesus, January 17, 1993

W E ARE THE LIGHT OF THE WORLD *and* the saviours of the world; so says Jesus. He ought to know, and we ought to trust him on this if we want to get back to where we belong. But this can only be possible by *believing* it of ourself and of our brothers, *regardless of outward appearances*. This cannot happen unless and until we stop thinking negative, judgemental thoughts – about ourself and our brothers. Negative thoughts betray us and our brothers because they do not reflect the Truth. They perpetuate the lie; the insane game of pretending to be what we are not. We are like Jesus; he is our brother and the template, the model, for our true Being.

Few would agree that betrayal is a laudable quality. Most would see it as shameful, degrading, dishonourable; something we would hope never to do to anyone. Yet most of us engage in it daily, even hourly, toward ourself and our fellows. If we take a moment and think about this, it is not hard to see how *damaging* it is to ourself – mentally, emotionally and inevitably, eventually, physically – regardless of whether those thoughts are directed to ourself *or* to another. If to ourself, still we cannot help but broadcast them, undetected by bodily senses, out into the world and beyond.

There they are received, at an unconscious level, by all around us; human and *all* sentient life forms. If detectable by olfactory senses they would be experienced as malign effluvia, causing others to shun us. But since most of us are unwittingly, undiscerningly doing the same, perhaps we are inured to it; such as when we all eat garlic we do not notice it on another's breath.

Is there one amongst us who believes Jesus has negative thoughts? Indeed, why would he choose, or need, to have such, *ever*? For he *Knows* the outcome of the Great Rescue Programme, the final phase of the Atonement; the restoration of the fragmented mind of Papa's Son to sanity, wholeness, Oneness. He *Knows* it because he has eschewed the time-and-place perspective in favour *only* of the eternal view. We are like Jesus; he is our brother and our template for Being. In order for us to come to *Know* it, as he does, we have first to have *faith* that it is so, for faith shall be *replaced* by sight.

True, spiritual sight, or vision, requires, first, *belief* because it is our choice for *un*belief that has blocked our vision, replacing unchangeable, perfect-Love-engendered reality that true vision shows us, with temporal, changeable, conflicting, decaying illusions. Faith, or a little willingness to believe, enables the removal of that block. By steadfast faith, unwavering belief, infinite patience, we keep our mind *open* to the Light that the Spirit of Truth constantly shines into it for us, until we remember that we *are* the Light. Thus, faith enables the Light to *penetrate*, illuminating our mind with Truth, transforming believing into *Knowing*, of a certainty beyond all doubt.

It is easier to dispel betraying, negative thoughts – with which we sentence ourself to death – than ego would have us believe. In fact, it is as easy as pie, once we remember how. We simply remind ourself that they are not *our* thoughts. We have allowed an interloper, a 'virus' to invade our mind so that our vision has become double. This has set us ill at ease. But, like all *disease*, it is not real. In 1968

Jesus counselled me not to *fight* illness, not to resist it, but *allow* it to flow through me, over me, and it would be like water off a duck's back, and thus, gone more swiftly *because it is met with no resistance*.

To resist or fight *dis*ease means we are resisting something that is not real, merely a figment in our slumbering, distorted, split-off-from-Truth mind. Resistance gives it reality in that mind, for we would not resist what in Truth we *Know* is not real. Assuredly, Jesus was impervious to bodily ailments simply because he *Knew* neither bodies nor ailments are real. When we hold onto negative thoughts, believing them to be ours – which they are not because in Truth we are like him – we block our own, Christ-Minded thoughts from our awareness. Those alien thoughts are interloper-virus thoughts.

Negative, ego-virus thoughts betray us into believing the unbelievable, valuing the valueless, so they become real to us and afflict us with an endless array of maladies of mind and body. 'Endless' because we keep on making up more and more as guilt and fear, judgement and grievance – negative thoughts – reflect destructively back onto us.

That calls for vigilance and steadfast commitment, not to resist or fight them but simply observe them, impassively. We could say to ourself, 'I observe these thoughts, but I do not judge them and I do not own them *because* they are not real; they are therefore nothing and I choose not to judge *or* own what is *nothing*, when Papa has given me *everything*. Instead I choose Christ-Mind thoughts of Love, forgiveness, wholeness, blessing as *my* thoughts and *Know* this is entirely possible because I – with Jesus and *all* my brethren in the Sonship – am Papa's beloved Son: Christ.'

The function of saviour of the world is *already* ours, just as being the Light of the world is what we already are. *Accepting* that function *enacts* it and brings meaning, purpose and fulfilment into our lives, in a world otherwise *without* meaning, purpose or fulfilment. Being saviours of the world is not some grandiose, arrogant thing, and does not require special tools, qualities or any gifts of the spirit with which we are not *already* equipped. It is merely forgiving our brother and ourself for what we 'virus-thought' – misperceived

– he did to us and/or we to him, and *unconditionally* Loving and blessing him, ourself and every living thing, *open-endedly*. This is an attitude we must choose, accept, adopt until it has become Who we really *Are* (again), just like Jesus. When we have truly forgiven our brother and ourself we find *unconditionally* Loving and blessing him, ourself and every living thing, open-endedly comes effortlessly, naturally, comfortably, easily, joyfully, peacefully and above all, **lovingly**. This state of Being is **Atonement** and Atonement is a state of undisturbable inner peace of which the world knows nothing. As Jesus said to my friend, Steve, back in the 1970s, "My peace is in Atonement; Atonement is **without effort**."

Our brother is that politician who fiddled his expenses, took a bribe, voted for some commercial deal that threatens the environment; he is that preacher advocating terrorism and martyrdom, or promulgating the myth that God is angry and demanded a once and for all blood sacrifice as a propitiation for our sins; he is that banker who paid himself millions while covering-up malfeasance that cost his customers and/or tax-payers billions; he is that medic who missed a diagnosis that cost us or a loved-one their life …

Being *selective* about forgiveness is not, cannot be, forgiveness at all, because forgiveness starts and ends with ourself, by *re*cognising that in Truth – in the Sight of Papa – there is only *One* of us; in Truth there *is* no guilt; in Truth there *is* no time and place. Withholding forgiveness is giving reality to what we have made up, denying ourself the experience of reality. Holding unforgiveness toward just one brother ties us into a karmic entanglement with that brother, locking him and us together, keeping us imprisoned in a body, time and place, limitation, the illusion of mortality...

If that is our wish, so be it. Neither God nor Jesus will deny it us. If it is *not* our wish, they will Help us fulfil the *true* desire of our heart for eternal Life, limitlessness, Joy, Peace and Love beyond human imagining. But we must *desire* it wholly, unequivocally. That may sound unachievable to our ego-yoked mind. It *is* unachievable without that Help; but happily, all that is required of us is that we simply *desire* it and *ask* for it. All else is accomplished *for* us, in *response* to that desire.

Then all things are possible for us because we have joined our life with Him for Whom all things are possible, including, of course, saving the world.

Diary of a Christ Communicant

A.M. October 17, 2010

**Papa is everywhere. But everywhere is not of time or place; it is of Mind, and Mind is *within*. The illusion perceived as time and place is without, and that made-up place is without indeed; without Mind.
That is *why* it is insane.**

Orthodox Christians believe Jesus is our saviour. And so he is. But that is an incomplete perception, and their interpretation is based on the false doctrine of *sacrifice* as the path to salvation, which is not supported by the scriptures [For detailed explanation of this, see *"Seek ye First the Kingdom..."*, Part Two, Vignette 12: *The False Doctrine of Sacrifice as the Path to Salvation*]. He points the way to our salvation by making clear that not only is *he* our saviour but that we are our brother's saviour as he is ours also. In other words, we must all be participant in salvation, or Awakening, *along with Jesus*. This is because we are all One – along with him – *appearing*, illusorily, as many. We are not *really* many. This is a false perception, brought about by a false belief. It is impossible to be separate from Papa, or from our Self.

Papa is the very Life, the essence of *all* that has life. There is nowhere He cannot Be, so to imagine He is not 'here' is for 'here' to be nowhere. Nowhere does not exist, other than in vain imagining. To believe in separation from Papa is to believe in sin and guilt, and that this has brought separation because He is perfection. But sin and guilt are mistaken *perceptions*, brought about by the mistaken *belief*

121

in separation from the Source of All.

Where would you go to be separate from Papa, since He is everywhere? If He is everywhere, everywhere *must* be real. But everywhere is not of time or place; it is of Mind, and Mind is *within*. The illusion perceived as time and place is without, and that made-up place is without indeed; without Mind. That is *why* it is insane.

20: The Oneness of Every Living Thing

Let the Father's Will and His Love fill your Life Centres and work His wonders in you, for the uplifting of the children of Earth. Be not afraid; shrink not from this joyous place, for your guidance and protection are in your Atonement with Him and with me.

–Jesus, January 24, 1993

ORTHODOX RELIGIOUS BELIEF has it that animals don't have a soul. Such a doctrine (or *dog*ma!) cannot have been fabricated by anyone who ever kept – and loved/was loved *by* – a dog. The soul of every living thing – human, animal, vegetable ... and many would also say mineral – is the life force that animates it, and that life force is the *Universal* Life Force; the Creator Spirit; Papa. This had been my understanding for as long as I can remember, but in 1995 I had an experience that confirmed this beyond all doubt, as described in this extract from chapter 7 of *"Seek ye First the Kingdom..."*:

> When walking the dogs in the hills, with woodland and fields around me, I suddenly saw the Life Force coursing through every tree, leaf, blade of grass, wheat plant in the adjacent field, even the very soil in which all was growing. Everything that is, including the dogs and me, *was* this Force and It was all One, all connected to Itself as One, all connected *to*, receiving its livingness *from*, having its beingness *in* the Source of All; a Cosmic Umbilicus. Ever since then I have known of and from the certainty that we can have only when we have *experienced* such, that this

is the reality: we are all One with, or in, the Creator, the Source of Life.

This reality is not dependent for its existence upon beliefs, or doctrines or dogmas or rituals. What, however, will be highly serviceable to *experiencing* that reality, for the purpose of spiritual growth and awakening, is to harmonise our mind and desire/get attuned with the 'Good Husbandman' ("I am the true vine, and my Father is the *husbandman*." [Jn. 15:1]). This aligns us with the Mind of God, by the agency of the Holy Spirit and/or Jesus, and illumination can and will be given, in *response* to our sincerity, desire and commitment.

That illumination becomes a living experience and then we truly *Know* the Truth, and cannot be diverted from our Path back to God by somebody else telling us *their* truth, because this has come from the Source, through our own within.

Seeing animals as soulless, and therefore, different – *separate* from ourselves – is characteristic of the separation consciousness, which is concocted to keep us believing *we* are separate ... from Papa and from our whole, Holy Self. Will we believe what our body's eyes show us? They are contrived to attest to what we have *chosen* to believe: unreality, in our game of make-believe. Or will we believe what our eternal soul-sight will reveal to us – actually, restore to our remembrance – when we are *ready* to believe and are willing to ask, and trust, in faith?

Jesus reminds us in *A Course in Miracles* that the Creator Spirit, Papa, creates by extending Himself, and thus are His creations *like* Himself; that His Son is an extension of Himself, created to create as He creates, by extending *his* Self. His Self is Love, because he is like his Creator, and cannot be *un*like his Creator because his Creator can create *only* in His likeness. Yet in his fragmented, dream state, in which he is playing at *not* being his Self, *he cannot create at all* – because he has chosen to believe he has separated himself from his

Creator, Who Is his very *Source* of creativeness.

Instead, he can only make, or fabricate – project from his split-off-from-Truth mind – false *images* of darkness (darkness because they are unenlightened) that simply reflect the false, unreal image he has made of his self. Because the image he has made is false, reflections of it will also be false, and therefore, not reflect an *exact* likeness. Hence every human – and all other living things – being different in form, or appearance. These images are all in the without – where he has tried to make his home since the dawn of time – and are all separate forms, subject to the laws of entropy, destined to keep dividing, withering and 'dying'.

But the substance, the content, the reality *within* every life-form that appears in time and place, from elephant to bacterium, from oak tree to daisy is the eternal, indestructible, unchangeable Life Force that is the Source of all Being, Whose very *nature* is Love.

Projecting images of ourself into the *without* – as multifarious, ever-changing forms – distracts us from remembrance, awareness of the Life, the Love, the Light, the unchanging, unchangeable, eternal *Being* that is Papa's Son, *within*. And then, believing, perceiving the *form* as the reality, the life – onto which we must hang, and devote so much of our attention to preserving – maintains the illusion, the dream, the lie. These images are not, of course, just 'humans', which we believe – and thus perceive – we are, but all other myriad life-forms we see around us.

It is not Papa Who has created them all, because they are of time and place and He Knows nothing of illusion. Who else, then, has made all these life forms; taken little piles of clay and animated them with diverse shapes, sizes and colours? In all eternity there is only the Creator and the created. Both can create only in their *Own* likeness, so says Jesus. But these *forms* are made, not created, because creation is forever. Only one who is playing a game of pretend, of make-believe, could make what is unreal, temporal, and then forget he made them and that they are not real.

Then, one life form kills and eats other life forms, in the mistaken understanding that this is giving or perpetuating life, when it is merely perpetuating the illusion that we are a mortal body.

Is this saying an elephant is not real? Just as human *form* is not real, but the eternal Life Force, the Soul that animates it *is*, so is it with elephants and all other life forms. There is but One Life, and all are integral, intrinsic, indivisible aspects of that Oneness. If it were possible to kill *a part* of It, the *whole* would be killed, but death is an illusion which Papa's Son dreamed up and now we mistakenly fear. How can we fear what we have made up, other than by forgetting we have made it up?

We, Papa's One Son, dreaming of being many and diverse, in our upside-down, split-off-from-Truth mind, made all the forms and gave them all their functions – including their poisonous, killing, competitive properties. So insane is this whole set-up that it could only hold any semblance of credibility to a mind that has chosen to forget its true, *all-Loving* Being.

Now is the moment, the time, of the Great Awakening, in which Papa's Son is remembering who he *really* Is; that he is One, not only in Papa, but with *all* living things. This is materialising in the without *from* the within as the growing flood of loving human-animal interaction stories and videos on the internet readily portrays. And that is merely an *outer* example of the universal rejoining of the One Life, as a reminder that all who have eyes to see and ears to hear can discern more deeply the gathering momentum with which that rejoining is occurring as the third measure of meal continues to leaven, 'until the *whole* is leavened'.

> *'Papa, I am in need of nothing, for You have given me everything, that I may share it with, extend it to, my brothers – irrespective of the form they may take – that we may all have it equally and return to Oneness together in You.'*
> Amen.

Diary of a Christ Communicant

A.M. October 24, 2010

Extend the same forgiveness to your brothers as Papa extends to you. That's how you make it yours. There is no other way to avoid judgement and condemnation of oneself to continuing riding that not-so-merry-go-round of birth and 'death'.

Full or complete enlightenment or Awakening is the result of healing the split mind by the Holy Spirit, Who dwells in the higher part of our mind, and is our unbreakable connection to Papa.

Indeed so. That healing brings restoration to remembrance of Whole-Mindedness, which *is* enlightenment. The seemingly split-off part of your mind, which is ego's habitat, has absolutely no awareness or understanding of Whole-Mindedness because that is *Christ* Mind and is of eternity, just like Papa's, of which it is part.

Ego-mind denies this reality because what it does not know or understand does not exist for it, and it knows and understands *nothing* of reality. It is this upside-down part of the mind that is consciously engaged most of the time by most of the fragments, due to distraction from spiritual commitment and discipline. Any who think healing can be performed by their own self-will, or any device it has contrived in the dream world of time and place, are mistaken. Such ideas are destined to detain prisoners in the separation consciousness.

So will self-determination continue, without intervention from Christ Mind, until free will *chooses* to abandon that downward-spiralling path in favour of the Path Home, under My all-empowered care, guidance and protection. However, although there can be no intervention, because that breaches the Law of free will, the Call Home constantly conspires to produce *opportunities* for remembrance, including – and often, *especially* – in the darkest moments of the dream. This is not contra to the Will of the Creator because His Son *is* His Will, which cannot *but* be done. It only *appears* contra in the illusion of time, but is impossible in reality.

By making the conscious decision to co-operate with God-Self Will by surrendering ego-self will, many circuits of the carousel can be saved, and the distress of those still necessary can be commensurately diminished, because the direction of the journey will be *toward* the Light, instead of *away* from it. This is inevitable because surrender means the end of resistance. But any time the ego is allowed control of the reins again this will not be prevented *because* of free will.

At such times do not make the mistake of believing you have been abandoned by Papa, or His Voice, or Jesus. Hence the need for vigilance and steadfast commitment. For this, forgiveness is an empowering tool. Extend the same forgiveness to your brothers as Papa extends to you. That's how you make it yours. There is no other way to avoid judgement and condemnation of oneself to continuing riding that not-so-merry-go-round of birth and 'death'.

21: Choosing Between Reality Within and Illusion Without

Let your heart be heard in all matters, my son, for it is there to be your guide and balance; then shall the Living Word be given to reassure you of the rightness of your heart. This is Truth and this is Principle; hearken unto it and so shall all be well with you in the Way.

–Jesus, January 31, 1993

I F WE BELIEVE SACRIFICE is the path to salvation, we believe God is angry with us and therefore requires something to get Him to Love us again: sacrifice. That makes His Love conditional. And if we are created in His likeness it justifies our anger at ourself and our brothers for the sinfulness and shortfalls of us all. Happily, we are only *dreaming* all this; we have made it up, so it is not true. We could only make up what is *not* true because what *is* true is forever, unchangeably true. Nothing of time and place is unchangeable so nothing of it can be true.

Truth, reality, is within. Untruth, unreality, is without. Seeking Truth where it is not is but a fool's errand. Truth and Papa's Son are indivisible because Papa and His Son are indivisible. We cannot be separated from Him or from Truth, but can *pretend* we are. If we *live* the Truth it will set us free, restore us to wholeness and to Oneness in Him. The freedom that living the Truth brings us includes total, unwavering inner peace, stillness, tranquillity; limitlessness; invulnerability; joy beyond human imagining; boundless, perfect, unconditional Love *for*, and Oneness *with*, all.

All this and immeasurably more – *everything*, in fact – is *already*, inseparably, freely, 'without money and without price', ours, so we need not strive for it. Striving for what is already ours is denying – blinding ourself to – what we *have* and what we *are*, keeping us in the illusion of scarcity. This can only happen by our freewill choice to *forget* the Truth; by pretending we are somewhere other than our true Home, and something other than our true state of Being. Denying everything is with us is our choice to be *without* everything. Everything is to be found only in eternity because 'everything' can include only that which is real.

If we perceive ourself in time and place – the without – we are bringing into our own experience the illusion of *being without* because none of what we might believe is ours here is either real *or* ours. That does not mean everything is not *available* to us while we still appear to be embodied. While we believe that is a state of limitation so will it be. Jesus, on the other hand, during his seemingly embodied state, was not limited by it because he *Knew* limitation was a self-imposed state of *mind*, manifested by mistaken belief. Instead, he saw past the illusion to the Truth of his – and our – *unlimited* Being.

What was possible for him is possible also for us because we are his brothers in the Sonship; ONE, *illusorily* appearing as many because we *chose* separation. We are free to choose again and be restored to Oneness, limitlessness and all-empowerment. But to effect this transformation requires the retraining of our mind.

'Without' means bereft; lonely, lost and abandoned. So rather than *striving* for our inheritance we will serve ourself well simply by choosing anew; choosing – just as Jesus did – to remember it is *already* with us and has always been, *will* always be, can *never* not be. Choosing anew is all that is required of us, but we have to mean it. Unequivocally. Such a choosing can only bring an end to the misperception that we are without (i.e., not *within* the Kingdom), bereft. No-one will choose anything unless he sees it as desirable, so desire is the catalyst of change from dreaming of illusions to wakefulness to Truth.

We have been dreaming of unreality so long that our way of perceiving, describing and interpreting things is alien to reality. There was recently an interesting documentary about Isaac Newton on BBC TV. In it were described Newton's experiments passing white light through a prism, separating white light into the colours of the spectrum. This, so the narrative explained, caused Newton, and many since, to perceive white light as impure; a blend of the primary colours of the light spectrum, each of which must be pure in its own, *separate* right.

That is like saying that God – the Allness of everything – is impure because He comprises many facets (e.g., Love, Peace, Joy); that only the facets are pure, and the Allness, completion, is an adulteration of its parts, or facets, which must be separated out from the Allness for them to be pure. Yet, it is only when all the fragmented parts are rejoined from separation back to Oneness that wholeness (i.e., holiness), *completion*, is restored. To discern Truth we need to begin to look with our true, *whole*, joined, single vision, *not* split, separated, distorted sight.

We continue in the consciousness of separation and we affirm it by using the *lexicon* of separation. The ego reassures us, 'We speak as we find.' This is a misperception. Rather, we speak as we *believe* and it is the believing that causes the perceiving – or, more accurately, the *mis*perceiving. We believe in death so we speak of death. We speak of misery, of division, of loss, of sickness, of conflict as if real because we *believe* in them. Who would bother to speak of that in which he no longer believed? Is there one amongst us who can imagine Jesus saying he experienced misery, loss or illness? He understood that to speak of them as real *gave* them reality, when he *Knew* that *nothing* of time and place is real. He was here to speak of reality, not of make believe. He still is.

If we desire to be like him, let us, then, *co-operate* with him and with the Spirit of Truth when They counsel us to abandon illusion in favour of Truth. How can we remember – and *live* – the Truth that will set us free when our lexicon still contains the language of death, loss, misery, sickness, envy, judgement, grievance, limitation, guilt, fear, unworthiness; when we allow the spirit of reckoning (ego) to stand in the place of faith; judgement in place of forgiveness?

The language of eternity, of our *true* Being, is like a foreign language to ears long inured to that of time and place. Re-learning the language of Truth is only possible if we are steadfast in choosing to stop littering it with that of illusion, and allowing ourself – unawares – to believe the latter is true, is real. This requires commitment, focus, repetition, vigilance. The language of illusion is of change, uncertainty, questioning, doubting, limitation, scarcity, judgement, grievance ... The language of Truth is of Love, Peace, Joy, abundance, giving, certainty, acceptance, allowing, honouring, forgiving, surrendering, humility, generosity of spirit, affirming ...

Shared here is an extract from an April 2010 communing:

> ...Affirming is building, reassuring, strengthening. Practise affirmations for your focusing, centring, uplifting. Say: 'I Am ... Just as Papa created me; I Am ... loved, unconditionally and eternally, every moment; I Am ... forgiving of myself and my brothers; I Am ... Loving; I Am ... compassionate; I Am ... caring; I Am ... free'... You can add to the list as inspiration moves you; but *always* keep it positive and it will *always* be Truthful and uplifting. Remember: *doubt* is ego's dismantling device.
>
> All IS well. I Am ... with you always.

If the Spirit of Truth is with us always – which, assuredly, He is – *truly*, then, all IS well. Let us, then, live, and think, and speak, and BE in wellness. Wellness of mind. For wellness of mind can but assure wellness of all facets of our Being. And wellness is wholeness.

So shall we surrender old order thinking and speaking and living – or, more accurately, *'dying'* – and being, and accept and allow the outpouring of Papa's boundless Love and blessings to fill and overflow us with Peace and Joy unto perfect Life in Him everlasting.

Diary of a Christ Communicant

A.M. November 11, 2010

> **When we remember the Truth, the 'need' for a body, in time and place, in a vain attempt to hide from Papa, is seen as the error it always was. Then we are free to lay it aside, and return to Him in pure Spirit, with no need for further masquerade disguises, or embodied persona identities.**

William Tyndale (1494–1536) has been inspiring me with enlightened interpretations of Bible scriptures (see Vignette 26 in Part Two of *"Seek ye First the Kingdom..."*). Now, suddenly, he brings this further understanding: 'And though ... worms destroy this body, yet in my flesh shall I see God.' (Job 19:26).

This is affirming that it is possible to awaken from the dream of bodies only from *within* the dream of bodies. And if – *when* – 'the embodiment of the moment' does not afford us that Awakening, then, assuredly worms *will* destroy it. But that unenlightened soul will, inevitably, inescapably take another, and yet another body, until '... in my flesh shall I see God'. This does not imply we take a physical body with us into the Heart of Papa when we Awaken and remember our One, true Identity, and return to Him in the eternity of Heaven.

Why would we need to? Papa's Son is like his Father, Who, assuredly, is not a body, but pure, unencumbered-by-a-body Spirit. A body makes of us an image in every way *unlike* Him: temporal, limited, mortal... Yet His inviolable gift of free will means He allows us to continue in illusion until we are ready and willing to remember the Truth, the nature, of our eternal Being.

When we remember the Truth, the 'need' for a body, in time and place, in a vain attempt to hide from Papa, is seen as the error it always was. Then we are free to lay it aside, and return to Him in pure Spirit, with no need for further masquerade disguises, or embodied persona identities.

22: Two Sides of the Same Coin

All is well; the Joy of Heaven infiltrate and overshadow your Earth-life conditions, that you may have life abundantly and give of it to those who hunger and thirst.

Holy Communion, February 14, 1993

D ARKNESS IS NOT REAL. It is merely the seeming, or *perceived*, absence of Light. In like manner, fear is not real. It is merely the seeming, or *perceived*, absence of Love. Darkness and fear do not exist because Love and Light *do*. Oneness is a condition, a quality, an intrinsic property of Love and Light. There is nowhere They are not. Therefore, time and place are nowhere; they do not exist in reality, which is everywhere, *eternally*. In a mad moment Papa's Son made them up. That moment ended the same instant it entered his mind, but the causative power of the Mind of Papa's Son *seemed* to have a separating effect.

Yet because unreality *cannot* exist in reality, it was over in an instant, with no *actual* effect on, or interruption to, reality taking place. Still the idea of separation *seems* to continue to play itself out in a split-off part of the mind that manifests itself in the without as separated into fragments, each imprisoned in a body. This can be likened to a film, made long ago but being endlessly re-viewed. We can choose to stop watching, re-viewing unreality at any moment and it will begin to cease being experienced as reality in our mind. Then will we begin to remember that in like manner, guilt does not exist either. It is merely the *imagined* absence of innocence.

God is Reality. Believing that or not believing it makes no difference to what is unchangeable, unassailable, everlasting. Any creation of, or by, the Creator can therefore only be real, unchangeable, unassailable, everlasting. Therefore Papa's beloved Son, His creation, His *completion* ... cannot, *could not* exist in the unreality of darkness, fear and guilt, for this would only mean he could not be his Father's Son, his Creator's creation.

Then, as we make that choice anew – to stop re-viewing unreality, i.e., the 'past' – and *steadfastly* refuse to be drawn back into believing the unbelievable, we begin to focus our sight on our destination, our journey's end: Home, in pure innocence, to Love and Light, Peace and Joy far, *far* beyond human imagining. And as our journey progresses it becomes ever more clear – like the Light at the end of the tunnel looming larger and brighter as we near it – that in Truth there *was* no journey. We made up the idea of going away, being away and returning Home. We have *never* been away, even for an instant.

* * *

As our journey's end comes into view and the Light at the end of the illusory tunnel grows larger and brighter, we appear to be in an age of growing *spiritual* enlightenment (not to be confused with the era between the early 1600s and the late 1700s referred to as the 'Age of Enlightenment', which was an era of cultural and intellectual change). This manifests itself in every aspect of our awareness. Among these aspects is the exponential growth of scientific accomplishment. During the Victorian era there was a perception that man had nearly arrived at the place of all scientific understanding and development. This perception seems comical now, in light of the ever-accelerating rate of progress of new discoveries, inventions and technological achievements.

One may well consider to what this accelerating rate of progress can be attributed. To allow some Light to shine on this we need to recognise that embodied existence in the illusion of time and place is like one side of a coin, yet being *perceived* as the whole. The other side of that coin is the etheric counterpart of the so-called 'physical' world. Most in the embodied state have the misperception that we are separated from that realm, and those who have laid aside their body, thus – presumably, hopefully – ending up in that mysterious, unknown place: 'the afterlife'; *if* it exists …

For those who do not believe it, or perhaps are wavering, I am here to attest – from awareness of and blessed, loving contact with it through most of my embodied sojourn in time as 'persona Brian' – to its being equally as much a part of our experience in time and place as 'this side' of that illusory coin. Further, there are endless accounts of others giving similar testimony. Our brothers on 'the other side' are just as much our brothers as those appearing embodied 'here', and the healing, rejoining, restoring to Oneness with them is *of equal importance* to that of those appearing 'here'.

They love us and long for our acknowledgment of their presence with us. But their desire for us extends to something far beyond that: they are being of *practical help* to us in myriad ways, even when we have no awareness of their presence, let alone of that help. This is not just for our apparent easement as we labour, imprisoned in a body, but combining that aspect with that of our progress toward spiritual enlightenment.

An excellent example of that came to me in 1997 during encounters with our brother, Sir Oliver Lodge, the famous British physicist, (1851–1940), as described in Vignette 21 in "*Seek ye First the Kingdom…*", headed *Laser: Amplifying the Light for the Kingdom.* It is in the interests of those functioning from the place of the separation consciousness to promulgate the perception that all intercourse with those 'invisible' realms is to be avoided because it is, somehow, preposterously, *evil*; trafficking with Satan.

A scientific mind does not cease being that when it releases itself from its attachment to – even self-imprisonment, -restriction, -limitation within – a dense, 'physical' body. On the contrary, it now has access to immeasurably greater study, research, application and understanding of the so-called laws of time and place – physics, chemistry and biology – in its now less unencumbered state, than the dense, physical, financial, dogmatic, closed-minded and other self-imposed constraints upon its still-embodied counterparts.

So, any heart-centred, benign research endeavours for the common good can progress in the etheric realms at an exponentially more rapid pace, and those advances can be shared with their embodied fellows. This is happening around the world, every day, even though their embodied fellows may have no awareness of the source of their inspirational discoveries, inventions, advances. The researchers in spirit draw close to their embodied colleagues and overshadow them with a hint here, an idea there, a 'eureka moment' that suddenly comes to mind 'out of the blue'.

The acceleration of beneficial scientific progress has been occurring in recent decades because we are approaching the end of the 'tunnel of separation', and the 'veil' we placed, as part of the game of make-believe, between the two sides of the time-and-place coin is thinning – being shone away by the Light and the Love of Heaven. That same Love and Light is who and what we all, in our seemingly embodied state, also are, and thus can we choose to *contribute* to the Love and Light from our own within. This thinning – and ultimately, disappearance – of the veil is unstoppable, and will continue to gather pace as the healing, the restoration to remembrance of the Truth, the leavening, or raising-up of the Sonship of God to Oneness continues.

This does not mean we should throw caution to the wind, for all the while we believe/perceive ourself as being in time and place, the prince of time and place – the ego – still has the Way lined with pitfalls, including disguising malign artifices as 'benign breaksthrough'.

Only by vigilantly seeking guidance in Truth within, from One Who *Knows*, can we remain receptive to the Light being shone into our minds, that we may discern the difference, and thus continue to eschew darkness masquerading as light.

Diary of a Christ Communicant

A.M. November 12, 2010

Reality cannot be experienced in or from the perspective of the without. It can only be experienced within. This is possible, even when appearing to be embodied – in the without – simply by going within.

Papa is *I Am that I Am*. His Son, His Creation, is created in His likeness. We, who are One appearing as many in a dream of separation, are His Son, so we, also, are *I Am that I Am*. This is perceived as Synchronicity. (See Glossary.)

Synchronicity seems exceptional – impossible – to the mind that perceives itself as separated, but is normal to the mind that is attuned to the Spirit of Truth.

This is because there is no such thing as separation, so all is, in Truth, in reality, connected, *regardless* of outward appearances. Outward appearances are, as the term denotes, of the without, so have no meaning, no reality; they change, fade, disintegrate, as with any dream. Synchronicity is a sign, or symbol, of connectedness, which is normal, or reality. Reality cannot be experienced in or from the perspective of the without. It can only be experienced within. This is possible, even when appearing to be embodied – in the without – simply by going within.

When reality is *experienced*, symbols become meaningless because they merely *represent* reality in the consciousness of unreality. Synchronicity, being a symbol, does not exist in reality because all reality is connected. It does not, therefore, comply with the definition ascribed to it. The term is serviceable within the context of unreality only insofar as it may help an Awakening mind to understand reality – the connectedness of everything. When that connectedness is *experienced*, the symbol that represented it in unreality simply disappears – along with all the rest of unreality.

23: Moving from Bodily Sight to True Vision

Today we all rejoice in Heaven and Earth, for all is prepared that has been aforetime determined, and great works for the Kingdom and for the glory of the Father, and of His little ones, may now begin in earnest.

–*Jesus,* February 21, 1993

FROM TIME TO TIME people ask me how I see Jesus; what he looks like. In responding to this meaningfully, some care is needed, for we appear to dwell in a realm of illusions, and yet perceive them as real. We are so inured to perceiving ourself as a body, and likewise our brothers – all the other fragments of God's *One* Son, pretending to be what he is not – that distinguishing between Truth and illusion from this perspective can be confusing.

To try, we must switch back and forth between terminology – words, symbols – with which we are familiar, yet is misleading, and other, that represents reality, yet is *still* only symbolic because words can only *ever* be symbols, whether they are used to represent illusion *or* Truth. It can help, however, if we can first accept that we do not see with our eyes, but with our mind. Eyes were devised by a confused, upside-down mind to show us illusions in our game of make believe and persuade us that that which passes away is real, when, in Truth, only that which is eternal *can* be real.

Reality requires no bodily eyes for its cognition. Nevertheless, it takes *retraining* of our upside-down mind to enable it to discern reality without habitually engaging our eyes in attempting to do so, for when we do that, illusion gets in the way. Our eyes show us what is 'out there'; but there is, in Truth, *nothing* out there. So, we must retrain our mind to seek reality *within*. This takes time, and Help from One Who sees both Truth *and* illusion, and can help us tell one from the other during our switchover.

However, I have learnt that if we view any aspect of reality in relation to our life's experience as an 'equation', when we include *time* – as ego perceives it – in the equation there is likely to be stress, because the distortion that time introduces clouds our vision, preventing us from seeing clearly. This is because linear time is an illusion, devised to block, or veil, our vision of eternity. Including an illusion in a bid to see reality is a fundamental error. So, by choosing to exclude time from the equation, instantly the stress is removed. We could say to ourself: 'I know time is an illusion, so including it in any attempt to discern reality is bound to confuse me and cause anxiety because it will never make sense.'

By deliberately, *resolutely* choosing to omit time, peace can replace it. For example, we might say:

> 'I recognise that judgement and grievance are still part of who I experience myself as being, even though I have been struggling, striving to dispel those ego characteristics from my mind for a long time. I don't seem to be progressing and the clock keeps ticking, so what hope is there for me getting free and becoming enlightened during this lifetime?'

By rewording this consideration and removing any reference to, or relevance of, time, the whole deliberation can become peaceful. We could say, instead:

> 'I observe judgement appears to still be part of my identity, but I continue steadfastly to surrender this illusion into the care and power of the Holy Spirit, so I can *Know*, of a certainty beyond all doubt, that He *is* dispelling it – *because* I have *asked* Him, and He *always* responds freely, lovingly and *immediately* to our requests – according to His

perfect Love, wisdom and power. I am therefore *content* to leave it with Him. Thank you, Holy Spirit, for healing my mind.'

This change of approach can help us to stop stressing about it, and simply *observe*, as a passer-by, with no attachment to a result within an arbitrary, meaningless time-scale that we have unserviceably set. With this turnabout of our approach to ego issues, such as judgement, it is inevitable that, by not making time our enemy or our master, in due course we will notice that the issue has diminished significantly, and is no longer the monster controlling our life that it previously seemed to be. This diminution will continue, mostly unnoticed by our conscious mind, until it ceases completely to be part of our awareness, and inner peace has taken its place.

Of *course* we need to use our eyes – and take reasonable care of them – while we appear to be with a body, but we can, at the same time, choose to accept that they are not showing us *reality*. They merely serve us well while we proceed to remember that our body has one meaningful purpose only: to serve as a communication mechanism for sharing-by-*living* (not proselytising) the Truth of our Being, with all our brothers, as Papa's beloved Son. That is the way Jesus operated during his time with a body, so we know it can work for us also, if we so choose, *because* we are his brothers, and are, therefore, *like him*.

All that is a circuitous way of leading back to how I 'see' Jesus. The same way I – and all of us who appear to be with a body – see anything: with my mind. As stated above, our eyes are devised to show us unreality in a self-deceiving attempt at proving illusions are real. When we are sincere and steadfast in our commitment to choosing to see *reality*, and hand-over the reins to our Whole/Holy Self, the Spirit of Truth, He can begin to work His transforming works in us. This has to be a one step at a time process because if it all took place in an instant it would severely shock and disturb our equilibrium.

We are familiar with the concept of perceiving ourself and our brothers as bodies, and that is – at least to some degree – how I see him; but with my *mind*, bypassing my eyes in the process. It is more meaningful to speak of *having inner*, or *soul*, *awareness* of him – or anyone else from the Realms of Light – and this conveys to our mind immeasurably more of the subject than our eyes can ever capture. This is not something persona Brian (pB) took upon himself to effect, for he hadn't the faintest idea about any of this line of thinking. But, by the time I had reached early adulthood I had given my life into the care, guiding and protection of Jesus. This means I had given him full power and authority over all the affairs of my life, so he was able to begin the transforming, Awakening process within me.

Be assured that there is nothing unique, different, special or in any other way, unusual about pB in this. It is all entirely applicable and available to us *all*, without exception. A little willingness is all that is required of us, inextricably blended with faith and desire for it to be so. Those three words – willingness, faith and desire – are not something at which we can cherrypick on an occasional whim. They are symbols of a state deep within the heart-mind of us all which we are at free choice to accept, *or* allow ourself to be distracted, sidetracked from it by ego's dismantling tool: doubt.

In the early days it did seem that I was seeing Jesus in bodily form, and assumed, incorrectly, it *must* have been with my eyes, even though I was fully aware his form was of etheric, not physical, substance. Once we accept we see – have awareness – with our *mind*, it liberates us to begin seeing the Truth. Awareness of Jesus in bodily appearance, even without the mechanism of eyes being involved, is but a stepping-stone to the Truth of his – and our – Being. This is necessary because most of us are not yet ready for accepting the *whole* Truth of Being. That will be completed for all the fragments by the end of time, when all three measures of meal have leavened, at the end of the Aquarian, or *Kingdom*, age.

As my journey and relationship with him has progressed there has been less and less need for awareness of him in the sense of him being a bodily form – even an etheric one. More, I have an all-pervading sense, an awareness, an inner *Knowing* – in my soul, my mind, my heart – of his *presence*, his energy, his vibration, his joy, his Love, his humour, his peace, his fun, his ageless, timeless, all-*Knowing* wisdom; his caring, his absolute reliability and trustworthiness, all adding up to the complete package: his inestimable Self.

At the end of Matthew's gospel Jesus says: *I am with you alway, even unto the end of the world.* In order for us to have *awareness* of that he would *have* to show himself in bodily form. He does this to comfort, reassure, encourage us that he really *is* with us. His promise is to remain with us in *accessible*, discernible form until we are restored to awareness of our Oneness with him, so that when Papa takes the final step of lifting us to Heaven, in Him, forever, it will be *all of us*, as the *One* Son that we are, at the same instant.

Jesus is already in that state of fully Awake Oneness in Papa, but because he Loves his brethren totally, unconditionally, *Knowing* that we are all One with him, he waits, with *infinite patience*, to help us all return to that state of remembrance. That is Love and commitment, but it is also because he *Knows* it is a *Principle of Life of the Father*. As he said to me in 1968:

"I am attuned to all mankind all the time; there is never a moment when I am not with you all. All that is needed to complete the contact is for you to attune with me and we are together, at any time." He has also said to me (and untold others) thousands of times over the decades, "All is well." This is *entirely true*, because all that appears otherwise is *not* true, not real, and therefore, no-thing.

Thank You, Holy Spirit, for helping us to choose Love and commitment to living the Truth, the whole Truth and nothing but the Truth.

Diary of a Christ Communicant

A.M. November 28, 2010

**When you are at peace, then will you remember that
you are Love, and then you will *BE*, once more, in your
experience, your *awareness*, Love. This is happening –
even as you engage in any outer endeavours
– one step at a time.**

The perception of separateness is the cause of confusion. Bodily senses are devised with that in mind. Only going *within* can turn this around and restore us to peace.

When you are at peace, then will you remember that you are Love, and then you will *BE*, once more, in your *experience*, your *awareness*, Love. This is, even as you write these thoughts, happening, one step at a time. Indeed, as you sleep, eat, engage in any outward endeavours, the restoration of the fragmented Sonship to Oneness is inexorably unfolding. The next step for the Sonship in this process is *togetherness*, for togetherness is the portal to Oneness. The fragments are seeing this, experiencing it, participating in it, this reconnecting, reuniting in brotherly Love; and it is growing exponentially.

This is in accord, in principle, with Jesus' words to you in 1978, "Give me the pieces of your life and I will give you back the wholeness". Ego would place many obstacles – which are outward distractions – to this in the path. Do not wrestle with, fight, fear them. Simply *allow* them and engage them as need according to commitment to earthly circumstances dictates, all the while remaining focused upon, and committed to, the Kingdom *within*. It is within that you are *Known*, understood, guided, Loved, cared for. By this do outward considerations fall more smoothly into place.

The outer becomes subsumed into the inner until they

are indistinguishable as the process of togetherness in Loving harmony continues. Rejoice in this and welcome, embrace with your heart, all who approach you, are brought by Me into contact for kingdomly fellowship in the spirit of brotherhood. Even those who believe they have another agenda for contact can equally be Loved and embraced, by you *PCB-ing* and honouring them, and all who sojourn in time. Only in these ways, with willing commitment to forgive *all* illusions, can wholeness be restored out of brokenness.

24: Letting Technology *Serve* the Awakening

As the Word of Life goes out into the lives and conditions of the
little ones, so shall they go forward, lifted up by the prayers,
the blessings, the desire of those ahead on the Path to help those
behind, that all may go forward and become One with the Father.

–Jesus, February 28, 1993

T HE EGO LOVES TO PLACE STUMBLING BLOCKS in our path; obstacles to sidetrack us, cause us doubt, sabotage our faith and trust, harden our unbelief. For example, many find it impossible to accept the religious doctrines of the immaculate conception and the virgin birth, or that Jesus 'died' on the cross, because they cannot accept that resurrection from the 'dead' could be possible. These – and immeasurably more – are all delaying manoeuvres to distract us from the Truth of Eternity that Jesus came to restore to our remembrance.

If – *when* – we are committed unequivocally to the Truth of Eternity we do not need to concern ourselves with stumbling blocks. Jesus is not the slightest concerned with whether or not we believe in an immaculate conception, a virgin birth, or his restoring souls departed from their body back to embodiment, and other miracles, though institutionalised religions have belief in these – and other doctrines – as *prerequisite* to our 'salvation'. *His* intent is solely to help us remember the Truth of our Being, and to do this he said there were but two 'commandments' that would facilitate this: 1) Love God with all our heart, mind, soul and strength, and 2) Love our neighbour as ourself (Mt. 22:37-40).

Another delaying manoeuvre that has come to the fore in recent years is the idea that Jesus was not only married, but sired progeny. To many, encumbered by orthodoxy, the very idea of Jesus being married is an apostasy; and as for having children ... well, whatever next! But how would any of these ideas alter the Truth he came to share? Yet there are those who set off on the trail of his descendants, as if such would have to be imbued with spiritual enlightenment. Spiritual enlightenment is nothing to do with genetic inheritance; enlightenment, it hardly need be said, is of the soul, not the body.

Often, unenlightened souls incarnate through spiritually aware parents and enlightened souls through spiritually somnolent parents. None of these events is an 'accident', a 'mistake'. All are *opportunities* for growth. Chromosomes and genetic inheritance are affective only of *bodily*, not mind or soul, characteristics. Like everything to do with bodies, time and place and all in the world of illusion, they are flawed because they are not of God's creation. Jesus assuredly knew all that because he knew time and place is not of Papa's creation; so why would perpetuating his biological line have been on his agenda?

And if a line did arise from his supposed union with a woman – Mary Magdalene or any other – still his mission was *solely* to raise, resurrect, leaven the minds (not bodies) of the fragmented Sonship to remembrance of the Truth of Being of us all, unified-of-Mind as the One Son of our eternal, heavenly Father, created in His likeness, not some 'super-race' of bodies. That was – and remains – his intention. God is pure, limitless Spirit, and thus must all created in His likeness also Be. And nothing else. There can *be* nothing else because pure, limitless Spirit – Which is, and can only be, Love – is everything.

Nevertheless, Jesus was, and remains a pragmatist, and so is the Spirit of Truth, since They are of One, unified, Mind and one purpose. Jesus states in *A Course in Miracles* (Clarification of Terms,

p. 89, 6. The Holy Spirit, 1:1):

> Jesus is the manifestation of the *Holy Spirit*, Whom he called down upon the earth after he ascended into Heaven, or became completely identified with the Christ, the Son of God as He created Him.

He goes on to say:

> The Holy Spirit is described as the remaining Communication Link between God and His separated Sons … He never forgets the Creator or His creation. He never forgets the Son of God. He never forgets you. And He brings the Love of your Father to you in an eternal shining that will never be obliterated because God has put it there. (6.3, p.89).

> The Holy Spirit abides in the part of your mind that is part of the Christ Mind. He represents your Self and your Creator, Who are One … He seems to be a Voice, for in that form He speaks God's Word to you. He seems to be a Guide through a far country, for you need that form of help. He seems to be whatever meets the needs you think you have. But He is not deceived when you perceive your self entrapped in needs you do not have. It is from these He would deliver you. It is from these that He would make you safe. (6.4, p.89).

As pragmatists, They *Know* it is necessary to establish, manifest, the Kingdom of Heaven on Earth (KOHOE) – 'the real world' as described by Jesus in *A Course in Miracles* – to bring us close enough to Eternity that Papa can take that final step of raising us back into Himself there. This means transforming a fully dysfunctional, fear-filled illusion into a fully functional one: 'a happy dream', based in Love, forgiveness, co-operation (instead of competition, a device to maintain the illusion of separation). One could infer from this that understanding the human genome can be serviceable to the establishing of the KOHOE.

Replacing faulty genes – and all the myriad other technologies, extant and emerging – may *contribute* to transforming a fear-filled dream to a happy one but it still remains a dream; not an *Awakening* to the reality of Perfect Love and limitlessness in Eternity that is our heritage and destiny as Papa's Son.

So, though such medical and scientific advances may be beneficial to us while we appear to be in a dream of illusions, they will not fulfil our only true function within that dream as the saviours of our brothers, and thus of ourself, *through forgiveness*. If we believe they will, we are *distracted* by illusions rather than simply *using* them to serve our one, true function.

Diary of a Christ Communicant

A.M. December 3, 2010

You are as Papa created His beloved Son: pure, eternal, innocent spirit, in His own likeness. Thus can you *easily* forgive what seems to happen but in reality could not because it is all but a dream, and dreams are not real.

Ego's objective with bodies is temptation; not just by sex, but anything else of time and place – food, money, power … Yet even temptation is not its ultimate objective, for that is intended to engender guilt. It is guilt – conscious, but mostly *un*conscious – that entraps us, holds us, keeps us in the consciousness of fear, which is the reversal of the freedom that is Love. But because time and place and all associated with it, including bodies, are but a dream, an unreality, we are not – cannot be – guilty, and thus have no *cause* for fear.

Yet ego's wiliness and cunning don't stop there. It posits that we are guilty of bodily cravings and fantasising – thus 'proving' we are a guilty, sinful *body*, and thus, worthy of punishment by God. Hence, fear, and its seemingly endless perpetuation, keeps us on the not-so-merry-go-round; our attempt at hiding, being separate, from God.

Therefore, to move past that misperception, hold fast to the certainty of *Knowing*, beyond all doubt, that time and place is an illusion; that you are not a body; that you are as Papa created His beloved Son: pure, eternal, innocent spirit, in His own *exact* likeness. Thus can you *easily* forgive what seems to happen but in reality could not because it is all but a dream, and dreams are not real.

By continuing to believe a dream is real, and that the ego holds you in its thrall, you would endeavour to deny guilt by suppressing bodily desires. But suppressing the acting-out of bodily desires does not dispel them, because they remain in your mind. This can only cause conflict in your mind and *exacerbate* the feelings of guilt.

The obvious answer to all this is simply to remind yourself that you are not a body; that you have made it up as an integral aspect of the dream of separation, which is impossible, and thus you are eternally *innocent*; that all bodily cravings are illusory, and therefore, nothing. So, do not try to suppress them but rather, look *beyond* them to your greater, true Being, with My Help. And I, your *True Self*, will raise your focus of awareness to the Truth of eternal Being, which cannot but bring the experience of joy, peace and Love that are fulfilling beyond all temporal aspirations.

25: Engaging the Creative Process

Your awareness of the Oneness, the wholeness of Life in the Father Creator, grows apace, so that your experience of the reality and the livingness of being awake, alive, spiritually, opens up before you, giving you new vistas of the limitlessness of eternal Life.

–*Jesus*, March 28, 1993

THE IDEA THAT THERE COULD BE other than joy, peace and Love in eternity is, of course, meaningless. Happily, they are able to be experienced while we appear to be here in the dream of time also. At such moments those states of Being well up within us, often bubbling over in the form of laughter. This is joyful, healing laughter, for it helps us to forget, if only briefly, our belief in the lie of disempowerment to which we have been so inured. For most of us, such moments seldom endure for long, the world of perception distracting us with illusions of guilt, fear, misery, mortality.

According to Jesus, the tiny, mad idea of time, or separation from eternity, caused God's Son (us) to forget to laugh because he believed the idea was serious, being possible of happening, and thus, of causing real effects (*ACIM*, Chapter 27, pp.586–587, VIII.6). Yet, *either* there is an eternity of joy, peace and Love – Oneness in our Source – *or* there is time and place, in which, even if we can *momentarily* blot out fear, guilt and misery, death seems to us to be inescapable. Eternity is real; we merely imagined the unreality of

151

time and place, made it up, so can *unmake* it by imagining reality in its place.

Imagination is the creative aspect of our mind. The creative process *begins* with imagining. Nothing comes into Being without it first being imagined. Imagination is the process of forming, developing, begetting, causing, giving rise to *ideas* in our mind. From cause arises effect. Within the creative process it is inevitable that cause gives rise to effect. Jesus tells us that this is how the Creator created, caused, begot His Son; that His Son arose as an idea in His Mind, and that ideas never leave their source, though they can be extended *from* their source.

This simple axiom is demonstrable in the example that a person who imagines, gives rise to an idea can extend that idea into a product that can be given (or sold, in this world!) to others, so the product then becomes theirs, yet the *idea* remains forever in the mind that imagined, gave rise to, it.

The Truth of eternity is forever within, immovable from, the Mind of the Creator, Who created Truth, reality. That Truth is extended to, and remains, also immovably, within the Mind of His Son (us, remember). Truth is unchangeable, indestructible – hence its eternal nature – as is *all* that is created. The Truth is we – one, appearing as many in a dream, a made-up idea of separation – are perfect Love; unchangeable, indestructible, eternal. Exactly like our Creator.

God, it hardly need be said, has free will. He gave to, shared with, His creation, His Son, all that He Is, all that is His, at his creation; this includes, of course, free will. That free will empowers us to imagine whatever we choose. When we choose Truth in our imagining, the creative process is engaged. Like Papa, we, His Son, can only create in our likeness – Love. So when, with our free will, our imagining runs wild and we imagine the unimaginable, the unreal, the impossible, it *cannot* be created.

This shows the *perfect* Love of Papa; for if the impossible – the absence of Love, of Light, of freedom, of eternal Life, of peace, of joy – could be created it would be a *destructive conflict*, not a *creative process*. And there is no conflict, no destruction in Heaven/eternity, reality. To conceive of, beget, give rise to the unreal is, thanks be to God, impossible. So, the tiny, mad idea of the impossible and unbelievable was over the moment it seemed to arise. It only *seemed* to arise to a *confused* mind that had imagined it.

It could not *actually* arise because giving rise to is part of the *creative* process, which is Loving and eternal, not temporal, mortal, destructive. In order to appear to experience unreality, we *had* to forget the Truth of our Being, enter into a state of self-disempowerment, littleness, limitation … (all so absurdly complicated and un*real*) all 'qualities' that deny, veil, obscure, block our awareness of our Truth so we could 'believe' the unbelievable. There can be few who would disagree that such a state is lonely, fearful, distressing. Happily none of it is real, nor *could* it be real, because the *Principles of Life of the Father* are Papa's safeguard against unreality.

Unreality cannot, therefore, be created (created = eternal), but such is the power of belief of even the *split-off* part of the mind of Papa's Son that by *believing* – in its upside-down state – it is real, false images of **un**reality can be projected onto the screen, or veil, we placed over our true vision. This veil, fabricated from our choice for unbelief-in-reality, shows the unreal, projected 'diorama' of time and place – the without – which, in our state of *forgetfulness*-of-reality we perceive as real.

What is not *created* is entropic, or disintegrates; thus the *inevitability* of time and place coming to an end. This would mean the apparently-physical universe, in linear time terms, would (according to astro-physicists' calculations!) take trillions of trillions of years. But time, and all appearing in it, is merely an insane, meaningless dream, and the Voice for God, the Spirit of Truth, embodied in Jesus, the anointed messenger of the Holy One, came – and remains with us, readily, lovingly accessible to our within, until time is done – to show us, teach us, *by example*, the Truth of our Being.

We have two choices: we can believe the illusion of disempowerment in time and place – 'the human condition' – or we can, quite simply, choose Love. Choosing Love means we can experience the reality of peace and joy. Joy means laughter – joyous laughter – which, *like* a virus, is infectious and spreads to those around us. It *differs* from viruses in that it is healing. Because we are so conditioned, from countless illusory incarnations, in the consciousness of fear and disempowerment from Self we need Help in *reclaiming* our all-empowerment.

That Help is – *always* – immediately, freely available to us in the guise of Jesus and will enable us to reclaim, regain, God-given empowerment in our life. Because we have convinced ourself we are *dis*empowered, we need his strength and reassurance to restore our belief in the Self we, like him, *are*. So, first, we attune with him, reminding ourself that he says, "I am attuned to all mankind all the time; there is never a moment when I am not with you all. All that is needed to complete the contact is for you to attune with me and we are together, at any time."

Then, together with him, taking his hand – which he gladly, willingly, *lovingly* gives – for strength and support, and with the reassurance that joining with him brings to our otherwise enfeebled state of mind, we can say, with the certainty he imparts to us because we *Know* he is all-empowered, and he shares that empowerment with us by our joining with him, "Peace, be still", to tempestuous conditions. Those tempestuous conditions arise in our confused minds and spread from there to the weather, human relations in all their made-up (and thus, unreal) complexity at the interpersonal, political, religious, national and international levels …

We are well-versed in the *destructive* power of negative thinking. The world is a reflection of it, with wars, famines, pestilences, iniquity abounding. All this has arisen from misperceiving minds; *ours*. Think what the world can be like when we engage our minds – joining them with Jesus and the Spirit of Truth – in the *creative* power of forgiveness, Love, blessing, espousing good and eschewing evil … How can the result be other than the *real world*, or *Kingdom of Heaven on Earth*?

There is nothing, I repeat, *nothing*, stopping us from this change of mind except ourself. Thus must we begin with ourself, forgiving, blessing, Loving, embracing good and repudiating evil. From there it can but radiate outward to our brothers. This cannot happen without absolute, unwavering commitment because the ego loses no opportunity to distract us from this, our one and only true, meaningful purpose and function. We know this is within our power because Jesus demonstrated it and we are like him, sharing his Pedigree as Papa's beloved Son.

Papa's Son disempowered himself at the separation. But what Papa gives – and He gave His Son everything – *remains* given. Period. Therefore, all-empowerment is still with His Son, even in his seemingly fragmented, forgetful, self-blinded state. Now is the time for His beloved Son – us – to remember and *reclaim* our empowerment. Alone, this is impossible. With Jesus this is entirely possible and *easy. If only we can believe*. This is requisite because it is only our *un*belief that disempowers us.

Diary of a Christ Communicant

A.M. December 3, 2010 (part two)

The Truth is seen and understood from a greater perspective by those fragments of the Sonship who begin to stir to awareness of the Truth of Eternity. They begin to remember that time and place is but an illusion, and awaken to experience of a higher reality.

Suppressing, or *trying* to suppress the ego desires of seeming to be embodied in time and place clearly does not, cannot work, and as You say, don't try to suppress them but rather, look beyond them, to our greater, higher, true Being, with Your Help, Holy Self. However, the vast predominance of humanity is not ready to take such a discernment on board, so abandonment of self-control, self-discipline, would only lead to anarchy; a complete collapse of social, national and international order.

This is so at the time-and-place consciousness level of belief and perception and this is precisely what is happening at the switch-over time that occurs at the wind-down of one epoch and the commencement of the next. In this instance, this is the end of the second, *Jesus*, measure of meal and the beginning of the third, or *Kingdom*, measure of meal. Such a transitional period is dubbed 'the Chaos Time'.

But the Truth is seen and understood from a *greater* perspective by those fragments of the Sonship who begin to stir from their slumbers to awareness of the Truth of Eternity. They begin to remember that time and place is but an illusion, and awaken to experience of a higher reality. They discern that 'old-order' self-discipline endeavours to function according to the so-called 'laws' of time and place.

They observe that this is merely an attempt at maintaining control and order by suppression of the inclinations of a confused mind that still believes that time and place, and its 'laws' of limitation, scarcity, inequality, decay and 'death' are real. The *Awakening* mind begins to recognise that *none* of that is real. They see that instead, a *higher* order of Being – an esoteric, eternal, *perfect* order, which functions according to the reality of Love, equality, inclusion, the certainty that all is well – is in operation; an operation of freedom.

That higher order of Being is within all the fragments, without exception, because in reality the whole is in the part. It is the true Self; the *Christ* Self. And it is this Being which is now emerging from the chrysalis, and will have fully emerged for all the fragments by the end, and be the completion, the leavening, of the third measure of meal; the Aquarian, or Kingdom Age; the end of time and the restoration of Papa's beloved Son to Oneness and his ascension into the Heart of his Father, forever and ever.

Amen!!!

26: Waking from Slow Suicide to Eternal Life

*The steep places are where you go forward, leaving behind
unwanted burdens, no longer pertinent to the path ahead. Be
assured, my son, that leaving such baggage makes the journey
lighter, easier, more joyful.*

–*Jesus,* Easter Sunday, April 11, 1993

I N JOHN'S GOSPEL JESUS STATES: *I go to prepare a place for you. And if
I go and prepare a place for you, I will come again, and receive you unto
myself; that where I am, there ye may be also.* (Jn. 14:2,3). The inference
to be drawn from this is that he was going away, yet just before the
event referred to as the Ascension, he said to his followers: *I am
with you alway, even unto the end of the world* (Mt. 28:20). There seems
to be a contradiction here, but this is not because his *intent* was
actually contradictory. The seeming difficulty lies in reconciling
two perspectives.

One is the true, real, unchangeable perspective; the other is an
upside down, false, deceiving perspective. Believing time and place
are real means we are seeing everything upside down but *believing*
all that our bodily senses are telling us is right-side up, real, true
... So, when someone says the opposite of what we are *perceiving* is
reality, he still has to use some of our terminology, or language, to
get the message across. An example of this is when we say the sun
has gone down. We all know that isn't actually the case, but we use

the term anyway.

A small child sees it that way and believes it to be so because it *appears* that way and adults state it as so, even though *they* know it is otherwise. From the child's perspective, the sun revolves around the Earth. That same child perceives itself as a body, with a name given it at birth, and spends the rest of its embodiment believing that is its identity. Yet throughout history there have been an enlightened few who have known within themselves that none of this is actually so. However, when they expressed this discernment it made little impact on the consensus perception.

Jesus spoke to his friends and followers about eternal reality, but that doesn't mean he didn't Know it is a waste of time trying to explain to people what they are not yet ready to hear. He also Knew the time would come to each of us when we *would* be ready to hear with our *inward* discernment and accept esoteric Truth as reality, recognising what had previously been accepted as real to the outer, or exoteric perception is a result only of what we have been led to believe. To many that may sound too simplistic an explanation, insufficient to persuade them.

Yet, in a confusing, ever-changing world, when so many different perceptions are being made, and so many different, often conflicting explanations offered on a given matter, most choose to believe what they *want* to believe, so that is what they see. This is almost always without a willingness to consider *all* the relevant data. For example, we are told by institutions set up by governments to safeguard our well-being that pesticides, fire retardants, microwaves … are safe within certain tolerances.

But those tolerances do not take into account the *cumulative* effects on us over decades. Nor do they take into account the *combined* effects of a vast array of man-made molecules our bodies ingest/assimilate from our food and the environment at large, also over decades. Those combined effects are not simple, arithmetic effects, but logarithmic.

About a hundred years ago cancer affected around three percent of people in what is now referred to as the developed world.

It is now between thirty and forty percent and rising so rapidly that many are projecting it to reach fifty percent within a decade or so. Here is a statistical example:

In 1935 only one case of cancer had been reported in the last fifty years by the Inuit people of Alaska and Canada. After they began eating processed foods, their cancer rate exploded until it equalled that of the US by the 1970s.

For centuries religions kept the people in the dark and under their control by withholding spiritual, esoteric, mystical Truth and in its place preached false doctrines of guilt, sin, sacrifice, unworthiness, judgement and punishment by a wrathful God. Today, with that control all-but exhausted, governments and 'big business' are withholding from the people information about the damage caused by most of what we eat, drink, wear, sit on, walk on, sleep on, breathe, communicate with ... How many men walk around with their 'smart' phone in their trouser pocket all day? Prostate, testicular and bowel cancers have sky-rocketed since their advent. How 'smart' is that?

How many women use a microwave oven in preparing meals each day? Breast cancer has soared since the advent of microwave ovens, which sit on counter-tops, at or near chest level ... It goes on and on. In our choice to be separate from Papa, our mind is in an upside-down, confused, misperceiving state. In that state we have fabricated a false way of living that is killing us, and are so addicted to it that we do not *want* to hear the truth about it. So we pay government scientists to give us false information (half-truths are false) because we are so addicted to killing ourselves.

The vast mass of fragments of the Sonship of God is unready and unwilling to hear and believe the Truth of our eternal, invulnerable, effulgent, all-empowered Being. They choose to believe, instead, lies that not only keep us in spiritual darkness (with ever-increasing media emphasis on the body as what we are), but are leading – actually, have already led – us into a lifestyle that is killing us; a situation to which the populace has, so far, chosen to remain in blissful ignorance and denial. How good the ego is at fabricating aphorisms that in our blindness we accept as 'wise', such as "Where ignorance is bliss, 'tis folly to be wise". How can deliberately, blindly, *blithely* choosing to ignore danger be wise?

But all this is changing because Jesus did not go *away* – leave us to our own devices – to prepare a place for us. He has kept his promise to be with us 'alway' because his mind and spirit live within our heart-mind; including those who are unaware of his presence. His Great Rescue Programme – the leavening of three measures of meal (Mt. 13:33) – is now in the final phase of leavening; raising up, resurrecting, healing our split, sick, insane minds. He had to be where the problem is in order to heal it, and prepare a place for us – *that where I am, there ye may be also* – i.e., heal our mind, restore it to whole, holy, *Christ* Mind.

A necessary step in the healing process is exposing the lies and half-truths, so that we are then in a position to choose either to continue with ego's script for lies, doubt, fear, conflict, illness, 'death'… or choose freedom. That exposure is happening now, largely thanks to the internet, and democracy is arriving, nascent, on planet Earth. But only when we choose our will to be at One with the perfect Will of God are we *truly* free. The Will of God is that His Son be saved – *awakened* from his insane, ego self – and restored to eternal Oneness in Him. This, therefore, is our *true* will also, and our only meaningful purpose in being here.

> *Father, Christ's vision is Your gift to me, and it has power to translate all that the body's eyes behold into the sight of a forgiven world... The world forgiven signifies Your Son acknowledges his Father, lets his dreams be brought to Truth, and waits expectantly the one remaining instant more of time which ends forever, as Your memory returns to him. And now his will is one with Yours. His function now is but Your Own, and every thought except Your Own is gone* (ACIM, Workbook for Students, p.430, Lesson 270).

Let us today behold each other in the sight of Christ.

How beautiful we are! How holy and how loving! Brother, come and join with me today. **We save the world when we have joined.** For in our [joined, Christ] vision it [the world] becomes as holy as the Light in us (*ACIM*, Workbook for Students, p.457, Lesson 313).

I have a special place to fill; a role for me alone. **Salvation waits until I take this part as what I <u>choose</u> to do.** Until I make this choice, I am the slave of time and human destiny ['death']. But when I willingly and gladly go the way my Father's plan appointed me to go, then will I recognize salvation is already here, already given all my brothers and already mine as well.

Father, Your way is what I choose today... The memory of You awaits me there. And all my sorrows end in Your embrace, which You have promised to Your Son, who thought mistakenly that he had wandered from the sure protection of Your loving Arms (*ACIM*, Workbook for Students, p.459, Lesson 317).

Let us, now, spend a moment together, silently joining our minds as one, in Christ, our true, unified Being, and bless the world, *every living thing*, for our rejoining as one, in wholeness, holiness. Forever.

Diary of a Christ Communicant

A.M. December 5, 2010

When you commit to forgiving all blocks to Love's awareness, then will you *Know* again the true experience of Perfect Love, which is a never-ending orgasm of the soul; a thousand times a thousand more consummate than any such feeble, bodily substitute.

In the upside-down, illusory world of time and place, we may believe we know what love is, and most of us may feel we experience love when we 'fall in love'. But time and place is a reversal of reality – Eternity – and we, Papa's Son, made up time and place, to appear to be, and experience, what we are not. In Truth we are like our Father

Creator: Love. Perfect, unconditional Love; *totally* Loving. That means *no* judgements, *no* grievances, *no* blame games, *no* attack, *no* defence … ever. All the while we believe, and thus perceive, we are what we are not we are placing blocks before our *awareness* of Love being our reality.

> Love is beyond the capability, the possibility of experiencing, of being the all-pervading awareness and reality while those blocks are kept in place. They are guilt, fear; allowing intellectualisation, or rationalisation to come before reason.
>
> They will be immovable without first surrendering ego's leasehold on one's life to true Self, and hand over the reins, the helm, control of thoughts to Him. Judgement and grievance seem heavy blocks indeed, but Self has the tool for transforming them into lighter-than-air nothingness: forgiveness.
>
> By a little willingness to co-operate with Self and commitment to forgiving all apparent blocks to Love's awareness, Self will effortlessly remove them and wakefulness to Love will be restored. Then will be *Known* again the true experience of Perfect Love, which is a never-ending orgasm of the soul, a thousand times a thousand more consummate than any such feeble, bodily substitute. Then will all guilt, fear, judgement, unforgiveness, grievance, shame, scarcity, separation, death … be gone from belief, awareness, experience. Forever.

Papa: Thank You for giving us the Spirit of Truth, The Holy Breath, Your Voice – to be with us when we foolishly chose to leave You and venture into a far country – so that the voice of reason would always be available to us, to restore us to sanity and guide us Home again.

We choose now to eschew the voice of insanity and focus one-pointedly, steadfastly on listening only to our heart-mind, where our true Self, our true Being resides, along with You. Amen.

27: The Polarity Switch

. . . keep on as ever, for your awareness of the Light and the Living Word continues to grow apace, and this must be your strength and your shield from the wickedness of the world. Fear not, for I am with you, your guide in hostile territory.

–Jesus, April 25, 1993

THERE ARE THOSE WHO SAY the Sun and the Earth are undergoing a reversal of polarity and that this is the cause of the turmoil we are witnessing in this world. I am not privy to any inner revelation on this, but it seems evident that outer turmoil – including that in the Sun and on Earth – is but a reflection of *inner* turmoil, and the 'inner' is the fragmented, split-off-from-Truth, upside-down *mind* of Papa's Son. In the *Diary of a Christ Communicant, Part Two*, entry dated December 3, 2010, (see page 155, Chapter 25 of this book) the Spirit of Truth stated that this period of inner turmoil is dubbed 'the Chaos Time'.

He explained that this is happening at the switch-over time that occurs during the wind-down of one (linear-time) epoch and the commencement of the next. In this instance, this is the end of the second, *Jesus*, measure of meal (Piscean Age) and the beginning of the third, or *Kingdom*, measure of meal (Aquarian Age). The chaos is caused by the fragmented minds, which are what are *actually* undergoing the polarity shift, or reversal, and are being torn between harking back to the old (negative) order consciousness and Awakening to the New (positive) Order awareness of eternal reality.

The old, negative polarity is the consciousness of fear. Control and order were preserved *outwardly* using guilt, fear, judgement, condemnation and punishment. Not exactly the Kingdom of Heaven on Earth! Institutionalised religion operated thusly during the *Jesus* measure of meal. It remains to be seen how it will unfold as the Kingdom measure progresses and unfolds. The positive polarity we are moving into is *heart* centred, *r*ecognising that unconditional, perfect Love, forgiveness, peace, Oneness are eternally ours in the ever-present *Now*. The only control required for this is Inner Self control, which is perfect freedom.

The negative-polarity, self-disempowerment consciousness abdicated the perceived authority, guidance, protection and safety to other, *outward* authorities, which wavered between *church* – which falsely claimed (and still does) to be the Bride of Christ, representing God and Christ on Earth, and thus, to have power over the *souls* of the people – and *state*, which exercised self-serving power over the *bodies* of the people. Church and state wrestled for control over their *minds*, usually with inveiglements that mostly were thinly disguised threats of temporal and/or eternal punishment.

Many observed the flaws in this dualistic state of affairs, but most saw no way around it; uprisings against church or state were ruthlessly crushed, with brutal torture, slaughter, repression and retribution being freely meted. But there was a modicum of safety felt by those who toed the line. Yet that sense of safety frequently turned to uncertainty as conflict and jockeying for power broke out within – and between – church and state, not to mention one version of the church and another, rival version. This is the legacy of disempowerment by untold millions of fragments, accruing in the unconscious mind during embodiment and re-embodiment over millennia.

In recent generations the church has been losing its power over the people; perhaps because it can no longer (openly, anyway) threaten, torture, murder dissenters!? And the now-emerging lies, moral turpitudes, inner conflicts and attempted cover-ups have all-but sounded its death-knell. Still, millions place their trust for leadership and protection in governments. Yet threats, torture, murder, even genocide have lingered longer with all too many state authorities, and corruption and lying are pandemic.

Now, in this time of changing polarities, the lies and corruption in state authorities are also coming into the open, and people around the world no longer believe or trust their leaders, even rising up against them, including in the so-called 'first world'. The demise of the negative order is leaving somnolent souls feeling lost, not knowing who or what to believe and losing faith and trust in anyone to provide honourable, transparent leadership. Meanwhile, the New, *positive* polarity arises from the within of the Sonship, and ever more fragments are remembering that the only power for real leadership lies within each of us; that this can only work fairly when we function ubiquitously in unison, recognising and allowing the Truth of our spiritual equality. As the Great Awakening progresses and the move from negative to positive polarity proceeds, so does the negative polarity diminish, until completely dispelled. Then the positive power will be all there is, so there will be no more polarity involved; only the positive power that is perfect, unconditional Love.

The power of the positive polarity is our one, true Identity, the Christ Self within us all. As this continues Its ascendancy, more and more are remembering that *Self* control, and this will progress to awareness that this is freedom, comfort, happiness, fulfilment and Self empowerment because our true, Christ Self is *One* in the Source of All Being: Love. Now that *is* empowerment! Those who cleave to the old, negative polarity will find no comfort because it is fading away, disintegrating in chaos and turmoil, without direction. But when the moment is right, they, also, will be drawn to the positive, the Light, *because we are One*.

The role of each of us as the Light and the saviour of the world is to be truly helpful to our floundering, languishing brothers, responding to their calls for Love *only* with Love, by blessing and forgiving. This can but hasten their awakening, and in so doing, hasten our own because we are, *inextricably*, One. The ego that *seems* to be within our mind, masquerading as ourself, will resist this, telling us we are arrogant, blasphemous, heretical. Can we hear Jesus telling us this? He leads us to the Light, where we can be seen in our true Light *as* the Light.

If we *deny* we are the Light we are denying ourself our own Truth, our own reality. Most of us can acknowledge *Jesus* as the Light, and he tells us we *also* are the Light (Mt. 5:14). Now is the time of the reversal of our polarity from denying our Truth to *claiming* it – and *pro*claiming it to our brothers as their Truth also – by living and embodying it (*not* by proselytising). We have a template, an exemplar for this in Jesus. If – *when* – we have had enough of the negative polarity we can join the switch-over; we simply accept his empowerment within us by desiring, choosing to join our mind to his. This is easy because he's *already* in our mind, waiting with infinite patience for us to acknowledge it and accept his offer to join with him.

He will help us – he *longs* to help us – to become like him, but can only do so in *response* to our asking and our willingness to co-operate with him in this process. If we truly desire to become like him we will be helping him – and thus, ourself – by training our mind to *think* like him. Most of us are still – albeit, mostly unwittingly – using the ego's lexicon of lies when an immeasurably more serviceable and meaningful lexicon of Truth is freely available to us. We are free to start using that lexicon – *without money and without price* – right now, and abandoning the old, outworn, self-destructive one.

The old order, negative-polarity lexicon speaks of separation, guilt, fear, judgement, grievance, punishment, unworthiness, limitation, scarcity, frailty, death … Death, along with all its myriad other terms, is the great granddaddy of the ego's lies. Our body cannot die because it was never alive; it is merely a little mound of clay that we chose to animate for a span, a moment; and our soul was never born, is immortal, so can certainly never die.

As the Great Awakening progress and the move from negative to positive polarity proceeds, so does the negative polarity diminish, until completely dispelled. Then the positive power will be all there is, so there will be no more polarity involved. There is no polarity in the Heaven that is eternity, only the positive power that is perfect, unconditional Love.

The positive power, into which we are now ascending, led by Jesus and the Holy Spirit within us all, has a lexicon that speaks of perfect Love, innocence, worth, eternal bliss, peace, joy, eternal, abundant Life, completion, Oneness ... Choosing to abandon our mesmeric fixation with the negative-polarity lexicon and, with Their Help, *vigilantly* adopt the positive-power, New Order lexicon will inestimably hasten the collapse of time and our restoration to Oneness as the Christ Self – Papa's beloved Son – that is the true Identity of us all.

> God's memory is in our holy minds, which know their Oneness and their unity with their Creator. Let our function be **only** to let this memory return, **only** to let God's Will be done on earth, **only** to be restored to sanity, and to **be** but as God created us (*ACIM*, Workbook for Students, p.461; 11. What is Creation?, 4:5–6).

Diary of a Christ Communicant

A.M. December 9, 2010

> **In the apparently separated, or upside-down conscious-ness, one may believe one is judging another, but in Truth it can only be possible that one is judging – and therefore, condemning – oneself, since in reality all are but One.**

In this upside-down world, appearances are the seeming opposite of reality (since appearances are of time and reality is of eternity, how can it be other?). So when we see a fragment of the bewildered

Sonship behaving in an unkingdomly (unloving) way, the temptation is to react in an equally unkingdomly (judgemental) way.

> This is an absolute indicator of the degree of ego domination of the mind. All the seeming fragments of the Sonship of God are Love. All who are not *expressing* Love are *calling* for Love. I need not remind you that unkingdomly behaviour is a *call* for Love. Love can only respond to a call for Love by *expressing* Love. This is the *natural* way – *God's* way – of Being. To respond to a call for Love with judgement is upside-down; in opposition to God's way – and is, therefore, unnatural – and His perfect Son's, too, since His Son is like his Father.

> To not respond to a call for Love with Love is to pretend to be what one is not. By such pretence it is inevitable that the sight will be double [confused]. Hence Jesus' reminder that if your eye be single, your whole body shall be full of Light, but if your sight be double, your whole body shall be full of darkness, and 'If therefore the light that is in thee be darkness, how great *is* that darkness!' [Mt. 6:23].

> Judgement, therefore, it can be readily seen, obscures the Light that is the Truth of eternity, of which all are inescapably part, so it can be safely observed that judgement obscures the Light, or Truth of Being, of all who judge, causing all such to perceive themselves as not what they are. In the apparently separated, or upside-down consciousness, one may believe one is judging another, but in Truth it can only be possible that one is judging – and therefore, condemning – oneself, since in reality all are but One.

> Even an upside-down mind can see the absurdity, the unserviceableness of such an action, can it not?

28: Transforming Enmity into Amity

Whosoever shall drink of the wine of my Love, it shall be in him as a well of Living Water, springing up unto Life eternal.

–Jesus, May 8, 1993

I N THE EARLY 1990s, my brother had a falling-out with our parents, and all contact between them was severed for some while. The dispute was, in the grand scheme of things, trivial; ego was doing what it does best – breaking relationships, thus delaying the inevitable restoration to Oneness of the fragmented Sonship. After about a couple of years I said to him, "It would be a shame if the old folks pass on without a healing of this rift. The moment they are gone it will be too late for you to do anything about it, and then you will have the rest of your life to regret a missed opportunity." This is not, of course, *actually* true, but I knew that from his perspective it would be perceived as such.

He obviously thought about this for a while, and it was not long before he took the initiative and restored a loving familial relationship. A few years later, when our dad was in a coma, hours before he breathed his last, my brother and I sat with him through the evening, reminiscing about our childhood, family life, what our parents meant to us ... When it came time to take our leave, knowing this would be the last time we would see him, we bade our fond farewells and my brother kissed him lovingly, tenderly, respectfully, honouringly on the forehead. It was a touching act of filial affection.

I have no doubt my brother was, and remains, grateful that he patched up a senseless spat while the opportunity still remained, and afterwards, realised the utter meaninglessness of it and how much more glad and peaceful his mind was able to be than if he had allowed a petty grievance to hold sway over reason. Viewed from the Light of eternal reality, *all* grievances are petty, however 'justified' they may seem from the false, upside-down perspective of time and place.

Most of us have made, and continue to make, mistakes, errors, misperceptions, judgements, and have unresolved issues with ourself and various brothers. When we come to the end of our sojourn with a body, and lay it aside, we have the opportunity to enter into a period of reflection about the progress we have made toward the Light of our eternal Home in Papa during this moment of embodiment. Many of us, entering such a period of reflection, will likely have regrets over missed opportunities to fulfil our only *real* purpose for being here. That purpose is to *heal* the broken Sonship.

The Sonship cannot be healed without the committed involvement and participation of each and every one of us. One fragment omitted from the healing means the Sonship is not complete, which means *Papa* is incomplete; for Father and Son are One. Every missed opportunity for healing brokenness – transforming enmity into amity – means unnecessary delay for those involved and additional circuits of the carousel of birth and death.

We do not need to wait until we lay aside our body to enter into a period of reflection on our progress toward the Light during this illusory embodiment. We can begin now; for there *is* only Now. Delaying is of the ego; it is not of *our* true nature. Delaying may seem like a soft option, but continuing one moment longer than necessary in the consciousness of fear – when uninterruptible, eternal peace and Love are *already* ours, awaiting our joyful *acceptance* – is far from soft. And it is but fear – which we have made up, not Love, which is real – that causes us to delay.

Such periods of reflection, as with all aspects of our Being, will not serve us well if they are used for self-recrimination and regret at the opportunities perceived as missed in the past. The past is over; it was *never* real. The only reality is the eternal *Now*; the forever, unchanging always. Now is the opportunity to forgive, Love, bless and release all we have been hanging onto as a substitute for God. The only alternative is to choose more of the same illusions of separation – valuing the valueless – from Self, our brothers and our Creator. The modern idiom, of which I have no fondness, nevertheless seems apposite here: This is a 'no-brainer'.

To ensure we are making the best of such periods – *opportunities* – we will do well to engage the counsel of One Who is ahead of us on the Path, and therefore, has a larger perspective than we. Indeed, there is no reason for not engaging the input of One Who has *completed* the journey Home, and whose perspective, therefore, also is complete. Ego would have us believe 'Jesus is too busy to have time to concern himself with my little issues.' I can affirm absolutely that this is not true. Jesus functions from eternity, so time is no limit for him, and he is at peace, so has no concerns either.

When we join our life with his he can help us remember that what we perceived as concerns, when viewed with the eyes of Christ, are nothing. It cannot be overemphasised what he told me in 1968:

> "I am attuned to all mankind all the time; there is never a moment when I am not with you all. <u>All that is needed to complete the contact is for you to attune with me and we are together, at any time.</u>"

Clearly, then, joining our life with his is entirely possible and indeed, easy. All that is required is the desire.

Now is the time for us all to reclaim the Truth of Self as our own: our brotherhood with Jesus in the Sonship of God, and thus, our equality with him, both in his sight and Papa's. Further, we all have loved ones in spirit working in harmony with him for our succour, our easement, our progress on our journey. All are there for us, to be truly helpful, so that we, in turn, can be truly helpful to brothers in need of *our* help.

We have been told there is a veil between us, in our illusorily embodied state, and those who have laid aside their body. This is a lie, but because we *believe* it, it *appears* to be true. We made it up; God did not create it, so it is not real. If He had, it would be immovable; but He did not, so it *is* movable – by us. It is merely a feeble attempt at *hiding* from the Truth. Who, in his *right* mind, would want to hide from the Truth? God created Oneness – which is Truth – not separation, nor any of its spurious appurtenances. We are in the moment when the unreal – including the veil of separation – is disintegrating and Truth is returning to our remembrance.

We can now dispense with our shabby paraphernalia, the dross of self-deception, and venture into the Light that is *already* within us. That Light, which we *are*, just as Jesus told us, is in our mind. It is the Spirit of Truth and is, according to Jesus, *the mechanism of miracles. He recognizes both God's creations and your illusions. He separates the true from the false by His ability to perceive totally rather than selectively.* (ACIM, Chapter 1, pp.5–6, I. Principles of Miracles, 38).

By This Mechanism we can commune with the mind of our brother with whom there are unhealed issues, for He Is the Connecting Link between all 'separated' minds, re-establishing them (us) as the One Mind that is their (our) reality. This communing appears as temporary from the time and place perspective, but *leads* to permanence as we come to acceptance of it. By this Link, forgiveness can be established, thus effecting healing of brokenness, even when our brother is not in *conscious* awareness of, or even agreement with, it. Then, when the moment is right, that connection will be recognised and accepted as the true estate of all parties involved, transforming enmity back to amity.

Diary of a Christ Communicant

A.M. December 16, 2010

**When synchronicity happens, be assured that Heaven
is involved, synchronising events and circumstances for
your benefit; for the benefit of *all*. So gratitude
is appropriate.**

Synchronicity seems to be amazing, remarkable, astonishing … from the time and place perspective. It works for our benefit, controlled and operated from higher Mind. It seems a rare occurrence for those who are closed to eternal reality, dismissed as mere 'coincidence'. But as we open to acceptance of it, it becomes more and more part of our experience during our sojourn in a body. Synchronicity is a practical, beneficial demonstration that we are, in reality, all connected, because in reality we are all One. There *is* no separation.

Synchronicity is not of Heaven, but not of Earth, either. Ego does not understand it and therefore cannot use it. Synchronicity is a device, a mechanism, a process engaged by, or from, higher Mind – as you correctly observe – to effect and further Its objectives in the Atonement, based on the eternal reality that all is One; an invisible matrix of which ego is completely unaware. So it perceives it as coincidence.

Like forgiveness, synchronicity cannot be of Heaven because action and change are part of its observable effects, and there is no action in Eternity because all is already accomplished, so there is nothing to do; no action is required – all is perfect, complete, There. There is no doing, only Being.

Synchronicity is the manipulation, or co-ordination, *of* outer circumstances *from* within, to bring them into harmony with the outworking of the Great Rescue Programme. Ego does not understand the Great Rescue Programme *or* synchronicity but is suspicious of both.

When synchronicity happens, be assured that Heaven is involved, synchronising events and circumstances for your benefit; for the benefit of *all*. So gratitude is appropriate.

29: Soul Mates

. . . wrestle not with the prince of time and place, but heed my counsel to be at peace, so that you may become One with the Father's Life, opening up your channels of receptivity to the eternal reality.

–Jesus, June 27, 1993

THE TERM *SOUL MATES* has come to the fore in recent years, and even for those who do not perceive themselves as having one, it is widely recognised as being something deeper, more meaningful than simply having a spouse, a partner, a friend, though soul mates might well be any of these. But soul mates know that they require no label, certificate, licence; neither do they need acceptance or recognition by any worldly institutions or statutes. And, since there is no such thing as gender in our eternal reality, sex is incidental – one could say optional – in soul mate relationships.

Sex and money are two of the ego's main armaments in effecting division, so even when genuine soul mates enjoy rapturous sex, eventually they move past that as the main attraction and the *real* purpose of their relationship in time and place moves into the ascendancy. Nevertheless, the sexual attraction will very likely serve the key purpose of enabling other souls to come into embodiment, either to extend and strengthen – consolidate – the soul-family relationships here, or equally important, to provide opportunity for the healing of *broken* relationships.

The latter is *very* common, though in most cases the opportunity fails to achieve its intention, because the parties involved remain too engaged with this world's distractions of fear, scarcity and judgement, so forgetfulness of the objective holds sway. Karmic entanglements either get healed, saving time and incarnations, or they get even more broken and entangled than before, requiring yet more time and incarnations – *opportunities* – to be called forth for the healing to be effected. So myriad intentions get waylaid by ego's distractions, keeping us riding the carousel of birth and death.

Soul mate relationships, like every other kind of relationship, do not come about by chance. By way of example, two souls might decide to incarnate with a joint purpose. A re-connecting plan is pre-agreed, at least in broad terms; the details will be fine-tuned nearer the moment, with the help of other members of the extended soul family, who are also privy to the plan, 'pulling a few strings' from spirit. So the two incarnating souls are, in fact, part of a wider relationship, where scores or even hundreds – who have been in close and loving association for many incarnations – also participate.

When the couple 'meet again' in their embodied state there will be an inner Love *re*cognition, re-establishing the bond that was forged/agreed between them 'aforetime' (i.e., before they incarnated). For souls of opposite (or perhaps more serviceably defined as 'complementary') gender this will be experienced as 'falling in love'. This is simply to cement the bond that will enable their pre-agreed purpose together to be outworked to its completion – if there is sufficient commitment to prevent ego's distractions from derailing them from their purpose.

Outwardly it may seem only the two embodied souls are engaged in the soul mate relationship. But they may have agreed aforetime on some mission for the healing of brokenness, the bringing of Light into the darkness of separation, the furthering of the manifesting of the Kingdom of Heaven on Earth. This is the committed objective of untold millions of crystal (Christ-all) souls now incarnate or in the process of incarnating. Any souls on such

Kingdom-calling missions will be part of a large, extended, equally Kingdom-committed family in spirit, and all there to provide support for the soul-mates' objectives.

So, soul mates may seem just to be a couple, but actually they are only the tip of the iceberg. From a greater perspective we are *all* soul mates because we are all brothers in the Sonship of our Father. This will become more apparent as the Great Rescue Programme continues to unfold toward its inevitable completion. Meanwhile, hasty decisions, or entering into another embodiment without purposeful planning, or mindful consideration for selection of a *Companion of the Way*, is likely to lead to unserviceable choices for such a companion. Errors, based on interpreting ego signals as Holy Spirit signals, can –and usually do – lead to *further* brokenness.

Partners, or soul mates, sensibly, purposefully joining for a kingdomly mission may elect to stay as partners for numerous embodiments, but because unconditional Love is universal – not *exclusive* – such partners will intuitively know that they are free to make alternative choices for missions where a different partner would be more serviceable to a fulfilling outcome. That does not mean the end of one soul-mate relationship and switching to another in the way this world perceives it, for unconditional Love is far beyond that; and as already stated, we are ALL soul mates in the eternal context.

Soul mates join to support each other and help each other grow, such as by providing opportunities for forgiveness, learning/remembering patience, tolerance, acceptance … all of which lead to the extension of Love by helping to remove blocks to the *awareness* of Love's presence. That support – always agreed by both parties aforetime – can sometimes seem deeply distressing, such as when one chooses an early exit strategy (laying aside the body), leaving the other feeling bereft. This can serve to help the discernment that *attachment* to another – which is not the same as *Love* – can detract from the importance, the value, of reliance upon Self.

For only absolute reliance on Self – God-Self, Christ-Self *within* – will ultimately serve us perfectly on our journey Home to Oneness. How easy it is to get distracted from this Truth when seeming to be embodied in a world devised *specifically* to distract us from eternal Truth. Careful planning, pre-incarnation, with wise counsel, including from One Who *Knows* all Truth, will readily recognise this. So a strategy for countering misperceptions during embodiment will likely be built into the plan.

Very often one party will be seen by the other as wiser, cleverer, more advanced … and this can, in the world of forgetfulness of Self, cause dependency by one on the other, perhaps inducing a sense of unworthiness. Yet all are equal in the sight of God and of Christ, our true Being. Both parties in a soul mate relationship bring qualities that complement and support the other, enabling the purpose of the relationship to be advanced and fulfilled for *both*, and without which that may not have become possible. Thus, false pride and false humility can serve only ego's script, never Holy Self's.

Even if our senses suggest inequality in a soul mate relationship, it will serve us, the Spirit of Truth and the coming of the Kingdom of Heaven on Earth – the real world – well to remind ourself that in the sight of God and our own, Christ-Self, unless, or until, we are able to accept the equality of all as *eternal*, unchangeable Truth, we can in no wise enter the Kingdom. Not because Papa is barring us but because our own misperceptions are keeping us out of resonance with the perfection – the absolute equality – of Heaven.

Diary of a Christ Communicant

A.M. December 18, 2010

Time and place is the apparent opposite of eternity – reality – so free will means it is always possible to choose to experience reality, which is Truth, instead of unreality, which is merely an illusion, an attempt at self-deception.

The idea that there could be pain or suffering, guilt or fear in eternity – Heaven, reality – is absurd, comical, meaningless. Therefore, if we perceive ourself to be experiencing pain or suffering, we can say to ourself, 'I am experiencing unreality. That, therefore, must be nothing more than my *choice*. Therefore, I am free – because I have God-given free will – to choose again.'

Time and place is the apparent opposite of eternity – reality – so free will means it is always possible to choose to experience reality, which is Truth, instead of unreality, which is merely an illusion, an attempt at self-deception. Such a new choice may not always bring the change of experience desired *immediately*. This is because the choice to perceive the lie as Truth for so long requires that the mind – the source of all false beliefs and therefore all perceptions and experiences – needs retraining.

How strong, how steadfast, how unequivocal is the *desire* to choose anew? How great is the *commitment* to allow that change of mind in order to open it to the experience of freedom from pain, suffering, fear, guilt, judgement, grievance and death?

30: Adversity: Opportunity in Disguise

Now is the time for your eyes to be opened, and you shall see the glory and joy of our Father's House.

–Jesus, July 18, 1993

W HATEVER TURNS UP IN OUR LIFE is *always*, without exception, the perfect thing. But we – in our upside-down, back-to-front ego mind – tend, with stultifying persistence, to perceive so many of such arrivals as adversity. All the while that is our choice so will it be, to us, adversity. Thus are we preventing ourself from seeing the *Truth*. We have wrapped the perfect present, the exactly-right-for-the-moment gift that we have – with immaculate, unerring precision – called into our own presence, with the wrapping paper we have dubbed *adversity*, and then see the *wrapper* as the gift.

We, in our ego-conscious mind, fail to see past the wrapper, so do not discern the perfection beneath it: just what we needed to help us take our next step toward the Kingdom of Heaven *within us.* As soon as we perceive the adversity wrapper, fear, doubt, uncertainty take hold of us in an icy grasp and this puts our mind into 'tilt' mode, freezing it and disengaging reason and clarity from our awareness. The only way past this apparent impediment to our progress, this astigmatism, is to *ask* our true Self, the Spirit of Truth, to reveal to our awareness the perfection of the gift within.

In that frozen, fear-filled state of mind, remembering to do this is extremely difficult for most of us. It takes the greatest commitment, focus and determination – especially in the *nascent stages* of our Awakening to the reality of our Being from the dream of disempowerment, limitation and death – to break free from that grasp. In fact, by ourself this is not possible. But we have Help. That Help is not far off, unreachable; too lofty for our lowly, unworthy self to reach. Neither is It so high as to consider us beneath Itself to deign to help.

It is, indivisibly, Who we really *are*; It is *One* with us; all-empowered by God to restore us to remembrance of our God-empowered-by-Love Self. Being like Papa – perfect Love – He *always*, unfailingly responds to *every* call for help. Why would He not? That is the unvarying nature of perfect Love. It is only our unbelief – our doubt, our unwillingness to trust – that blocks our *awareness* of His response, His Help. And because we have God-given free will, if we *choose* not to believe, neither Jesus nor the Holy Spirit can, or will, force Their Help on us. They can respond only to our *asking*, in sincerity and spiritual humility, for Help.

In order to *receive* that Help to release us from our self-made prison of fear we must change our mind from unwillingness to willingness. Yet for most of us the fierceness of resistance to giving up the ego-leasehold on our mind, our life, makes that *seem* very, very difficult. Will it help if we remember that that resistance is not really *our* resistance but that of the ego-virus that we have allowed to infect our mind, taking it over and masquerading as our self, yet has only as much power over us as we ascribe to it? It will if we *allow* it to help; for we have freedom of choice.

So, we must *choose* to change our mind – surrender control of it to Holy Spirit/Self, and thus, *away* from ego – from unwillingness to willingness, unbelief to belief, and then, *with His Help*, see past the wrapper and become aware, by His inspiring us, of HOW the gift is the perfect thing. Despite outward appearances, everything that arrives in our presence is perfect because everything that turns up is an *opportunity*. But when we are so inured to the consciousness of fear, *any* change is likely to be perceived – even before we know what it is – as fearful.

How do we ask for that Help, when we are frozen with fear, panic, despair? First, by NOT trying to run away and hide. We have all noticed how often that is the reaction with people of our acquaintance. It may be understandable from the Earth-mind perspective, *but it definitely does not work*. It simply reaffirms our belief in adversity. In Truth there is no such thing as adversity. We made it up, just as we made up guilt, fear, littleness, disempowerment, death... Instead, we could try taking a deep breath and counting to ten, which could help us regain a modicum of equilibrium.

Olga Park used to say 'Jesus works through a crisis.' He doesn't *have* to work through a crisis; he would much rather work with us through our *joyful willingness* to work with him. But you have to admit that a crisis (even imagined!) has a way of getting our attention. And so, having got our attention, we might say something like:

> "This situation that has turned up *seems* to be adversity, causing me to feel fearful. Of myself I can do nothing, so I am now choosing to ask for Help to see it clearly, objectively, truly, because I am reminding myself that fear is not, *cannot be* real, however much it *seems* so at this moment. But that is ego's perception and I am NOT ego. I am holy/wholly Self, and it is my unwavering choice to see this gift I have called into my presence – the perfect thing at the perfect moment – for the *opportunity* it brings me to remember my true Being by unburdening myself from illusions.
>
> "I cannot, at this moment, *see* the perfection, the opportunity, because my vision is not yet clear, but I *trust* that my true, *limitless* Self sees truly. Therefore there is no need for me to *see* in order for all to be resolved – only to *trust*. So I choose, right now, to ask Him to reveal

the purpose of the gift, and <u>in faith and trust</u> *await* His answer, His solution, to be given in His own way and His own, perfect timing. And if I do not become aware of His answer immediately I will still wait and remain in trust, remembering that time is an illusion, believing His answer will be made known to me when the moment is right, according to His perfect wisdom and Love, because it is *by* my belief and trust that this becomes possible, since it is only unbelief that blocks my awareness. Meanwhile, I remind myself not to be fearful, doubtful, panicky, as that is not the real me, but ego, masquerading as me. In my true Self I *Know* that <u>all is well</u>, for with God all things are possible, if only I can believe; and, *by* my faith and trust, I AM restored to the safety, peace, joy and certainty of being Loved, guided and protected."

Whatever turns up is always the right thing at the right moment. To see it otherwise can only *keep* us in the slough of despond that is the illusory world of time and place; the world of seeming adversity; the dream of 'death'. Asking Help in choosing to accept each opportunity as such can only assist us in remembering that we only *dream* this miry place but in Truth we are safe, at Home in the Celestial City.

Diary of a Christ Communicant

A.M. January 5, 2011

Purification is to be gladly welcomed, for it is a gentle, Loving process, as are all things of Papa; a clearing out of upside-down, bewildered, confused minds, cluttered with false, unserviceable, imprisoning beliefs.

Jesus reminds us "Miracles are everyone's right, but purification is necessary first" (*ACIM*, Chapter 1, p.3, Principles of Miracles, 7). Most people either don't believe in purification – or *say* they don't, because of fear – or are fearful of it being some sort of painful sacrifice, loss or punishment! So, either way, it amounts to the same thing: misperception.

Purification is to be gladly welcomed, for it is a gentle, Loving process, as are all things of Papa; a clearing out of upside-down, bewildered, confused minds, cluttered with false, unserviceable, imprisoning beliefs. How can such remain when there is one seed of desire for the ability to receive right-minded, *Christ*-Minded thoughts, awareness, understanding? For misperceptions, illusions, block the filter of a mind that desires Truth, rendering impossible the choice for Truth while retaining illusions. Either one holds sway *or* the other; both together cannot be.

As well you Know, Papa is perfect Love, and He created His Son in His likeness, so His Son is perfect Love, too. This was perfectly demonstrated by Jesus. From a time and place perspective, perfect Love extends the qualities of caring, compassion, forgiveness, infinite patience, tolerance, surrender, healing, perseverance, restoration, redemption, salvation …

But in eternity, Heaven, there is nothing to forgive, no-one to redeem, to save, to tolerate, to heal … because all is complete, perfect, and has always been. Yet qualities such as these are the foundation stones of completion, and without them the *ascent* to completion – Heaven, the true and only Home of Papa's Son – is not possible.

Who, then, remembering this, would desire to serve both God *and* mammon?

31: Love Believeth *All* Things

The Word by Jesus is as Mine, for it is the Living, eternal Word.
We are One by the Word of Truth and Life, and the words that he
spoke are My words of Life and Truth. By these shall you, and all
My little ones, be made free from bondage to time and place.

–Papa, August 1, 1993

I N PAUL'S FIRST LETTER to the Corinthians he states, in his famous, beautiful treatise on Love, 'Love ... believeth *all* things ...'
(1 Cor. 13:7).

We appear to be in a cynical, unbelieving state of consciousness,
demanding 'proof' of what we do not see before being willing to
believe it. Yet it is the veil, or blind (a truly apposite term) of *unbelief*
that *prevents* our vision from being restored. Unbelief, or lack of
faith, in eternal Truth, therefore, rendered us sightless; caused our
soul vision to be substituted by bodily eyes that show us what
we have *chosen* to believe: unreality, a world, a dream, of 'death'.
Judgement arises from unbelief ... unbelief that this person or that
person – or we, ourself – are the Light; perfect, just as God created
us.

In this world judgement is considered 'wise'. Yet judgement
without command of *all* pertinent details *cannot* be wise, but rather,
foolish. Insane, in fact. Here is what Jesus has to say about this:

Judgment was made to be a weapon used against the

Truth. It separates what it is being used against, and sets it off **as if it were a thing apart.** *And then it makes of it what you would have it be.* It judges what it cannot understand, because **it cannot see totality and <u>therefore judges falsely</u>**. Let us not use it today, but make a gift of it to Him Who has a different use for it. He will relieve us of the agony of all the judgments we have made against ourselves, and re-establish peace of mind by giving us <u>God's</u> Judgment of His Son. (*ACIM,* Workbook for Students, p.456, Lesson 311).

For any unfamiliar with the totally benign, Loving (*not* fearful) nature of Papa's judgement of His beloved Son (us), here it is, as stated by His *Anointed Messenger,* Jesus of Nazareth:

This is God's Final Judgment: "You are still My holy Son, forever innocent, forever loving and forever loved, as limitless as your Creator, and completely changeless and forever pure. Therefore awaken and return to Me. I am your Father and you are My Son." (*ACIM,* Workbook for Students, p.455, Lesson 10: 5).

Just about every day we are likely to encounter someone making statements with which we do not agree. Ego is then in there like a shot, proclaiming in our head that he is wrong; doesn't know what he is talking about; I am here to put him straight … And when he doesn't agree with our pronouncements, how easy is it for us to dismiss him as an ignorant, misguided fool? Such are not, cannot be, the observations of Papa's beloved, perfect, all-Loving, all-embracing, all-forgiving, all-blessing Son.

Most of us would prefer to be thought of as that Son, yet still those judgemental thoughts crowd in, spontaneously, uninvited, so it seems, and even though we may not like them, or ourself for allowing them to arise within us, there seems to be little or nothing we can do to prevent them. They *seem* to be uninvited, but somewhere along the line we *allowed* them in. This was due to forgetfulness of our Truth. That forgetfulness began at the moment we accepted the myth of separation from Papa as reality. That was a long time ago. And we reaffirm that forgetfulness every time we take another body.

Forgetfulness is the engine that drives the carousel of birth and death. For, by forgetting Who we really Are, we make up and act out all manner of erroneous ideas about who we are, and religionists call them 'sins'. This is a game of make believe, and to give greater plausibility to that game, we don costumes; we masquerade as 'this' character, or 'that' persona. And when each 'act' (incarnation) comes to its end without a satisfactory outcome we feel compelled to try another, and yet another costume. We seek fame and fortune, power and glory because we believe they will bring us happiness, fulfilment.

Little do we realise, in our state of amnesia, that we already have all those things, but we set them aside when we left Home for a far country to start a career on the stage of make believe, play-acting that we are what we are not. But in every act we keep fluffing our lines, engendering confusion and misperception, and getting reactions that we didn't anticipate, causing us to become even *more* confused about our identity. And the more we play-act, the deeper we move into forgetfulness of our *true* Identity and the more convoluted, sinister and fearful becomes the plot.

That other player (our brother), keeps altering the plot, making it harder and harder for us to remember our lines and which way the story is *supposed* to be heading, so that it ends up way off base from our intended direction. And it's all his fault. So our role-playing would have us believe. But a closer look shows us that it is we who have forgotten our lines and that is causing our brother to appear to us as not playing the role we thought we had assigned to him. So, how can it possibly be right, or sane, to accept Paul's counsel that says 'Love believeth *all* things …'?

By choosing, steadfastly (as distinct from intermittently) – even when deluded ramblings and judgements emanate from a brother – to see *past* what we inwardly *Know* is unreal, and therefore doesn't exist, to his *true* Self, we can recognise the Christ Identity within him. And in so doing, with practise and unwavering commitment, we begin not to even take any notice – and especially not to be *affected* by – the nonsense that issues forth, *Knowing* this is not who he really is. We can do this because we have *chosen* to accept Truth in place of illusions. Thus do we see only the face of Christ in him and remember it is a reflection of our Self.

The unreal does not exist; it is *no*-thing. We can choose to continue believing in *no*-thing and remain feeling miserable, lost, lonely, guilty, fearful, misunderstood, aggrieved, or we can choose to believe *all* things. Love believeth *all* things ... That is our true, God-given, *natural* estate, in which we can only be happy and peaceful. Not too hard, really – especially as, when that is our choice, the evidence, the witnesses to reality come immediately in to attest to us its Truth. Why? Because we have lifted *the veil of unbelief*, allowing Truth to enter into our awareness; something our unbelief was previously denying us.

So, we can overlook the judgements, grievances, conflict, misperceptions and thus be kept from the pitfall of believing such are our brother's nature. For what we believe of our brother is what we believe of ourself, regardless of our lack of *conscious awareness* of it, or however vigorously we may deny it. How easily, how quickly does a mind enthralled by ego's yoke, ego's lies, forget the Truth. Here is a reminder from Jesus in the long ago, from Luke's Gospel, chapter 6:

> *But love ye your enemies, and do good, and lend, hoping for nothing again; and your reward shall be great, and ye shall be the children of the Highest: for he is kind unto the unthankful and to the evil. Be ye therefore merciful, as your Father also is merciful. Judge not, and ye shall not be judged: condemn not, and ye shall not be condemned: forgive, and ye shall be forgiven:*

These statements have been perceived as meaning *God* will judge us and condemn us if we judge and condemn; that *He* will forgive us only if we forgive. But He knows nothing of judgement or condemnation, nor even of forgiveness. In His sight there is nothing to judge or condemn, and therefore nothing to forgive. For He is but Love; unconditional, *perfect* Love. No-one judges, condemns *or* forgives us save ourself, by our own thoughts and acts of judgement or forgiveness – of our brother or of ourself, for in Truth we are One. When we see that we set ourself *and* our brother free.

Diary of a Christ Communicant

A.M. February 1, 2011

> **"Thank You, Papa, for *always* hearing me, Loving me and for giving me everything, including Your Voice, the Spirit of Truth, to heal my mind of all misperceptions. I gladly, willingly, choose always to listen to His guiding, so that He can bring me safely Home to You."**

Here, even in prayer, we seek answers to questions pertaining to matters of time and place. But Papa is not *in* or *of* time and place. He Is, and *Knows* only of, Eternity. Chapter 6 of Matthew's Gospel says it all, in which Jesus exhorts us to: *Take no thought for your life, what ye shall eat, or what ye shall drink; nor yet for your body, what ye shall put on … for your heavenly Father knoweth that ye have need of all these things. But seek ye __first__ the kingdom of God, and his righteousness; and all these things shall be added unto you. Take therefore no thought for the morrow: for the morrow shall take thought for the things of itself.*

> *"Seek ye First the Kingdom…"* and, *"Thy will be done on Earth as it is in Heaven"* are the keys, the very foundation stones to prayer, for these focus the errant mind on Atonement with Papa and His Kingdom. Prayer is an attunement, not a pleading. For what shall one plead, when one already has everything? Rather, enter into that place of mind – within – where is *awareness* of that abundance.
>
> When Jesus went off by himself to pray, or *commune*, with Papa, he entered into the Oneness with Him, away from all time and place considerations. In that state of

Oneness, nothing, I repeat, *nothing*, matters. For it is your *within* – where you encounter true, eternal Being – that is affected; uplifted, restored, illumined by that *real* prayer.

Then, when you are raised up to the exalted state of awareness, all to do with time and place is seen in its true perspective. When in the state of communion with Papa there is a harmony – a Song – of thanksgiving, of Love, between Father and Son, back and to. From that song of harmony, communion, Atonement (of thanksgiving, blessing and Love) there will come a loving 'echo', which will be, will bring, the answer to your apparent, specific needs.

So, having laid the foundation stones of our prayer, we can then add the superstructure of gratitude and Love, such as "Thank You, Papa, for *always* hearing me, Loving me and for giving me everything, including Your Voice, the Spirit of Truth, to heal my mind of all misperceptions. I gladly, willingly, choose always to listen to His guiding, so that He can bring me safely Home to You."

32: Communing with the Mind of Christ

Concern yourself only with the Kingdom of Heaven upon the Earth ...so that it may fill you ... and spread beyond, purifying the contaminated waters[1] *of Earth and transforming them into many founts springing up, clear as crystal, a symbol of the Life Eternal which flows in them.*

–Jesus, August 8, 1993

I T IS NOT POSSIBLE TO HAVE awareness of reality with our bodily senses. They are devised to show us only what we chose to see *instead* of reality – the temporal, which passes away and therefore is not real but a momentary mirage. Reality is God, God is Spirit and Spirit is eternal. Bodily senses cannot discern spirit. Discerning reality is a mystical process, a *soul* awareness; nothing to do with bodily faculties, such discernment is of the within, and bodily faculties are attuned only to the without. As long as we are unwilling – which is fear in disguise – to go within, we will remain without.

To suggest lack of awareness of the reality within is anything to do with unwillingness may seem harsh; judgemental even. Yet unwillingness, always a product of fear, can present itself in various guises, masking the unconscious fear of reality, which is Love, because God *is* Love. We can know unwillingness is fear-driven because the only counter to fear is Love, which is what we really are. And Love is *always* willing; willing to share, to extend itself; accepting of all things because Love *Knows* that ... *nothing real can be threatened, nothing unreal exists* [and that] *herein lies the peace of God. (ACIM,* Introduction).

This ego-self-imposed block to our awareness of reality is totally understood by the Spirit of Truth and by Jesus, which is why he taught in parables. Parables, or allegories, are symbols which *represent* a Truth that cannot be *directly* discerned – due to unreadiness – and are devised to help bring at least *some* degree of clarity to those unaware of, or only nascent in their Awakening to, spiritual reality.

So, in the introduction to the *Service of Mystical Communion with Christ*[2] (SMCC) – given from spirit to Olga Park by John of Patmos, 'the disciple Jesus loved' (to whom we refer as 'the Teacher') – all who *truly* seek after God (whether embodied or disembodied, it makes no difference) and *earnestly* desire the coming of the Kingdom of Heaven on Earth are invited to draw near, and commune *together* upon the bread and wine of eternal life and Truth as revealed in Jesus. In order so to do, all are further exhorted to *ascend unto the Hill of the Lord,* and *rise up unto his Holy Place* ...

There is much symbolism here, of necessity, to describe an invitation to participate in a mystical experience of spiritual reality that is beyond the awareness or understanding of a mind engaged with, focused upon, matters solely of the without, or unreality. So, a few quick explanations: bread is a symbol of spiritual Truth – 'the Living Word' – because bread nourishes us bodily, and spiritual Truth nourishes our soul, vitalising, raising it up, enlivening it, opening our mind to greater awareness of eternal reality. Wine (and its imbibing) is a symbol of conviviality, lightness of heart and spirit, celebration, goodwill, relaxation, and ultimately, Love; the New Wine of the Kingdom is *Christ* Love, which Jesus exemplified for us.

When consecrated – i.e., blessed – the bread and wine are imbued with a higher, spiritual vibration so that, when ingested, they act as conveyances – or at least, contributors – to heightened awareness of reality within us. And *the Hill of the Lord* symbolises a state, or place, to which we desire to ascend, in our mind, for communing with that higher awareness: the Mind of Christ. The following extract from *"Seek ye First the Kingdom..."* gives, by way of an example, an indication of how symbols can help in raising the awareness and experience of the Light:

During a Communion Service in August 1992, we were, in the dual consciousness, on Mount Moriah, the 'Hill of the Lord', in Jerusalem – the City of Peace – where the temples, first of Solomon and later, Herod, stood. We were looking down across the Jordan Valley, where millions of fragments of the Sonship, from all races, colours and creeds were streaming toward the Hill of the Lord, where we were in the presence of individuals, drawn by the Light engendered by the Service, who seemed to symbolise spiritual, or some other form of natural leadership of each respective group, or race. Among them were Winston Churchill, along with Martin Luther King, and Jack and Bobby Kennedy. I heard Jack whisper to Bobby, 'This is what I have been praying for.'

Mohandas (Mahatma) Gandhi also was there. He is a *great* light, effulgent as the sun, and his power and Love filled me to overflowing. He stood facing me, smiling a smile of indescribable, rapturous joy, and with great happiness at what is taking place. He was inches away from me and he stretched out his arms and touched his fingertips to mine. The surge of spiritual power – which is Love, joy, peace and the wisdom of Eternity – that flowed from his fingertips into mine and through me, was immense, *overwhelming,* as if I had been plugged into the National Grid. I will never forget the radiant, uplifting power, beauty and glory of his smile.

The Teacher said, "Brian, give freely to all who are drawn – there is no difference in the soul of man; all are One, brothers and sisters in Christ Jesus our Lord, and children of One Father Creator. All are here in the Earth conditions that they may come into Oneness together in full and joyful brotherhood, and go forward to the House of the Eternal Father … It is necessary for each one … to come to the place of spiritual growth whereby the … Father's Will be done in the lives of all the children of Earth.

"Peace and joy be yours, that you may give freely to all who will receive of this precious gift of the Father. This is the path to eternal Life."

Words, being symbols of symbols, do not convey the magnificence, the ineffable joy and clarity – the free gift to us all – that is communing with the Wholeness, the Holiness, of the Christ Mind when ours is broken and fragmented. But in 1978 Jesus said to me, "Give me the pieces of your life, and I will give you back the wholeness." Those words, it hardly need be said, were not just for persona Brian, but for *every* broken fragment of Papa's beloved Son. There are, and can be, no exceptions to this Truth. And he *can*, and lovingly, earnestly *desires* to do this for each of us, restoring us to Oneness with him.

The ego thinks it is in control of our life, and guards this misperception fiercely. It is not. It has control only over 'death'. Yet death, like its inventor, does not exist. Our limited, made-up self, in its confusion, cannot distinguish between the ego's script for death and the Holy Spirit's script for Life. So, first we give our life, totally, unreservedly, *trustingly* into the all-Loving, all-caring, all-empowered control of the Holy Spirit. When He has freed our mind from the ego's control it is automatically released back to Self – Christ – control, in which all things are possible. Just as exemplified by Jesus.

Let us join as one, in the true brotherhood of the Sonship, for blessing the world, forgiving the world of dreams of death, and ourselves for our part in its arising, and the release of all from its thrall, back to the freedom of eternity that is our heritage, and is *already* ours, without money and without price, merely awaiting, with infinite patience, our acceptance.

Diary of a Christ Communicant

A.M. February 11, 2011

I create by extending Myself. This is the only way creation is possible, because I Am all there Is ... There is only My Self with and from Which to create, so I extend My Self. I extend My Self in you, Beloved, so you are like Me in every respect, aspect, detail.

Papa, thank You for creating Your Son in Your likeness...

> ... I can create *only* in My likeness, for all is Holy. Holy is whole, and wholeness is complete; perfection. There is nothing yet to do. All is accomplished, and that which is complete is whole; is One. My creation is My extension, My offspring, My Son; like his Father in every detail, eternally.

We, Your Son, are no more human than butterflies are caterpillars. He had a mad moment of believing what he is not – a limited, mortal body, imprisoning a limited, finite mind. But he is metamorphosing back to his true, soaring, limitless, infinite reality.

> I create by extending Myself. This is the only way creation is possible, because I Am all there Is. There is nothing else, so there is nothing else with which to create. There is only My Self with and from Which to create, so I extend My Self. I extend My Self in you, Beloved, so you are like Me in every respect, aspect, detail.
>
> I Am Perfect Love, and therefore you, My Son, are Perfect Love also. This is your True Being. So Be it.
>
> Perfect Love is eternally, unchangeably Who I Am, and so Perfect Love is eternally, unchangeably, Who you are. There is nothing else for you to Be, for that is all there Is. There is nothing else to Be, for to Be is the eternal present, the everlasting gift that I keep giving; and, because you are like Me in every way, *you* keep giving. Like Me, you give by extending your Self, Which is Perfect Love.

Because you are Perfect Love, you cannot change, forever, for if you could change from Perfect Love you would become imperfect, and imperfection cannot be eternal, so would come to an end – would cease to Be. That would mean that *All That Is* would cease to Be, because you are like Me and I Am like you. Then there would be nothing, and nothing cannot have Being.

1. This refers to peoples and their assorted cultural and religious conditions which are ego-driven rather than Holy Spirit led.

2. For further information about SMCC, please visit: www.members.shaw.ca/communion/

33: Exchanging Thinking for Being

There is yet much rescue work and many lost sheep waiting alone and bereft, separated from the good Shepherd. So shall we work together that all may be brought into the fold ... All who will, let them join with me in gathering in the harvest, for now is the time of readiness.

–Jesus, August 15, 1993

I N THE AUTUMN OF 1970, not many days before Theresa and I left Canada to return to live in England, we made a final visit to our spiritual mentor, Olga Park. To our joy and delight, Jesus overshadowed Olga and engaged with us, speaking through her voice, though with discernibly different tonal qualities, in precious, inspiring, Loving, easy conversation for some twenty or thirty minutes. During that fellowship I mentioned something about what people might think of this cherished moment with him. In nearly half a century of one-on-one journeying and communing with Jesus I have only encountered him expressing his Christ Love light-heartedly. Except once.

His response to my comment was the one and only exception. He said, emphatically, in a voice that exhibited a tinge of frustration, "People *don't THINK!*" In the time and place consciousness we have handed over our thinking to an alien illusory interloper called the ego. The ego's thought system is not ours, though most unwittingly believe it is. It led, and is still leading most of us into outer darkness, forgetfulness of Self as the Light, the Love, the Life, the Truth. Just like Jesus. It is anti-Life, anti-Love, anti-Christ, and has filled our minds with thoughts of guilt, fear, darkness, conflict and death.

The still, small Voice for God within us will lead us back to the Truth of our Being, to all *Knowledge*, when we are ready to listen to His Voice in place of the ego's. That seems an insuperable task to our self-limited mind. Happily, He, the Holy Spirit, *Knows* this, and is able to help in an entirely practical way: all that is required of us is that we *desire*, we *choose*, to hear only His Voice within us. All the rest is accomplished *for* us by Him, enabled by our little *willingness* for it to happen. That willingness motivates our co-operation. He will then restore to our remembrance all *Knowledge* of eternal reality.

Some words of encouragement and reassurance on all this from Jesus, to help assuage doubts and uncertainties:

> Your Friend [Holy Spirit] goes with you. **You are not alone.** *No one who calls on Him can call in vain.* Whatever troubles you, be **certain** that He has the answer, and will gladly give it to you, if you simply **turn to Him and ask it of Him.** *He will not withhold all answers that you need* for anything that seems to trouble you. He knows the way to solve all problems, and resolve all doubts. His certainty is yours. You need but ask it of Him, and it **will** be given you. (*ACIM*, Workbook for Students, p.487, Epilogue, 1:2–9).

The ego, that knows nothing and doubts everything, will fill our head with doubts about this, seeking to dismantle our faith that this could be true, *'because nothing like this has ever happened so far, so why is that suddenly, miraculously going to change?'* This is where a leap of faith is called for, giving a little willingness for Him to enter our conscious mind, past those ego barricades to Truth. Here is some more illumination from Jesus (*Diary of a Christ Communicant* entry dated May 4, 1997) for our strengthening in Faith, Trust, Obedience to the inner Voice, and Commitment (FTOC):

> My son, it is to the act of Asking, Seeking, Knocking (ASK-ing) that your heavenly Father, Papa, [or Holy Spirit]

responds freely, lovingly, <u>immediately,</u> with His giving. It is *not* according to your <u>faith</u> but your *<u>desire</u>* that He responds. It is according to your <u>faith</u> that you are able to *<u>receive</u>* His giving. Your <u>faith</u> is something that Papa will grow in you as you *<u>ask</u>*. The more you ask, *believing* – having faith – the more you will receive and you will grow in your expectation of receiving that which He is *<u>always</u>* giving.

You expect the sun to rise every day because it always does. That is faith. Easy. As you ask more and more of Papa [or Holy Spirit], *believing* He is giving it, so will your faith in receiving *grow*, until it is as your faith that the sun will rise.

It is by/with this faith that I came into the Earth life, believing, trusting, that Papa would give all that I asked. These things which I did shall you do – and receive – also, and greater things than these. <u>Believe</u> and you shall <u>receive</u>. <u>Ask, *believing*</u>. It is Papa's *<u>good pleasure</u>* to give to His little ones – all of them, including you... *Only believe.* You know He is giving you the Kingdom ...

If you do not receive *immediately* it is more to do with your growth in faith than Papa's giving [or, of course, our *paucity* of growth in faith, which is because we are shackled by guilt, fear, doubt, unbelief, sense of unworthiness ...]. Be at peace and let your certainty be that He is <u>giving</u> so that your faith in <u>receiving</u> may grow. All is well, my son. Rejoice, for the Kingdom *is* at hand.

When we are restored to all *Knowledge*, thinking is no longer necessary. Then, there is only stillness, quiet, the eternal bliss that is our true, unchangeable *Being*, as One in Papa. Then will be – as the Spirit of Truth said to me on December 5, 2010: *Known* again the true experience of Perfect Love, which is a never-ending orgasm of the soul; a thousand times a thousand more consummate than any such feeble, bodily substitute. Then will all thoughts of guilt, fear, judgement, unforgiveness, grievance, shame, scarcity, separation, death be gone from your mind, awareness, experience. Forever.

Many might consider it impossible *not* to think; to have no thoughts at all … about the weather, bills, job security, health, that yummy bar of chocolate … But who can honestly recall any thoughts at all when engaged in passionate love-making; when in those moments of 'any such feeble, bodily substitute'? Assuredly, when we are experiencing 'a never-ending orgasm of the soul; a thousand times a thousand more consummate …', who could – or would wish to – be distracted by any thoughts at all? Joy is not a thought; peace is not a thought; Love is not a thought; ecstasy is not a thought.

The only reality, in our true, eternal, unchangeable state, is *Being*. Thinking, then, is not our true estate; *Being* is, and that Beingness is Love. Love is uncontainable. It simply has to express itself, extend itself, share itself. Love knows no limits; it is *boundless* in its expression, its extending, its sharing, its giving. Forever. Knowing the Truth of our eternal Being is enough to make the intrusion of our petty thoughts, personal desires and unholy judgements seem, well … petty, doesn't it? It is enough to make us want to leave them all behind and return, without unwarranted delay, to our right mind.

For it is in our right mind, our whole/holy mind, our *heart-mind* – Christ Mind – that we *Know* the Truth of our Being and it is There that we experience this ineffable, indescribable Love. Under ego's misdirection we made up bodies; they are illusions, projected from a confused, upside-down, split-off-from-Truth mind. We do not sense with our bodily faculties. *All* sensation is within the mind. The hell that is apparent separation from Papa – the temporal – is sensed within that confused, split-off part of our mind; and the Heaven that is our *Oneness* in Him is experienced, *Known*, only in our whole, holy, Christ Mind.

Meanwhile, we believe, and therefore perceive, that thoughts of separation and death are our own. How *can* they be when we are the Christ, the perfect, all-*Knowing*, innocent, all-empowered, all-Loving-for-all-eternity holy Son of our Father Creator, created in His exact, nothing-left-out likeness? Can there be one amongst us who believes, even for a moment, that Jesus had the kind of thoughts we have believed are ours? He *Knew*, and lived, *only* the Truth. How many of us can truly say that of ourselves?

However hard this may seem to us, it *is* doable. He whom we know and love as Jesus did it, so we can *Know* it is doable. The incentive greatly outweighs the disincentive. The incentive is peace, freedom from the fear of death and *all* illusions of time and place. The disincentive is more turns of the carousel. Indefinitely. The correct choice, the correct outcome is inevitable – eventually – because that is our true, inescapable nature and Destiny. How long it will take is our own decision. Yet even that is already made, even though we have no conscious awareness of that being the case.

This is because that Destiny is *already* within us, and has always been; can never not be, regardless of outward appearances or beliefs to the contrary. They are simply that: outward appearances. Neither 'outward' nor 'appearances' are real; they are temporal, and, changing every moment, pass away. Yet still our ego-mind clings to unreality; to death. We have allowed it to veil from our awareness the Destiny within us. When we choose anew and allow our Higher Self to restore us to full remembrance, complete *Knowledge* of our Oneness in Papa, we will joyfully embrace *Life*. And all memory of separation, fear and 'death' will be erased *immediately* from our memory. What more apposite response to such a joyous thought might we give than "*Alleluia!*"?

Diary of a Christ Communicant

A.M. February 12, 2011

… I am Your host, Papa; I welcome You into my heart and into my mind. I will not to allow ego to divert or distract me from my journey Home to You.

34: Accessing Help in Escaping the Carousel

That which is within shall become that which is without for all
who follow me and walk the path of Life, which unfolds at your feet
with each step. I am your guide, and the Living Word shall lead
you onwards and upwards, unswervingly. All is well.

–Jesus, August 22, 1993

U NLESS WE DECIDE – CONSCIOUSLY – for eternity, we have
decided – *un*consciously – for time and place. There can be no
alternatives. We *already* chose, unconsciously, for time and place, a
very long time ago; so long ago that we have forgotten that choice.
It may not seem like that is *our* choice because the ego-controlled
part of our mind, that is split-off from our whole, Christ Mind,
distracts us with myriad sidetracking irrelevances and questions to
keep us unsure, unaware, confused, doubtful, bewildered … about
our One, true Identity.

This is why, if we desire to escape the carousel of birth and
death, guilt, fear and misery, it will serve that desire extremely well
to choose *consciously* for our restoration to fullness of remembrance
of our true, innocent, all-empowered-by-Love Self; Papa's One beloved Son, the Christ.

Some might say, "How can I choose for eternity when I am – or
appear, so persuasively, to be – stuck in time and place? There are so
many challenges, hazards, uncertainties to my very existence that

even if I wanted to, I haven't time to focus on the 'great unknown' called eternity. I will attend to eternity when (or if) I find myself there. Meanwhile, I haven't time to think about it because I have to devote all my attention to treading water, just to stop myself going under in this rat-race of a world. Besides, it is not ALL bad down here, so I'll simply have to take my chances."

Others might say, "I have no need to worry about eternity; I chose for it years ago, so I am okay. Meanwhile, I just get on with the day by day things the universe brings to me." Let us consider the serviceability – or otherwise – of each of these perceptions.

The first is just what the ego wants for us, a loop that will keep us on the carousel. Time and place is *devised* to keep us distracted from Truth, and the only alternative to Truth – i.e., eternity – is … you guessed it: time and place, aka the carousel of birth and death. The perception of linear time is a self-entrapment that keeps us going round and round in the consciousness of fear because it has a way of getting us to believe it is running out. And there is so much to do before it – and we! – expire(s).

So we must rush to get everything done that it seems is being thrown at us or we will be found wanting, and therefore, unworthy of any 'greater reward' there just *might* be awaiting us at the end of the line – or, hopefully, sooner. The more we allow ourself to become sidetracked by the cares, the struggles, the fears, the judgements … the deeper we get into the wilderness, or expressed alternatively, outer darkness; away from the Light of Home. And the ego throws in just enough jollies to make it seem worth soldiering on, ever in hope.

But that is not so for hundreds of millions – perhaps billions even – of our brothers who have *no* jollies and whose daily existence brings no hope; only despair. And our next turn of the carousel, the next throw of the dice, may just as readily make despair *our* lot. Assuredly, it has already done so in more than enough of our past (in linear-time terms) incarnations. Even when our 'present' lot appears to be tolerable enough – at least for the time being – no-one knows what 'adversity' lies just round the corner. And if we believe this is all there is, 'death' is the final curtain. *Then* what!?

A sobering perspective, in which all those distractions may seem no bad thing after all. But they will not get us *Home* to where we really belong, where all is ineffable, unceasing ecstasy; eternally. Papa is Calling us Home, *right now*, yet the most eloquent, evocative words – mere symbols – attempting to describe our true, eternal Home are meaningless to those of us who choose to attune their minds only to the temporal. However, these graphic words from page seven of Gary Renard's book *The Disappearance of the Universe* can give a hint:

> ... imagine the very peak of a perfect sexual orgasm, except this orgasm never stops. It keeps going on forever with no decrease in its powerful and flawless intensity. The physical act of sex doesn't even come close to the incredible bliss of Heaven ...

I attest to the veracity of this statement because I experienced it when Jesus manifested to me in his glory in 1967, as described in chapter two of *"Seek ye First the Kingdom..."*:

> This feeling of all-pervasive, all-inclusive Love was complete, permeating not just my body but my entire aura in an orgasm of the soul, immeasurably more intense than any such physical experience. I was blinded by a waterfall of joyful, rapturous tears and every part of me was alive, electrified, as never before.

This event took place thirty-five years before Gary's book was published, and the account recorded at the time, clearly obviating collusion or plagiarism.

The second perception (above) is one that opens itself to self-defeat because, as our brother John (author of the fourth Gospel) said to me in November 1994:

> I know I do not need to caution you to be constantly vigilant against the wiles of the enemy [the ego], or to maintain your armour of defence against its 'darts of

destruction'. The greatest threat of breach to such armour is <u>complacency</u> ... You know that the cloak of the Lord's protection – living in him and *always* keeping your heart and life open to his presence – is the *whole* armour, and that no further contortions of mind or body are needful for such protection [though chapter 6 of Paul's letter to the Ephesians expresses the various aspects of such armour poetically].

He went on to say:

Let this serve you well in reminding, renewing and restoring you in Christ humility, Love, desire to serve. And thus shall the desire of your heart be fulfilled in joyous fellowship of Heaven. And thus shall there continue to be much rejoicing in Heaven, echoing and reverberating in the Earth, as it becomes illuminated with the Light of the Kingdom, banishing away the darkness forever.

This 'joyous fellowship of Heaven' of which he speaks is freely, lovingly available to us *all*, right here, right now, *if only we are willing to believe*. Orthodox Christianity speaks of 'the Communion of Saints'. Here is what Wikipedia says about it:

The communion of saints ... is the spiritual union of the members of the Christian Church, living and the dead [sic], those on earth, [and] in heaven ...

They are all part of a single "mystical body", with Christ as the head, in which each member contributes to the good of all and shares in the welfare of all ...

This clearly indicates that we are free to commune, not just with Jesus but with *all* our loved ones in the Realms of Light, or more generically, any who have laid aside their body and are now in the etheric counterpart of the ('physical') Earth. Yet, many professing to be Christians are nevertheless of the view that communing with any in spirit other than Jesus is strictly *verboten*, based on Deuteronomy 18:10, 11, which has God forbidding *divination* or *necromancy*.

This seeming dichotomy authorising communion between embodied and disembodied souls on the one hand, yet forbidding it in the Torah, is cause for an interesting – some might say absurd – contradiction within current church canon. Yet, there is a very simple way past this unserviceable convolution: If our desire for communion is sincere, transparent, only for the help and blessing of all, and particularly when committed into the care, guidance and protection of Jesus and/or the Holy Spirit, then assuredly it will be beneficial – and therefore, *desirable* – for all.

The whole mission and purpose of Jesus is the reunion, the rejoining of *all* the fragments of the Sonship of God as *One* with him and in Him. *All* can only mean embodied (at any one moment) *and* disembodied. If we are 'forbidden' (by those with no knowledge or experience of mystical or spiritual reality, yet spuriously claiming authority and leadership in these matters over the rest of us) communion with our loved ones in spirit, how, pray, can we be rejoined with them? And this cannot be got around by saying 'Ah, that will be in the future, after the Rapture ...' because, as we all know, in reality there is *only* the eternal moment of *Now*, in which there is no past or future.

Therefore, let us all consciously choose to join, NOW, in loving, glorious, joyful, blessed reunion and communion, to help prepare us for, and hasten, our journey Home together, as One.

Diary of a Christ Communicant

A.M. February 21, 2011

You *are* the Light. Jesus tells you so. Welcome the Light and you welcome wholeness. Thus shall you be healed because the Light will illumine your mind when it believes it is in darkness.

Healing is about wholeness, and wholeness is holiness. Who can envisage holiness not being whole, or complete?

Yet, so, so many of the little ones, lost in the wilderness of forgetfulness of their true Identity, want wholeness while choosing – albeit unconsciously, and therefore by default – to remain broken, separated or fragmented. How's that for a split, conflicted mind?

Wholeness is rejoining. Papa's little ones, in their restored-to-Oneness state – the Christ – are the Word of God. I, the Spirit of Truth, Am the Voice that reminds them of their reality as the Word. The Word is whole *because* It is the Word of God.

It is not my desire to shut out the Light.

Fiat Lux! The Light and the Word are one and the same. You *are* the Light. Jesus tells you so. Welcome the Light and you welcome wholeness. Thus shall you be healed because the Light will illumine your mind when it believes it is in darkness.

35: Who am I? Why am I here?

*Unless you can receive of me that which it is the Father's joy
to give to you, your freedom of citizenship in the City of Peace
cannot become complete. Let not anxiety to reach the journey's end
diminish the joy of the journey, nor distract or cloud your vision
and cause you to stumble from the path.*

–*Jesus*, August 29, 1993

IN 1967 I VISITED a gifted clairvoyant in Brighton named William King. He told me that the vast majority of people spend a whole incarnation without ever knowing – or even wondering – who they really are, or why they are here (or appear to be!). This is, of course, just the way the ego wants it, for thus does our escape from the illusions of misery, fear of 'death, judgement and hell' get delayed.

And the ego has 'secured' its position by persuading us that there is no point in asking God about these crucial matters because He doesn't speak to us any more – except, *perhaps*, through the Church, and their answers don't satisfy many people with enquiring, discerning minds. They wouldn't, would they, since the institutionalised Church is an ego construct? This is not a judgement against clergy *or* members of such churches, all of whom are Papa's beloved, innocent little ones – as are we all. It is the institutions they blindly follow and serve, with their false creeds and doctrines of Jesus being a blood sacrifice, demanded by God, contra to the scriptures, that serve their followers ill. For a full explanation of this, see Vignette 12 in *"Seek ye First the Kingdom..."*

So, to what are most people turning for answers? Science. Yet, sadly, however adept 'science' may be at investigating the *without*, it is singularly lacking in the ability, or the will, or belief, to investigate the *within*.

This, in spite of Jesus telling us two-thousand years ago: *The kingdom of God cometh not with observation: Neither shall they say, Lo here! or, lo there! for, behold, the kingdom of God is within you* (Lk. 17:20). Assuredly, any amount of investigating the without will leave us bereft of answers to the Truth of eternity – the Kingdom of God *within* – and our relationship to it and the King. The without is nothing but a mirage, devised to distract us from reality. Studying the without can only bring *information;* never *Knowledge*, for Knowledge is of reality, Truth, eternity, changelessness, peace, joy, Love.

Increasing numbers in recent generations have turned instead – in an endeavour to 'find the within' – to hallucinogens, to take them 'on a trip to nirvana'. But hallucinogens are another tool of the ego to drag us into an even deeper pit of despair. This is because so many users have little thought for spiritual humility (self-depreciation is no substitute for it), or the will to place themselves within the care, guidance and protection of Jesus – who, assuredly, knows more about the within, the Kingdom of Heaven, than any other soul who has ever walked the Earth – or the Spirit of Truth.

Few of such 'seekers through hallucinogens' have sought – or found – true enlightenment. More have sought self-gratification. Enlightenment is of eternity; self-gratification can only ever be a fleeting moment in time, always leading onto, and down, the slippery slope to oblivion. And, to borrow the words of Jesus, a *faithless and perverse generation* (Mt. 17:17) is disinclined to believe other than in what its bodily senses were devised to tell it, eschewing the wit to seek more deeply within. But I attest that **A**sk(ing), **S**eek(ing), **K**nock(ing)[1] brings dividends inestimably beyond any earthly reward.

The very last thing the ego – lurking in part of our mind that is split-off from the part wherein dwell Papa, Jesus and the Spirit of Truth (showing just how 'big' our mind/the within really is, and that it can never get crowded in there because the within is beyond limit) – masquerading as our self, wants is for us to ask who we really are, or why we appear to be here.

So, to any who wonder a) who they are or b) why they perceive themselves to be 'here' in time and place, ASK: Who am I; why am I here? Of course, we are blessed beyond human cognition that Jesus has given us the most clear, complete, unequivocal answer to these questions in *A Course in Miracles*. For any unfamiliar with this, the most priceless document ever to bless humanity, a) we all are the eternal, innocent (i.e., guiltless), perfect, all-empowered-by-Love Son of our Father Creator, and b) we, like our brother Jesus, are here to save the world. Of course, the ego will call this arrogance, blasphemy, heresy, apostasy.

Here is what Papa has to say about this, as recorded in the small hours of the morning:

> To Know Me, you must first know your Self. To see Me, you must first see your Self. For when you have seen your Self you have seen Me, because you are created in My exact likeness. Until you have seen and *Known* your Self you can in no wise see and Know Me. To see and *Know* your Self, you must *Be* your Self. Jesus is your exemplar for this, demonstrating, showing, *Being* Love, gentleness, humility, forgiveness; limitless, empowered by Truth; free of ambition or concern for self.
>
> You are My beloved Son, the Christ, just as Jesus. Accept this Truth unto yourself and acknowledge it; honour it, Be it, live it. Love it, own it, *allow* it. Let there be an end to denying it. For by not acknowledging and living it you *are* denying it. Instead, give a joyous *welcome* to it. Let nothing in you deny your acceptance of the Truth and you shall *Know* the Truth; and it shall set you free because you can only *Know* it first by believing it, then by living it, and thus,

experiencing it.

You have no difficulty acknowledging you are My Son. That, therefore, means you are *the Christ*, the One eternal Son of the One eternal Father. Deny this and you are but denying Me. How can this not be 'blasphemy'? If you are My Son – and you *Know* you are – how then can you not be whole, holy, complete; free of limit, guilt, fear?

Your goal is to see *only* the face of Christ in your brother, and you Know that can only be a reflection of your Self. Therefore, until you can acknowledge and attest that you are the Christ how can you expect to see His face in him? If this is your objective you should be able to look at a reflection of yourself in the mirror and say to it, "I Am the Christ, the blessed, holy Son of my eternal, holy Father, exactly as He created me. This is the Truth. So *Be* it." Let there be an end, once and for all, to Self denial. How else can you return Home to the Truth of your Being: Heaven; eternity; Me?

There is no other – save Papa – to whom we need declare ourself as Christ. But if we are unable, as yet, to acknowledge it to *ourself* – and to Him – how can we be other than holding on to at least *some* illusions, *some* pretence, *some* make-believe, *some* confusion, *some* doubt as to our true Identity. Heaven is about Truth, the whole Truth and nothing but the Truth. Holding on to the least illusion is withholding ourself from our true Home. There is no chance we can dispel all illusion by ourself, but *every* chance – certainty, in fact – that we *can* with the Help of Jesus and/or the Spirit of Truth.

Just a little willingness is all we need. They accomplish all the rest for us, with our willing co-operation.

Diary of a Christ Communicant

A.M. February 22, 2011

You are remembering Who you are. This is good. This is just as it is intended. The Plan is working. Since it is the Plan of Papa, who could imagine it otherwise?

Prayer is an attunement, or At-*One*-ment, not a pleading. We perceive ourselves as so separate from Papa, so deep in the wilderness, so lost in outer darkness, so far from the Light; so little, limited, vulnerable, mortal; Papa so remote, that pleading is about all we can muster. This indicates how much we are in need of mind retraining.

> As well you are aware, this is not how Jesus sees his brethren. He sees them as whole; the Light, equal with himself. Is he fantasising or are his brothers? You accept Jesus as Christ, the Living Word of God. If he sees his brothers as equal with him, *all* must be the Christ also.
>
> So, you are the Christ, the Word *of* God; I, the Spirit of Truth, Am the Voice *for* God, sent by Him to accompany His beloved Son as he dreamt he was sojourning in a far country, to remind him continually, unceasingly that he is the Living Word of his Father, created in His Own likeness. That likeness is pure Spirit. Spirit is Light, Love, Life.
>
> You are remembering Who you are. This is good. This is just as it is intended. The Plan is working. Since it is the Plan of Papa, who could imagine it otherwise?

---

1. This is from Mt. 7:7,8, in which Jesus says: "**Ask**, and it shall be given you; **seek**, and ye shall find; **knock**, and it shall be opened unto you: For every one that asketh receiveth; and he that seeketh findeth; and to him that knocketh it shall be opened."

36: Our Greatest Joy and Blessing: Communing with Universal Mind

. . . in your spiritual growth you are a little one. All that is asked of a little one is co-operation so that those responsible for his development can lead him forward.

–Jesus, September 5, 1993

T HE VAST, SOMNOLENT MASS of the fragments of the Sonship still confuses the brain and the mind. This is so even for many within the circle of neuroscience and other august spheres of learning and endeavour. Yet, the brain is merely a transfer mechanism for messages/instructions from the mind to the body. It is not devised to be a *source* of thought processes – including memory – and is thus incapable of such. The brain, like the rest of the body, is temporal and therefore not of God. The mind is eternal, abstract and limitless, and therefore *is* of God. Yet the brain is lionised by confused, misperceiving, upside-down minds.

The reason for this confusion is adherence – conscious or otherwise – to the thought system of the ego. It wants us to believe we are a body; temporal, limited, mortal. If we see past that perception to the idea of mind being, somehow, more than – beyond the finite construct of – the brain, it might get us thinking 'outside the box'. And if part of us is not to be dismissed as corruptible, that would *be* outside the box. And that would be fearful to the ego. But there *is* no box; no limit to Papa's Son. How can he who is created in the likeness of his infinite Father Creator be other than limitless?

Of course, having unlimited free will, we are able to *imagine* being limited; restricted to the confines of the box. And by such imagining it thus can *appear* to be the case. But because such imagining is not with the *whole*, complete, undivided, holy Mind of our true Self, the Christ, it is not *creative* imagining. Creative imagining can only be powered by *Limitless* Love because that is what Creation is. But in our illusory, self-limited, divided, separated, conflicted state of mind we have thrown away our creative power. And as Arten says to Gary Renard in *The Disappearance of the Universe*[1]:

> Being without the power of God, all your mind can do
> is seemingly divide and subdivide and then attempt to
> glorify the result.

Further down the same page (126) he continues:

> In fact, you are able to awaken to the perfect Oneness
> of Heaven exactly as you did [or were] before. But your
> mind must be trained to be dominated by the thoughts of
> the Holy Spirit instead of your ego.

Creation is eternal because it is real, and therefore, changeless, and it is real because it is of God. Anything not of God is temporal, constantly changing, and corruptible. The ego thought system is corruptible because it is founded in guilt, and guilt is destructive. It is the very source of fear. Would we want guilt and fear to be eternal?

Hiding them in our unconscious mind does not mean they have ceased to be with us; that we have dispelled them from our being. We can know this of a certainty if we are not experiencing the peace of God (which passeth human understanding) uninterruptedly and uninterruptibly. Whether we are consciously aware of it or not, guilt and fear are with us if mortality is our belief – and thus, our experience – for they are its cause. Guilt and fear cease to exist or have any effect on us when we *Know*, remember, Who we really Are because Who we really Are is created in perfect Love and innocence. Immortally.

Meanwhile, even if we deny it consciously, at an *unconscious* level we believe we are guilty. And until we choose to follow the Holy Spirit's script for living we keep re-minding ourself we are guilty. We even construct religions to preach our guilt at us. But Papa is Calling us *Home*, and so we are moving inexorably toward the place of remembrance that we, His Son, are innocent. And innocence has *nothing to fear*. This is why it is so important to consciously choose to abandon the belief in guilt and its promulgators/witnesses. But that is not enough to free us from the ego's clutches.

The ego is firmly ensconced in our unconscious mind, and to dispel it from there we need Help because we are *unaware* of what lurks there, accrued during myriad other embodiments, in which there will inevitably have been murder, mayhem, hatred and all manner of other spiritual darkness, of thought, word *and* deed. Because such may be perceived as 'in the past' does not mean they are 'gone and forgotten' and can have no impact upon our 'present' embodiment. That is just what the ego would have us believe, thus lulling us into a false sense of having escaped their consequences.

But those illusory events are stored in the illusory part of our mind that seems to be split off from our whole, holy, innocent *Christ* Mind, as 'seed memories'. And all the while we do not consciously choose to repudiate, renounce the ego and its script from pulling the strings, pushing the buttons in our conscious mind, the Spirit of Truth – the inner link to our true Being – is powerless to provide the Help that He is so ably equipped to give. We must ASK Him to Help us, and *mean* it. He *Knows* our heart and mind, and if it is not our *sincere* desire to receive His Help, He cannot give it.

This is because we are endowed with free will, and the Holy Spirit always honours that. By asking His help we *authorise* His intercession. This is not an outsider horning in on our act (the ego has done that, and persuaded us *it* is who we are). Rather, this is our true *Self*, Who Knows us *totally* and can Help us totally. He *Knows* the content of our unconscious mind. All of it. So, how do we activate this Help, to gain the benefit of it? This *Diary of a Christ Communicant* entry dated November 17, 2008 says it all:

Hello, Papa.

Hello, My son.

I Love You. You *Know* that, and I *Know* You Love me. That gives me peace of mind. I *Know* You Love me. I don't just believe, or hope; I *Know* of a certainty beyond all doubt.

*Love is all there Is, so it is impossible that I could **not** Love you. It is impossible that I could not Love My creation – ALL My creation.*

I feel ready to move up a level in communing, functioning *from*, awareness *of*, spiritual reality – my reality; to move beyond the bodily limitations.

The way forward is by relinquishment of control from the lower to the higher; from 'little me' to 'Big Me'.

I am aware of this, but don't know *how* to move up a gear in that process.

*That is because it is not a **doing** process but a **being** process. 'Doing' is taking control. 'Being' is letting go. Big Me, higher, true Self **Is**. Is-ness is able to transform littleness from limitation to fulfilment; from crawling to soaring. This is a function of Spirit and requires no thought processes; merely an **allowing**. I assure you, you have surrendered – mostly! – to Big Me, and that transformational process **is** proceeding.*

*You have left behind the crawling activity and are now in the chrysalis. This requires no **doing** thoughts, only **being** thoughts. These are not so much thoughts as remembrances. **Remembrances** of Who you are, Where you are. There is nothing to **do** because it is already done. All was completed at your creation, by Me. Creation is the only 'doing' and that is accomplished.*

*All you can meaningfully 'do' is extend My creation – and you **are** My creation, My Son – and that is by Love. Is Loving 'doing'? How do you 'do' Love? You cannot 'do' Love, you can* *only 'be' Love. And Love can only **Know** Itself by extending Itself. Love is all you need to remember and to be. Freedom from all that shackles Love is achieved by forgiving what has never restricted Love but only **appears** that way. Forgiveness re-empowers you to see past illusions and they then disappear, My beloved.*

Thank you for reminding me, Papa. Another step forward.

Another step allowed; not taken, but given, and received.

In this world of unreality – loneliness, separation, division, guilt and fear – our greatest blessing can only be communing with the Mind of Papa, or of His beloved Son, the Christ, or of His Voice, the Spirit of Truth; Universal Mind. How can it be otherwise; how else can we be restored to wholeness, since there is but One Mind and One Spirit, and This is our true Being, our *One* Self?

---

1. Renard, Gary R., *The Dissappearance of the Universe*
©2004 Gary R. Renard, Hay House, Inc., California.

37: Qualities that Connect Us to Eternity

Now is the time for great rejoicing. Draw near unto me; let your communing continue, for it is the Open Door through which you, and all who will, shall enter in and partake in the marriage of Heaven with Earth and the great banquet celebration which accompanies it.

–Jesus, October 3, 1993

A LTHOUGH WE APPEAR TO BE EMBODIED in a finite, fear-driven consciousness, there are things we can experience in time and place that are not *of* eternity but that connect us *to* it. One is compassion. Most of us feel it at one time or another. It connects us very powerfully to distressed brothers in the fragmented Sonship. But although compassion is an *aspect* of Love it has no place in eternity because there is no distress there. The more connected to Love we become, while still *seeming* to be embodied, the more we experience compassion for our brothers in distress. Jesus exemplified this:

> ... when he saw the multitudes, he was moved with compassion on them, because they fainted, and were scattered abroad, as sheep having no shepherd (Mt. 9:36). [Does this not perfectly describe today's multitudes?] ... and he healed their sick (Mt. 14:14).

Another is forgiveness. There is nothing to forgive in eternity, but without true forgiveness our remembrance of Heaven cannot be restored to us because *unforgiveness* blocks our awareness of What and Where we *really* are. True forgiveness is impossible without a little willingness first to acknowledge that there is *actually* nothing to forgive. This means recognising and accepting *the* Truth as *our* Truth; that what we have *believed* is happening in time and place cannot be *truly* happening because time and place does not exist. It is *merely* a dream, and dreams are not real.

We can only replace the belief in time and place with the *re*cognition of eternal, uninterruptible Love, Peace and Joy by willingness to forgive what we have *believed* is real – guilt, fear, hate, conflict, death … That willingness *authorises* the Holy Spirit, our Higher Self, to shine the Light of eternity into our split-off-from-Truth mind, replacing confusion – caused by our choice to go out into outer darkness, i.e., the darkness of the without – with clarity. The shadowy misperceptions about what we had thought were reality then simply disappear; cease to occupy any part of our mind – which is the only place they ever seemed to exist.

Love and fear cannot co-exist in our mind, which is the source of our awareness. They are mutually exclusive. If we allow one, awareness of the other is erased, or blocked from our memory, like magnetic signals on recording tape. When we place the signals of separation – with all their crepuscular messages of fear, darkness and death (the 'opposites' of Love, Light and Life) – on record (i.e., believe them to be real) they cover over what is *permanently* embedded in our Mind, hiding our awareness of it. As we re-view these false, shadowy signals over and over they *seem* to be our experience but *cannot* be reality because only Love is real.

This is like watching a horror film and getting caught up in the belief that its story is real. This is not something God has done to punish us for our 'sins'. We have done it to ourself, and God allows it because He gave us free will. That is the measure of His Love for and trust in His beloved Son – us. How could an all-*Knowing* God have trust in a Son who has made such a mistake? Because he *Knows* His Son has made only a momentary error of *perception*, and it is not real; He *Knows* His Son is, in Truth, innocent; that an error of perception is not a 'sin', and thus is not deserving of punishment.

The Son emerges from the cinema into the bright Light of Day, hears the birdsong, sees the flowers, smells their perfume, feels the warmth of the sunlight, and the illusion of the images of horror projected onto the screen in the darkened cinema are readily erased from his memory – gone and forgotten – as he experiences the joy of Life restoring him to peace once more. And he gives thanks as he skips light-heartedly home. In like manner we can release the phantasms of our confused, upside-down minds and reconnect with reality; commence our journey Home to Papa.

We are all connected; to each other and to our Creator, as One. We all have moments of that connectedness even while separation – from each other and Him – is our *imagined* experience. This is because that connectedness, that Oneness is immovably stored in the memory, the hard-drive, of our Mind, our very Being, and lapses – gaps – in the flawed, overlaid imagining of unreality enable that connectedness to come through. We even have a word for this phenomenon: synchronicity.

The New Oxford Dictionary of English defines synchronicity as *"The simultaneous occurrence of events which appear significantly related but have no [outwardly] discernible causal connection."* They *appear* not to have a discernible causal connection only to the mind that has closed itself off from the *Light of Spiritual Discernment* (LSD). The connection is, nevertheless, irreversibly there. How can it be otherwise, when in Truth we are all, eternally, irreversibly One? Now is the time, the moment of the *re-connection* of the fragmented Sonship. Or, to be more accurate, the moment of restoration to *remembrance* of the unbreachable connectedness of the Sonship to Itself and Its Creator.

So, synchronicity is another experience we can have in time and place that is not *of* eternity but that connects us *to* it, *re*-minds us of it. When we are restored to remembrance of our true Oneness, or connectedness, that will be our *uninterrupted* awareness. That was the state of mind of Jesus during his embodiment two millennia ago and is our inescapable destiny because he came to restore us to it. Meanwhile, the nearer our restoration gets to that place of remembrance, the more synchronicity occurs in our Earth-conscious experience.

As the leavening of the third measure of meal gathers momentum, and time-collapsing events increasingly occur, people are being brought together, reconnected by what, to a forgetful, unbelieving mind, seem like 'astonishing' acts of synchronicity. So astonishing that closed minds label them 'coincidence', 'chance', 'fluke', or some other 'elaborate theory of men'. Yet those whose minds begin to open, awaken to the Truth of their Being, have an intuitive *Knowing* that they belong together; have been together through many incarnations, united in a common, kingdomly purpose.

Re-united, their commonality of purpose strengthens their singleness of vision and commitment to the Great Rescue Programme as they find mutuality of encouragement and affirmation. As forward progress into remembrance continues into the Light, and co-operation with the Spirit of Truth in the outworking of our birth vision grows, so do misfortune, confusion, fear, judgement, grievance, unforgiveness … diminish until synchronicity is seen for what it really is: emergent connectedness; Oneness; unity.

Diary of a Christ Communicant

A.M. March 1, 2011

… Humility is peaceful and joyful because it is our true nature, in which we are fully aware that we have everything. There is no requirement to defend or justify ourself; we simply *Know* what we are. Humility is full, complete, lacking in nothing, requiring nothing. In contrast, arrogance is empty, lonely, seeking recognition and approval, and never lastingly achieving what it vainly seeks. It is bluff and bluster to cover fear and lack of self-worth.

38: Becoming Like Jesus

It is possible for that which you experience, and of which you have awareness, to be transmitted from, or reflected by, your aura – which is more greatly refined and enlightened by understanding and commitment – into the realms of lesser understanding. Even as I lead and you follow, do you also lead by my example and others will be drawn and follow.

–Jesus, October 17, 1993

HERE IS A POWERFUL QUOTE by Jesus in *A Course in Miracles*: If you want to be like me I will help you, *knowing* that we are alike. If you want to be different, I will wait until you change your mind. I can teach you, but only you can choose to listen to my teaching. How else can it be, if God's Kingdom is freedom? (*ACIM,* Chapter 8, p145, IV.6:3-6).

There is one way and one way only we can *appear* to be different from him and that is by *pretending* to be different. In Truth he is Christ, and as, in Truth, we *are* like him, so we also are Christ. We have been pretending to be different since the seeming separation from our Christ-Self and our Creator. Not a pretty sight. Happily, even in Pretendville the game is drawing to a close, and that is inevitable, inescapable. Not because Papa is an autocrat but because we can only play make-believe for so long before it becomes impossible to not return Home to our right mind.

When we observe the world with our bodily senses it seems we are a very long way from Home. Those who are consciously aware, or starting to become aware, of the unreality of time and place are still a tiny percentage, even though that percentage increases day by day. The vast mass of humanity continues to surrender its will to the ego script of littleness, disempowerment and vulnerability. This manifests itself as guilt, fear, conflict, and in the dependence on medicine, body-part replacement, technology... instead of the Holy Spirit's script of God-Self empowerment, inner *Knowing*, wholeness, invulnerability, immortality...

Of course there is nothing inherently 'wrong' with technology – it is neutral – and when committed to the Spirit of Truth for use within the outworking of His script for the raising up, the leavening, the restoring to wholeness of our self-limited, misperceiving, upside-down mind, it can serve His purpose very well. But it will also serve *us* well to remind ourself from time to time that ultimately, the all-empowered-by-God Mind and Spirit of our true, eternal Being – Papa's Son, the Christ – has no need of telephones, computers, surgery, drugs, aeroplanes, cars, TV ... *anything* temporal, and that thus symbolise unreality.

Slavish dependence on any or all such as a *substitute* for our God-given true, unending completion, happiness, wholeness, peace ... is a *self*-deprival of our creation-right, heritage and thus, our certain, inescapable destiny. Such substitution is born of the choice for forgetfulness, which arises from guilt and fear. Joy, Light, Life, Love, Truth, freedom ... all arise from our free choice for remembrance, not of our perceived differences, indiv*iduality*, but of our *likeness*. Here, the ego will do all it can to make little of such a suggestion. So be it. It *wants* us to argue against our likeness – to Jesus and all our brothers – and thus continue to give specious reality to the differences that make up the illusion of separation. But who would argue, get into conflict, about what he *Knows* (or even *believes*) does not exist?

The Holy Spirit does not engage in conflict, nor does Truth need defending. As Jesus says in *A Course in Miracles*, it simply *is*. Hence he made no attempt to defend himself before the Sanhedrin or Pilate. Most of humanity is not yet ready for Truth, but all will come to readiness in due season because Truth is our eternal nature and reality. Meanwhile, we have taken/made bodies and the physical universe – the without – as a hiding place from Papa within, to escape from His wrath and punishment. How absurd, how comical is that? A God of unconditional Love being wrathful, vengeful, jealous, angry, judgemental, condemnatory, punitive …

We have made a god of duality, in our own misperceived likeness, and then try to hide from him by pretending we cannot experience awareness of his presence or that of his anointed emissary. This is hardly surprising since we have persuaded ourself his emissary is coming 'to judge the quick and the dead', who will then be cast into the fires of hell by that self-made god. Ego-enthralled minds proclaim we can have no way of knowing whether God and His emissary – Jesus – are really there, or even whether there is any such thing as 'life after death'.

All this pretence of not Knowing is fear-driven. *Everything* is either Love- or fear-engendered; there are no other possibilities. Papa is not fearful *because* He is Love. Jesus is Love. *We* are Love. Only Love is real. All the rest is made up, and because it is not real it *has* to come to an end, and with it, darkness, confusion, limitation, scarcity, *dis*ease and 'death' – all the illusions we have imagined in our dream of separation.

We try to separate ourself from the worst excesses of hate, conflict, oppression, famine, slavery, civil war … but we are One, so the only way to return to Love is for us all to return to Love *together*, as the One we are. Can the dream of separation end by remaining separate? Assuredly we are dreaming if we are happy to buy 'cheap' clothing – and whatever else – made in sweat-shops by people working nineteen-hour days, six days per week, for a pittance. That is a symbol of separation as unserviceable to the healing, the re-unifying of Papa's Son with his Self and his Father as any other symbol.

Yet, we cannot save the world from without, which is what the ego wants us to try to do, because it knows that for every 'wrong' we 'right', every disease we cure 'out there' another will arise to take its place. We can only save it from our own within, by Loving, blessing, forgiving our brothers and ourself. That will be perceived as a cop-out by the ego and it *is* if we don't follow Jesus' counsel and *Love* our neighbour as ourself, just as he did in the long ago, and still does. We can only Love our neighbour as ourself if, when, we remember that he *is* our Self, because we are, *truly*, One.

When we remember that we *are* One our behaviour will, *automatically*, spontaneously, fall into line with that remembrance, and we will start to *feel* that, *experience* the reality of it in our heart. And we will realise that we *are* becoming like Jesus.

Let us join, just for a moment, as the *One* we really are, to bless the world – every living thing, including the tens of billions of animals being factory-farm reared each year as a mere *commodity*, without Love, tender care or compassion, then brutally treated and slaughtered every illusory, linear moment, to provide a pathetic substitute for the nurture of our *true* Being by Papa – forgive the world and forgive ourself, thus hastening our return Home, together, as the One-with-*every*-living-thing we are in Truth.

Hence Jesus' words, "Inasmuch as ye have done it [anything – Loving or unloving – it still applies] unto one of these, the least of my brethren, ye have done it unto me." (Mt. 25:40). How characteristic of the ego to dupe Papa's befuddled Son into believing 'brethren' applies only to humans, when every living thing is equally part of the same, *One* Life. This ego-subterfuge enables its murderous blood-lust to be carried on right under our noses with most of us hardly even noticing, and 'thinking' it's all perfectly all right. Happily, we are in the time when this is all changing as more and more fragments begin to waken from their slumbers and realise this is not who we all really Are.

Diary of a Christ Communicant

A.M. March 7, 2011

**What Papa creates is real because it is created in His
likeness: Perfect Love, and cannot change or it would
become *other* than perfect, and therefore could not be
of Him. How can Perfect Love – Papa – create other than
what is of the nature of His Being?**

When we look at the illusions we have made, they appear to our
sight because we *believe* them to be real. But our bodily sight is
flawed, devised to show us our temporal misperceptions in place of
eternal Reality. Eternity is Light, but time and place, being unreal,
is darkness, because the Light is not present; we have blocked it
out. We see as through a darkened glass, and what we perceive is
shadows. All the while we choose to see those shadows as real so
will they *be* our reality because what we believe, we see.

But they are *not* reality to Papa, so He doesn't see them. He
sees only what is real. What is real is eternally, *unchangeably*
real. If what is real is eternal and unchangeable, what is
constantly changing, fading, disintegrating cannot be real,
for it is *contra* to reality.

What Papa creates is real because it is created in His
likeness: Perfect Love, and cannot change or it would
become *other* than perfect, and therefore could not be of
Him. How can Perfect Love – Papa – create other than
what is of the nature of His Being? Re-read what He said to
you on February 11, 2011, to re-mind yourself. [See *Diary of
a Christ Communicant* at the end of chapter 32: p195.]

39: To Fear or to Love: Our Only Choice

Our heavenly Father is ever ready to respond to the spark of awakening desire in us to go forward, and the pattern of unfoldment in time and place is ever moving in such a fashion as to present opportunities for us, His little ones, to respond accordingly.

–A Christ-server from the Realms of Light, October 24, 1993

W E HAVE ALL BEEN RIDING the carousel of birth and death for countless aeons. Most of the fragmented Sonship still *seems* to have an indeterminate number of further circuits to make before Awakening to the remembrance that we can escape and return *Home* to the perfect peace, joy, Love and freedom that is eternity. But there is something with which we can all, without exception, consciously choose to engage that will foreshorten the number of further circuits by a quantum factor.

Now is the moment in the Great Rescue Programme when time is being increasingly collapsed, by and for increasing numbers of us. We can actively, knowingly, consciously take part in its collapsing, for ourself and for our brothers, known and unknown, loved and unloved; feared and hated, even. This can happen without our brothers even being aware of our committed endeavour, because by participating for ourself we *include* them, since, in spite of contra appearances, we are One. The contra appearances are caused by fear. We all desire to escape from fear; *fear is perpetuated by unwillingness to forgive.*

As Pursah (visiting from Spirit) says to Gary Renard in his book *The Disappearance of the Universe*:

The law of forgiveness is this:

Fear binds the world. Forgiveness sets it free (*ACIM*, Workbook for Students, p.468, Lesson 332).

> The world feels solid to you [i.e., all of us who believe illusions are real] because fear binds it [and binds us to it]. **It doesn't feel solid to me because I have forgiven the world, so its touch is no more solid than your dreams are for you at night.** Yes, I feel *something* – but only enough to be able to function while I appear to be here. It's very gentle. *That's* **why the nails didn't hurt J as they were being driven into his flesh.** Being guiltless, his mind could not suffer – and someday you will attain the condition where you cannot suffer. That is the destiny the Holy Spirit holds out to you when you forgive the episodic fantasies of your bodily addicted ego.

That was no idle promise by Pursah. It is a *certainty* for us all, *guaranteed* by Papa. All the while we *believe* we are here, we are *making* it our reality, and while crucifixion may not be widely practised in this era, we are all crucifying *ourself* in myriad forms, some slowly, over decades and multiple incarnations, some much quicker, overlapping the slower forms. The nails we are driving into our own flesh, and the crown of thorns we are placing on our own head are unforgiveness, judgements, grievances. For all the grievances, judgements, unforgivenesses inevitably reflect back to us, and we find ourself on the receiving end, sooner or later.

This can manifest in mental and bodily illness, 'accidents', theft, assault ... All are forms of self-judgement and self-punishment. Yet we can avoid all such without lifting a finger by *choosing* <u>unconditional</u> *forgiveness*. This means we make the conscious choice to forgive **everything** – past, present and future – regardless of what it might appear to be, whose 'fault' it might appear to be, what appears to be done to whom.

This is because forgiveness is an all or nothing thing. Partial forgiveness is not forgiveness because it is not *true* forgiveness. How could we be at peace about God if He was partial in His forgiveness? And we and God, in spite of outward appearances to the contrary, are One. In order to become restored to awareness of that Oneness we must be willing to *believe* It and commit to willingness to *live* it. Then, truly, are we set free – from our own, self-applied chains.

The Spirit of Truth, our whole, higher, *real* Self does all the rest, but *cannot* until we so choose and surrender the outcome into His able care. This is because He honours our God-given free-will. When we give Him the reins of our life *things start to happen*, things start to change. There is plenty to change in the mind, the affairs, of any whose life has been under ego's yoke.

At first it may seem scary because it is so different, and the ego, masquerading as ourself, does not like change. It wants more of the same: self-crucifying, albeit slowly, so we don't realise its intent. But under Holy Spirit-Self care, guiding and protection, all is *always* for our highest good and that of all with whom our life interacts. When a change of direction – to the Light – is sought, it will always require a sorting out, and ridding ourself of ego 'stuff'. This is where Faith, Trust, Obedience (to the Voice for God, our Higher Self, within us) and Commitment (FTOC) comes into its own. Trust is difficult, seemingly impossible even, in this world of lies, but not in the Spirit of Truth.

From the perspective of linear time, waking up to reality, returning Home to Oneness in Papa is not a sprint, but a marathon. Some of us may be so nearly ready to Awaken in this 'present' act that it will happen; for most of us, more acts will be needful. But, as stated in chapter 28 of this book:

> ... When we come to the end of our sojourn with a body and lay it aside we have the opportunity to enter into a period of reflection about the progress (or seeming lack thereof) we have made toward the Light of our eternal Home in Papa during this moment of embodiment...
>
> ... (Yet) we do not need to wait until we lay aside our

body to enter into a period of reflection … We can begin *now*; for there *is* only Now. Delaying is of the ego; it is not of *our* true nature …

Such periods of reflection between embodiments provide the perfect opportunity to initiate the *further* collapsing of time by asking guidance in planning our next act more wisely, carefully, purposefully. The vast mass of fragments proceeds haphazardly from one act to the next, blinded by guilt and fear, with no enlightened idea, plan or purpose, drawn by myriad uncontrolled, undisciplined emotions, feelings, desires, lusts … Yet by choosing to plan, with the help of wise counsel from the Realms of Light, we can cut short the number of acts needed to arrive at the place of wakefulness from the dream of separation.

Even a carefully, wisely planned reincarnation means re-entry into total forgetfulness, but will not countervail such purposeful planning, for two reasons:

1. We bring the memory of the plan (and everything else) with us, in seed, or dormant mode, and the circumstances into which we have *mindfully* chosen to incarnate will trigger flashes of remembrance, controlled by our higher, Holy Spirit Self, a bit at a time, *as required*. That is possible because we have purposefully chosen aforetime to co-operate with Self during embodiment.

2. We will have also included within the planning the *intent* to accept the help, care, counsel and protection of a guide, or guides, from the Realms of Light who have helped us with the planning.

All this falls within our free choice: to follow the lead of the Spirit of Truth … or not. The only alternative is for more of the same … the open-ended continuation of the dream of limitation, littleness, guilt, fear, death.

Thank You, Holy Spirit-Self, for clarity, that today and every day our decisions may increasingly involve Your input, until we are fully restored to remembrance of our wholeness, our Oneness.

Diary of a Christ Communicant

A.M. March 13, 2011

> **The choice for power in time and place in lieu of empowerment with eternity is the choice for disenfranchisement of that same empowerment for good, for healing the world – and Oneself in the process – that Jesus, your brother and template for true Being, chose.**

By placing ourself under (within) Christ authority we are accessing Christ-empowerment, just as Jesus did. This is the true nature and Being of us all.

But most of the fragments of the Sonship still worship at the altar of power in matters of time and place – a reversal of their true, eternal Being. Compare the empowerment of Jesus with the 'power' of the CEO of some corporate conglomerate, who exercises arbitrary power and authority over the lives and fortunes of thousands of employees. How often does this power fill those employees with hate, envy, fear of a boss who can change – upheave – their lives at the stroke of a pen, and will do so when the accountants, or shareholders, tell him he must close a factory, slim-down the workforce. Is this empowerment?

In a few short years that CEO will be replaced and forgotten, other than for the legacy of privation he enforced – by circumstances beyond his control – upon the pawns in the ruthless game of power-mongering for 'survival of the fittest'. Who sees power over rather than empowerment with is misperceiving indeed.

The choice for power in time and place in lieu of empowerment with eternity is the choice for disenfranchisement of that same empowerment for good, for healing the world – and Oneself in the process – that Jesus, your brother and template for true Being, chose.

40: Freedom through *Self*-Forgiveness

My son, it is the Father's good pleasure to give the Kingdom to His little ones... It does, however, depend on the willingness of those little ones to <u>receive</u> these good gifts.

–Jesus, October 31, 1993

LIFE IS SPIRIT AND SPIRIT IS LIFE. There is but *One* Life and that is Papa, the *Creator* Spirit. Our life is part of, One within, Him, indivisibly. If we were to be separate from Him – a total impossibility in Truth – we would not have life and therefore would not, could not, exist at all. It is only in our mind that we have chosen to *believe* we are separate from Him. When we choose to stop believing in separation, and choose instead to remember our Oneness in Him, we will be immediately restored to that awareness. Jesus will help us if we are willing to *ask* him sincerely, from the heart. He Knows and *responds* to that sincerity.

We cannot accomplish this restoration to remembrance of our true, innocent (i.e., guiltless), whole Self, Papa's beloved Son, the Christ, alone. This is because most of our misperceptions of separation are hidden in a part of our mind we cannot consciously access. They all stem from the one misperception that we are guilty of breach of the *Principle of Life of the Father* that is the eternal, indivisible Oneness of all Life, and because we believe we have broken God's Law we believe we deserve to be punished by Him. This, in turn, gives rise to fear.

Because of this mistaken idea, we believe, and thus perceive, our experience is of the opposite of Life: 'death'. Life is wholeness, is Love and Peace and Joy. Uninterruptibly, forever. So our mistaken belief, being the *opposite* of Life, brings us what we have called into our own, illusorily-separated presence ... fear, anxiety, brokenness, doubt, scarcity, loneliness, misery, sickness, 'death'. All this – or nearly all of it – is so terrible we cannot countenance it consciously; hence its submersion to the part of our supposedly split-off-from-Truth mind that is *unconscious*.

Unconscious does not mean non-existent. It means we have pushed it under the rug in a vain attempt at *pretending* it is not there while we endeavour to make something worthwhile out of nothing, and *call* it a life. But what lurks in the deep cannot remain there indefinitely, and from time to time something fetid rises to the surface of our conscious mind to cause us fear, ruin our moment, our day, our life. Much of the time we have no knowledge or understanding of the cause, projecting blame for it onto brothers or other 'outside' circumstances.

This is barely touching the surface of the black hole into which we seem to have sucked ourself, yet it suffices to indicate why we haven't a hope of escaping from its pull without *Help*. According to the bewildered, ego part of our upside-down, back-to-front mind, help is for wimps, losers, no-hopers; we must never surrender to receiving help, for that shows our weakness, our inadequacy, our failure. And if we do, we can use that as a 'valid' reason to pile on the guilt. Yet only when we are prepared to surrender the reins of our life to One Who is *all*-empowered-by-Love-and-Light can we escape from darkness.

As stated in chapter 39, when we give Him – Jesus and/or the Spirit of Truth, it makes no difference; They are our connection, within our mind, and thus, *accessible*, to sanity, wholeness, Oneness – the reins of our life *things start to happen*, things start to change. There is plenty to change in the mind, the affairs, of any whose life has been under ego's yoke. Its yoke is guilt, fear, pain, suffering, judgement and 'death'; more burdensome than most of us have any desire to contemplate. Yet, as recorded of Jesus in the long ago:

> Come unto me, all *ye* that labour and are heavy laden, and I will give you rest. Take my yoke upon you, and learn of me; for I am meek and lowly in heart: and ye shall find rest unto your souls. For my yoke *is* easy, and my burden is light (Mt. 11:28-30).

As we judge, so are we *self*-judged, and as we forgive so are we *self*-forgiven. Who else is there to judge – or forgive – us other than ourself? Only *we* believe we have done anything worthy of judgement *or* forgiveness, and that is only within an insane dream of separation from Papa and our own true Being: Christ. The only thing Papa *Knows* of separation is that it is impossible, so He has neither desire nor cause to judge us. And because He *Knows* His beloved Son is guiltless, He Knows there is nothing to forgive. Since His Son is exactly like his Father, he *also* Knows similarly.

Yet we *believe*, mostly at an unconscious level in our upside-down, split-off-from-Truth mind, that we are guilty, so *deserve* to be judged. And, believing it, that is what we are doing: judging, condemning and punishing *ourself*. Who else will punish us? Papa certainly won't; neither, of course, will Jesus. This is why the most important thing we can do if we wish to escape the carousel of birth and death – death by myriad forms of 'self-crucifixion' – is to forgive *ourself*. And because we have projected our self-perceived guilt onto our brothers 'out there' – but who are simply a reflection of our unconscious *self*-perception – we experience a need to forgive them also.

By forgiving ourself we *are* forgiving our brothers, and when we forgive our brothers we *are* forgiving ourself, because in reality there is but One of us, appearing, *illusorily*, as many. All the while we judge ourself and/or our brothers we will see ourself and them as separate – because that is our belief, and what we believe, we perceive, so it becomes our 'reality'. When we have forgiven ourself and our brothers for what, in Truth, none of us has *ever* done, we will have seen past the illusion of separation to the Truth of our Being as One.

When we have forgiven ourself (along with our brothers) ALL that we *believe*, in our unconscious mind, we have done, all the 'sins' we have (actually, not) committed over untold incarnations, and that there is, therefore, nothing left to forgive, we will have become *fully* self-forgiven (remembering that neither God, nor Jesus, nor the Holy Spirit judge us). Thus are we released into innocence, to freedom; restored to remembrance of our guiltlessness; our wholeness/holiness; our true, eternal, all-*Knowing*, all-empowered-by-Perfect-Love Being: Papa's beloved Son, the Christ.

Now can we see how escape is impossible *without* that Help. Help from One Who sees ALL our 'secret sins and hidden fears' – *Knowing* they are not real – and brings them to the surface of our awareness when He sees we are ready to forgive and release them, in a gentle way that does not overwhelm us. These are presented in the form of circumstances, encounters, events in our 'present' act, or embodiment. Those with whom we have had a karmic entanglement in 'former acts' are brought, by synchronicity, into our presence to provide a forgive-and-release-back-to-innocence opportunity.

Truly, this indicates that there is no escape, *save* by forgiveness. It may seem absurd to think we must forgive what *in Truth* we have never done, but it is necessary because, deep in our unconscious mind – functioning within a dream of *reversal* of Truth – we *believe* we have done it. It is that mistaken belief that must be corrected, and this can only happen with that wondrous Help. From there it must ALL be brought to the surface, *faced*, consciously forgiven and thereby are we released – from the fallacious belief in guilt – back to innocence. Then we are One again, and returned to *awareness* that we are at Home in Papa. Forever.

Diary of a Christ Communicant

A.M. March 14, 2011

… Thank You, beloved Papa, for taking up Your abode in me, just as Jesus, Your anointed messenger, promised You would do for *all who Love him and keep his word* (Jn. 14:23). I gladly, joyously welcome You into my heart-mind, *Knowing* Your presence there is forever and forever. Amen.

41: Attuning Our Mind and Life with Truth

You shall become empowered in your Earth vehicle by the reality of the Living Word and the spring of the Waters of Life which wells up in all who Love me above all else.

–Jesus, November 7, 1993

PERCEIVING OURSELF AS A BODY, in time and place, indicates brokenness. Perceiving myriad others as bodies, in time and place, separate from our self, further *affirms* that perception of brokenness. That brokenness arose within us, and *seems* to continue to proceed all the while, and I am prompted to repeat ALL THE WHILE we choose to deny our true Identity as Papa's One, perfect, innocent Son. It does not *actually* continue to proceed because it was over the same instant it began, but we keep re-viewing it in a vain attempt to make the unreal real, and also to make it better. Trying to make the unreal real, let alone better, is vain indeed. Brokenness is separation, or fragmentation, from wholeness. Wholeness is our true estate. Yet, neither God, nor Jesus, nor the Holy Spirit can restore us to wholeness without our conscious *willingness* for it to happen.

That shows the absoluteness of the gift of free will with which Papa endowed His Son at his creation. If it is our perceived – erroneous – will to be separated, broken-off from our Source and from our Self, we are denying ourself eternal wholeness, freedom, all-empowerment-by-Love. It hardly needs stating again here that this choice is not the will of our true Self but that of the ego, which continues, *with our compliance*, in that choice; a total *reversal* of every quality of our *true* Being. There is one failsafe way to dispel the ego from our driving seat and *keep* it dispelled: unite with Jesus.

> When you unite with me you are uniting **without** the ego, because I have renounced the ego in myself and therefore cannot unite with yours. **Our union is therefore the way to renounce the ego in you.** (Jesus in *ACIM*, Chapter 8, p.147, V. The Undivided Will of the Sonship, 4:1, 2).

Sounds like a doddle, but the ego has something to say about that, putting up terrific resistance to our uniting with Jesus. It will assure us we are lowly, guilty, sinners, 'down here' and Jesus is 'up there', far beyond our unworthy reach. It will tell us we must be prepared to go through all sorts of doctrinal hoops, including that we must believe that Jesus' death on the cross was a once and for all time blood sacrifice, required of an angry God, as propitiation for our sins, and unless we believe this we will be judged by Him as guilty and sentenced to burn eternally in the fires of hell.

Such doctrinal chicanery is confusing, misleading, fear-engendering and not true. As stated in "*Seek ye First the Kingdom…*":

> It is not the death of Jesus on the cross that 'makes us at one' with God but his *life* – and his demonstration of Life's indestructibleness by/through his resurrection – and leading us back to God by reminding us who we really are: eternal, immortal Beings of Light, God's perfect Son, all One within the Sonship.

We are already halfway to uniting with Jesus without even trying; before we even have any awareness of it! For, as he told me in 1968:

> "I am attuned to all mankind all the time; there is never a moment when I am not with you all. All that is needed to complete the contact is for you to attune with me and we are together, at any time."

How, then, do we attune with him? By simply *desiring* so to do; by making that our *choice*. We will serve ourself immeasurably well also by ignoring, not reacting to, the ego's frenetic resistance; by *refusing to believe* we are unworthy, guilty, sinners ...

Jesus, believe it or no, *Loves* us; is our friend and wants us to accept that *we* are *his* friends. Friends do not judge. They look past 'imperfections, mistakes, errors, faults, foibles', recognising them as nothing, choosing instead to see only the best in us, as do we in them, knowing those are their *real* qualities and thus make them *truly* lovable. How can we join, or unite, with Jesus, when we seem to be in a body and he does not? We do not unite *bodily*, with anyone, but with our *mind*. We unite with Jesus as we do with *any* we love or desire to be with, embodied or not: by mind-to-mind communing.

This does not have to be anything elaborate, any more than communing mind to mind with any other loving friends, who simply love us for being true to ourself, and thus, true to them. How can we be true to ourself if we are lying to our brother? We certainly cannot commune with Jesus if we are lying to him about ourself. What would be the point? The whole objective of uniting, communing, with Jesus is to help us *renounce* the ego in us. The ego is 'the father of lies', so trying to kid Jesus by carrying on the game of pretend with him will get us nowhere; he's on the wavelength of *reality*.

We are so inured to the game of pretend – which is lying by another name, because it is denying the Truth – that when our endeavouring to commune with Jesus is nascent we will likely be stuck for words. This means *nothing* to him. He is not interested in our words but in our heart – the seat of our desire, our sincerity, our very soul, and thus, our Truth. He wants us to enter into the sanctuary of our inner being, which is our heart, where he dwells within us. If we are sincere in our desire for communion with him – and thus, with Papa – we *will* encounter him there. If we *are* not, we *will* not.

Not because he is not there; assuredly he *is*. But our sojourning in the world of make-believe is intended, by the ego, to cause us to lose our way back into that sanctuary, so long have we been out of it, lost and alone in a far country. The ego is our thinking, or intellect, or calculating, reckoning 'head-mind'. We have allowed the spirit of reckoning to stand in the place of faith. Reckoning and faith are mutually exclusive. We either base our life in faith or in reckoning. We cannot successfully engage both, though most of us try. Faith is our pathway to Truth, in which we surrender our life into the care, guiding and protection of Jesus and/or the Spirit of Truth, our whole, holy Self; reckoning is the slippery slope to oblivion, led by the duplicitous ego. For any who don't believe that, take a look at this world, which outwardly descends deeper into chaos of every kind, hell-bent on oblivion – because most political, financial, educational and religious decisions are based not in faith but in reckoning.

Our true, faith-focused mind is our *heart*-mind, and most of us have lost the way to connect with the heart-mind, the Truth of our Being, which is, of course, Love, which is, of course, Papa. When we are *safe* in the heart of Love, no calculating, or reckoning, is necessary, precisely *because* we are safe. That is how it was with Jesus, including during his embodied state, so we can *Know*, of a certainty beyond all doubt, that it is achievable by us during *our* embodied state, because we are his brothers, with all the same attributes, the same Pedigree. *If only we can believe*.

We are lost in a world of unreality, having handed the direction of our life to the wrong guide, that has *deliberately* led us into 'outer darkness'. We do not feel safe without the Light. Every step we take in the alien, hostile world of time and place, blind, without the Light of eternal Truth, is potentially fraught with danger, so we feel the *need* to calculate the risk. But Jesus has repudiated the ego and is thus enlightened within; he is our true, illuminated guide on what is otherwise a perilous path out of the 'wilderness of sin'. He will guide us unfailingly. *If we are willing to follow his lead*.

Head-mind endeavours at communion with Truth (I am the Way, the TRUTH and the Life; no man cometh to the Father but by me ~ Jesus [Jn. 14:6]) cannot succeed. We unite with him not with our head-mind – mistakenly used by what Jesus described to me as 'the clever, the proud and the scornful' (i.e., not the humble) – but with our heart-mind. So, we have no need for calculations, or reckoning; only faith, a true and sincere *desire* for joyous, loving fellowship and for his care, guiding and protection in our seemingly separated lives, for our restoration to Oneness with him in Papa.

Only therein is to be found freedom from loneliness, guilt, fear, confusion, doubt, scarcity, darkness, illness, limitation, 'death'... and in their place Joy, Peace, Love, beyond all Earth-mind imagining. Eternally.

Diary of a Christ Communicant

A.M. March 21, 2011

Now is the pivotal moment for Papa's Holy Son ... the moment he can choose the onward and upward Path to the Light, or continue the downward and backward descent to darkness.

There is no need for forgiveness when we Awaken because then we *Know*, we see, that in *Truth* nothing has ever happened warranting forgiveness. That is where Jesus is. All that *appears* to warrant forgiveness has only been within illusion, and therefore is not real; has never *actually* happened.

Until we Awaken we perceive – in our self-blinded-to-reality state, through a glass, darkly – grievances, with judgement.

So true forgiveness is a way of reminding oneself of misperception. This prevents the conviction that misperceptions are true from settling into a solid foundation; they are undermined by forgiveness.

There are those who say it is their Christian duty to judge their fellows. Such claim to be followers of him of whom it is recorded, "I judge no man" [Jn. 8:15], and, "I came not to judge the world, but to save the world." [Jn. 12:47]. Do they believe such dualistic thinking is the way to the Kingdom-of-all-inclusiveness? Yet it is from such insanity that the Great Rescue Programme will resurrect their minds.

Now is the pivotal moment for Papa's Holy Son ... the moment he can choose the onward and upward Path to the Light or continue the downward and backward descent to darkness.

Only true forgiveness can be the deciding factor. Unwillingness to see past the misperceptions of 'sin' means remaining in the *belief* in sin.

42: Taking Advantage of Opportunities

Eternity is where you belong, my son; keep your sight focused on that and let neither fear nor baubles distract you from the Way. Now is the time of fulfilment of those whose eye is single.

–Jesus, November 28, 1993

WHEN THE EGO ATTACKS, which it does all the time, even when we are unaware of it – if we do not engage with it by defending ourself with a counterattack, it runs out of steam. This is because it is our defence, or counterattack, which *fuels* its attack. Stop fuelling it and it grinds to a halt. Even better, *actively* forgiving what comes up before us *actively* empties its tank. Ultimately, when *all* in our unconscious mind is forgiven that will be the *complete* undoing of the ego, which can but mean Awakening to remembrance of our Oneness and our return to the eternity that is Heaven.

The ego believes in war; the Holy Spirit *Knows* – and IS – peace. It's plain to see which the world is following. The ego is at war constantly but the Holy Spirit – the inner connection to our Higher, Whole, Christ Self – does not engage with it. By choosing with the Holy Spirit, i.e. not engaging with judgement, grievance, conflict (thought, word or deed, it makes no difference) we are saving ourself from more of the same – further fear-filled, self-limiting imprisonments in a mortal body; further circuits of the carousel of birth and death. In Gary Renard's book, *Love Has Forgotten No One*[1], Pursah says:

If you're thinking right-minded, or forgiveness thoughts, with the Holy Spirit, you have to be headed in the right direction. That direction is Home to God. If you're thinking judgemental and condemning thoughts with the ego, then you keep yourself away from God.

She goes on to say:

The freedom, or free will, that exists for [people] during those dream lifetimes is the ability to choose the Holy Spirit's interpretation of everything instead of the ego's. Whether or not they do that and achieve real healing will determine the nature of their in-between lifetime experience [i.e. after laying aside their body and before their 'next' incarnation], as well as which lifetime they will experience after that!

And then she makes a statement that we will ALL serve ourself very well indeed to take on-board, to heart, and commit earnestly to applying:

That's why it's so important that you <u>don't wait</u> to practice forgiveness. Don't wait until next year. Don't wait until your next lifetime. Your future is being determined by you right *now*, depending on the choices you make: on whether you choose the Holy Spirit's interpretation of what you're seeing or the ego's.

And, finally:

... it's crucial to take advantage of the lessons that are presented to you on any given day. Those are the lessons the Holy Spirit wants you to learn ... and you do so by practicing true forgiveness ... then you won't have to repeat the same kinds of patterns all over again in your next dream lifetime.

Most of the fragmented Sonship is deceived by the ego into thinking that the reason adversity keeps on showing up in our experience is because we must deserve it; it is God punishing us for our wickedness – in this and/or other acts. We are sinners, and God has sent all those horrible people, accidents, misfortunes, health issues … to torment and punish us. That is the ego's interpretation, and it keeps us going round in ever-decreasing circles. Now let us consider the Holy Spirit's interpretation:

He brings these things up from our unconscious to our conscious mind so we can forgive them and release them. *He* will then dispose of them, *permanently*, so we don't have to keep re-experiencing them, in one form or another. He can only dispose of them when we authorise Him accordingly – by our forgiving and releasing them – thus releasing ourself, one forgiveness episode at a time, back into the innocence which is our true, eternal state of Being.

The ego perceives different *forms* of the same forgiveness opportunity as unrelated, and that we are so sinful, so guilty we *deserve* myriad attacks from all these 'different' people, events, illnesses … But we can choose, with the Holy Spirit, to see them not as punishment for innumerable sins, but the opportunity to correct the *only mistake* we *seem* to have made.

Needless to say, that one and only error is believing we are separate from Papa. All else stems from that and can all be dispelled *by correcting that one false belief*. The mechanism for correction is forgiving ourself, our brothers and the world for what in Truth (i.e., eternity) has *never* happened. That retrains our misled mind into the *remembrance* that none of it happened, that we therefore *cannot* be guilty, so there is *nothing* to fear. But all those dream-lifetime experiences are stored in our unconscious mind, where we cannot access them with our limited, split-off-from-Truth, *conscious* mind.

They are there, inaccessible to us because they are so fearful to us that we have entered into a state of *denial* of their existence. *Denying* what seems to be real does not *dispel* from our mind what we have *believed* to be real, so it has to 'go somewhere' – away from our *conscious* awareness. Thus is it consigned to, buried in, our *unconscious* mind; seemingly out of sight but not *actually* out of mind; like twilight shadows that seem to appear from nowhere to scare us in our state of confusion. This would keep us indefinitely in the hell that is the belief we are separate from our Source.

But the Holy Spirit sees into our unconscious mind, even though we cannot, and he *Knows* what is there is not real in Truth, only in our belief. And when we are willing to *trust* Him to free us from our self-made hell – without scaring us to death in the process(!) – and restore us to the reality of Heaven, He will bring up from our unconscious storehouse-of-hell one illusion at a time, as much as He *Knows* we are ready to *see* is not real, and can thus forgive. Our *willingness* to forgive what has *seemed* so real, yet in Truth is not, empowers, authorises the Holy Spirit to restore us to *remembrance* of our innocence.

There are vast, unfathomable amounts of guilt and fear dream-experiences stored in our unconscious mind, accrued from untold dream-life incarnations, so there is a lot to be brought to the surface for us to forgive, thus enabling our release back into innocence, one step at a time. Happily, the Holy Spirit sees all, *Knows* all, is all-empowered for this task, and will not, cannot fail. All He asks of us is that we trust Him. He will perform ALL the rest *for* us.

Then we can get on with the only real reason we are here: saving the world. The ego would have us believe this is arrogance of the first magnitude, because 'saving the world' is a *grandiose* scheme, far beyond the ability of our littleness and limitation. But our steadfast, unwavering commitment to forgiveness releases us from littleness and limitation (just like Jesus) and we, inevitably, become like him. Thus, saving the world is a simple thing, which we all can do (just like Jesus), starting right now (there *is* only now!), without lifting a finger or costing a penny.

And, by consciously choosing to join together, as the One we all really are – which forgiveness not only *enables* but restores our vision so we will *want* to join, there no longer being any reason for not so doing – we can more *powerfully* collapse time together, *sooner*, obviating untold repeat ego-moments of guilt, fear and 'death'. Since joining is of the mind, in which bodies have no part to play, we can do this wherever our body appears to be or whatever it seems to be doing.

Mind-to-mind communion is an anywhere, anytime process. Communion means *common union*. Common means *shared by all*.

Diary of a Christ Communicant

P.M. March 28, 2011

Faith will dispel doubt, but one must *hold fast* to faith, in trust that it will endure and restore true Sight – eternal, spiritual vision – if there is but a little willingness to *be* steadfast.

We are totally safe within Papa. Who, or what, could assail us There? That is Where we *are*. There *is* nowhere else. He Loves His Son. He created him perfect. Any idea to the contrary is not of Papa, so is not real, and therefore, not worth vainly trying to keep, to hold onto. The idea that He would expel His Son from Heaven, when he is perfect, makes no sense. Who amongst us can believe *any* idea of Papa's could make no sense?

> What Papa creates is eternal, perfect and thus, unchangeable. What is constantly changing can only be temporal, therefore cannot be real, so *must* be made up. What is made up cannot be of Heaven, the only reality. Time and place is made up, is not real, is not eternal, and thus, not of Heaven, not an idea of Papa's.
>
> Who could seriously believe He could create imperfection, in which everything that appears to live can do so only by the 'death' of other living things, and that grows old, withers and 'dies'?
>
> Papa's Son dreamt, for an infinitesimal moment, that something that is not who he is has persuaded him that it *is* who he is, and that he is in a place and a state that, in Truth, he is not: separated and fragmented. In that momentary dream his true Self remains quiescent to his time-and-place-focused consciousness because he has free

will to choose to be thusly focused, and Self honours that free will. In this consciousness his experience is of being alone, separate, isolated, fearful, different, guilty, doubting, uncertain, vulnerable …

None of this is true; not now, not ever. Yet he will remain in this perception all the while he doubts the Truth. Doubt is contra to certainty. Doubt is the great dismantler of faith, which is the only way he can be restored to certainty. Doubt is not easy to dispel when one is inured to it. Faith will dispel doubt, but one must *hold fast* to faith, in trust that it will endure and restore true Sight – eternal, spiritual vision – if there is but a little willingness to be steadfast. And best of all, to be comforted by the certainty that one is *not* alone, without Help, never has been, never will be, never *could* be.

1. Renard, Gary R., *Love Has Forgotten No One*, ©2013, Gary R. Renard, Hay House, Inc., California.

43: Inner Peace through Forgiveness

Not by striving and toiling to extract more shall the harvest increase, but by opening to the munificence of the Father and by giving freely of this bounty shall it increase and be sufficient for all the little ones.

–Jesus, December 5, 1993

TWO THOUSAND YEARS AGO Jesus, famously, calmed a storm that was about to swamp the boat he was in with his friends. Mk.4:39 states that he spoke the words 'Peace, be still'. He says in *A Course in Miracles* that *speaking* the words means nothing, but *believing* them means everything. He further reminds us that the works that he did (in the long ago) we shall do also, and greater works than those, *if only we can believe*. This is so because he is at-*One* with Papa, and believing in him connects us with Papa *via* him, until we are fully restored to innocence, to wholeness, Oneness *with* him, *in* Papa.

Here we have the key word, *believe*, which occurs well over thirteen hundred times in *A Course in Miracles*, along with its derivatives such as belief, believed, believing, etc. Nothing happens without believing. Believing is of the mind. This is where the miracle takes place, for only when we first are willing to believe – which is cause – will the effect, the manifestation of the miracle, occur. Miracles become part of our experience when we remember that we are cause, not effect. Papa is First Cause and we are created in His exact likeness, so we must *also* be cause. Jesus remembered this. Now is *our* time to remember it, too.

We are cause of the dream of time and place, including the weather. The turmoil in global weather is an outer reflection, or projection, of the turmoil in our upside-down, turbulent mind. Stilling the tempest on Lake Galilee was easy for Jesus because he *Knew* he was coming from the place of cause, not effect, and that cause was/is peace. He was at peace within because he was at-One with Papa. We are causing the turbulent weather because our mind is not at peace, having chosen to follow the ego's script of separation, which can but lead to chaos. Yet all we need is to choose the Holy Spirit's script and we begin to become right minded; miracle minded.

The ego-script – the *cause* of time and place, (i.e. the illusion of separation) – is fear driven; the *effect* of the belief in guilt. The Holy Spirit-script – also cause – is Love driven; the effect is peace; *inner* peace. Love is peaceful and cannot cause conflict, or turmoil; can only instil peace. And when we have peace, joy is inevitable. We have all these qualities of Love within us because we are the *Son* of Love. Love, peace and joy are the true estate of our Being, whether we believe it, experience it, understand it, or not. Being willing to forgive – i.e. let go of all judgement and grievance – enables us to experience inner peace. Experiencing inner peace cannot but cause us to believe it, and what we believe, we perceive – in our brothers and every living thing, regardless of outer appearances to the contrary, which mean nothing because appearances, all the while changing, fading, disintegrating, *are* nothing.

We are making the conflicted global weather, a reflection of our conflicted beliefs about ourself, so we can *unmake* it by choosing, consciously, to follow the Holy Spirit's script. Some while ago a big, powerful storm blew across southern Britain and on to mainland Europe. Gloucester was right in its trajectory. Theresa and I have been practising the 'Peace, be still' example of Jesus for several years now, and each time damaging storms have threatened, we have chosen, by faith, by believing, to remember who we really are – *Cause* – and this has produced the stilling *effect*, every time.

We are ALL at free will to so choose. There is nothing unique or 'special' about Theresa or me; we are ALL the same as Jesus. There *was* some wind and rain overnight in this area, but it was negligible in its effects. Further afield the wind and rain was many times greater, causing widespread damage. The media reported the effects, with the usual ego terminology, describing 'victims' of such conditions 'happening *to* us', over which we have no control. It is unbelief that is causing us to victimise ourself, and that is something we *can* change, starting right now.

As Theresa and I were told from the Realms of Light in 1969, *"Prayer is an attunement* [At-*One*-ment], *not a pleading."* We do not, *cannot* reach our Source, or First Cause, by entreating, *or* demanding, what Papa has *already* freely given His beloved Son. It is by *attuning* our mind with His that we become One with Him, where all is Love, Peace and Joy; eternally, uninterruptibly. Imagine how such Atonement can transform the heart-minds – where miracles arise – of us all, and thus, miraculously transform the meteorological, political, ideological, economic, environmental and all other climates.

All that is required is a change of perception, a shift of focus from ego-driven, wrong-minded perception that we are each a separate identity – what Sigmund Freud might have appositely described as an *id-entity* – to our Holy Spirit-Self, right-minded perception. And that automatically takes us to miracle-mindedness. That shift is the start of our healing; the dispelling from our unconscious mind of guilt, caused by the false belief that we separated ourself from Papa.

Whatever appears to be wrong with us – bodily ill-health, broken relationships, scarcity … – all are *opportunities* to allow healing of our unconscious mind by forgiving what we have hidden there over innumerable incarnations. Guilt, arising from feeling separated from Self and from our Home in God, *blocks* miracle-mindedness, or, one might say, whole-mindedness. Jesus could perform miracles because there was no guilt in his unconscious mind. He *had* no unconscious mind, because it is a device, a receptacle made to hide guilt from our awareness, yet keep us burdened with it. He *Knew*, had remembered, he was innocent, so had nothing to hide. Thus was he fully God-conscious.

When we have allowed Holy Spirit-Self to bring all our unconscious guilt, our secret sins and hidden hates to the surface of our conscious mind – there to be forgiven so we can be released into innocence – we will be fully restored to Oneness in First Cause: Papa. Just like Jesus. In Lesson 121 of the *A Course in Miracles* Workbook, Jesus offers us a very serviceable mantra, counselling that we tell ourself every hour for the day of practising that Lesson:

> *Forgiveness is the key to happiness. I will awaken from the dream that I am mortal, fallible and full of sin, and know I am the perfect Son of God.*

Ego would have us believe we must be, somehow, impossibly, 'perfect' *before* we can engage with holiness, and thus, with our divine, whole, inner Self. Nice ploy to keep us trapped in belief in our unholiness. Except it is, of course, entirely untrue. Why? Because we are *already* perfectly innocent and always have been; can never not be, other than in fantasy. And fantasy is not real. So, time to get real. Let us then say, believing:

Holy Spirit, I choose to be totally trusting in You and Your healing of my mind, and restoring me to completion of innocence, Knowing that in that there is no fear; only peace. Thank You.

Diary of a Christ Communicant

P.M. April 2, 2011

The idea of not being totally at peace in Heaven is, of course, made up, so is not true. Therefore the perception of not being at peace indicates the belief in separation, which is preposterous, an error, because separation is impossible.

The word 'Gospel' means *good news*. We have to *share* good news; we cannot keep it to ourself or it withers. Everything that 'turns up' we have actually called into our own presence, and is *actually* good news, a gift, an opportunity. How we *perceive* that gift affects what we do with it. If we perceive it as adversity it is *still* a gift for which we will serve ourself well to choose to see past the *apparent* adversity, for each is *always* an **O**pportunity to **T**ransform **A**dversity into **F**ulfilment (OTAF).

All who are attuned to the ego's script are in the consciousness of fear, and will react with fear to opportunities that are outwardly disguised as adversity.

The idea of not being totally at peace in Heaven is, of course, made up, so is not true. Therefore the perception of not being at peace indicates the belief in separation, which is preposterous, an error, because separation is impossible. Engaging in thoughts and activities that promulgate that misperception is equally preposterous. If there is enough self-honesty to examine such daily thoughts, endeavours, commitments, beliefs … it will quickly show their falsity. From that platform can the choice *for*, the change *to*, right-mindedness readily be made.

44: Unburdening from Unconscious Guilt

My son, your desire is well known to me. Give it to me, offer it up and commit it to me. ...my purpose is also as your heart's desire – for the children of Earth to know Eternal Truth and to let me gather them unto the Father by my Love for them.

–Jesus, December 12, 1993

CHAPTER 43 STATES:

Jesus could perform miracles because there was no guilt in his unconscious mind. He *had* no unconscious mind, because it is a device, a receptacle made to hide guilt from our awareness, yet keep us burdened with it. He *Knew*, had remembered, he was innocent, so had nothing to hide. Thus was he fully God-conscious.

The essence of *A Course in Miracles* and its explanation about perceived sin, or guilt (for who could feel guilty if he did not believe he had 'sinned'?[(1)]), and how to be released from it and restored to Oneness in Papa is to be found in this paragraph:

[True] Forgiveness recognizes what you thought your brother did to you has not [actually] occurred. It does not pardon sins and [therefore] make them real. It sees [instead that] there *was* no sin. And in that view are all your sins forgiven. *What is sin, except a false idea about God's Son?* [True] Forgiveness merely sees its falsity, and therefore **lets it go**. *What then is free to take its place is now the Will of*

God. (*ACIM*, Workbook for Students, Part 2, p.401, 1.)

The false sense of guilt arising from the 'original sin' that we split from Papa was/is so terrible, so unbearable that it had to be hidden away from our conscious awareness. What better place to conceal it than in a partitioned section of the already split-off-from-Truth, upside-down mind. That split mind has caused us to believe that what we perceive ourself as being – a little, limited, separate, mortal body – is what we are. That partitioned-off section is the unconscious mind. But that section, or box, cannot be hermetically sealed, and its contents – guilt, fear, judgement, grievance, hatred, jealousy, conflict, karmic entanglement … leak out, a bit here and a bit there, up into our conscious mind.

It is so utterly abhorrent to us that we try to rid ourselves of it by projecting it onto other people, circumstances, events. But that does not work because, as made clear in *A Course in Miracles*, ideas do not leave their source; *they are reflected back to us,* and perceived as an endless round of attack and retaliation. Like Pandora's Box, all the evils we have experienced – on the giving and receiving end – over untold acts in the dream world of time and place are hidden, stored, preserved in our unconscious mind. It could be posited that this box has myriad compartments, one for each unloving, unkingdomly dream event.

These dream events will keep re-arising from that box and replaying into our conscious mind, one or another at a time. And because the time, place, events, people seem to be different each time it is replayed, we perceive them as unconnected to what it is actually, simply _re_playing. Previous events, hidden from awareness in the unconscious-memory box are thus unable to be consciously perceived as replays of the dream of separation. If we are following the ego's script of guilt, fear, hatred, scarcity, murder, *disease*, mortality … each replay adds *further* to the seeming darkness inside the box.

But when we have had enough of riding the carousel of misery, birth and death, which *appears* inescapable, we can call upon infallible, all-*Knowing*, all-wise, all-empowered Help. Yes, it's our elder brother, Jesus, who saw through the illusion, awakened from the dream and fashioned (see Vignette 27, "*Seek ye First the Kingdom...*"), and now presides over, the escape ladder – true forgiveness – from our self-made hell of seeming separation. Once we make that choice to *ask* for Help, Jesus – and/or the Spirit of Truth – takes control of our life and turns it around; we are no longer heading into outer darkness but back toward the Light.

The Holy Spirit, totally benign, trustworthy and Loving, then has charge of our unconscious mind – *because we have asked, authorising Him thusly*. This is the end of our unwitting, blind compliance with the ego's pulling of our strings, causing us to feel that we are at the mercy of malign, 'random' events that keep 'punishing us for our guilt'. Holy Spirit shines the Light of eternal Truth into one compartment – one unconscious-mind stored 'event' – at a time, when He sees we are ready to face it, forgive it and release it into innocence. The contents – guilt, fear, judgement, grievance ... – are all aspects of darkness.

But darkness – in all its aspects – is *still* nothing. It does not exist. It is the apparent *absence* of something real: Light. That shining of the Light into our unconscious mind raises it to our conscious awareness, where, when we are willing, we can choose to see it for what it really is – nothing – and let it go, releasing us from its grip into the freedom of innocence by the process of True Forgiveness. The alternative is reverting to ego script, when it will be adduced as evidence of our *guilt*, which – with ego's fear-filled perception – causes us to go into denial or projection mode, ensuring it will have to be raised again in another time, another illusory circumstance, another circuit of the carousel.

However, if we remain steadfastly with the Holy Spirit's script, we can give thanks for the perfect *opportunity* He has provided for us to forgive ourself for imagining, dreaming the darkness of that event, and forgive our brother if we have perceived he has 'trespassed against us'. This act of true forgiveness then frees us from the chains of guilt, fear, unforgiveness that have bound us to that *dreamt* situation. The dream is then *dispelled* from our mind and we are released by Him (our Higher Self) into innocence of any imagined karmic encumbrance to that fictitious event.

Holy Spirit could, and *would* bring ALL the unconscious guilt – 'dark stuff' – to our conscious mind at once, for dispelling and our release to *complete* innocence and thus, restoration to full, *immediate* remembrance of the unity of the Sonship and Its Oneness in Papa. However, in His wisdom, and with our best interests at heart, He does not do this because most of us have *so much* dark stuff, accrued over myriad acts, festering in our unconscious mind that it would produce an unbearable trauma. So, once we have placed Him in control of healing our mind, best to *leave* Him in charge.

He *will* lead us fully back to the Light as rapidly as He *Knows* we are able to progress, in a balanced way, ensuring the *minimum* – if *any* – trauma. This is why it is so important, *vital* to our well-being, reassurance, peace of mind … that we *co-operate with Him* by placing ourself totally, unreservedly, unremittingly in His care, guidance and protection – *without needless delay*. Who, in his right mind, would choose to *prolong* unnecessary misery? When He has shone away ALL the imaginary dark stuff from our unconscious mind, there will *be* no more seeming darkness.

In its illusory place there will be *only* the *Light* that IS eternal Truth in our mind. Then, and only then, will we be truly enLIGHTened. Here are some alternative terms that are synonymous with, indicative of, Light: Perfect Love, Life eternal, Truth, Innocence, Peace uninterruptible, Joy unending, Wholeness, Holiness, all-empowerment, all-*Knowingness*, absolute freedom, Glory, Heaven, happiness, Oneness, immortality, limitlessness, plenitude … add your own discernments to the list. In a word, it means *everything*.

Diary of a Christ Communicant

P.M. April 11, 2011

> **It is inevitable that Papa's Son will, in due season,**
> **choose to return to his Father, but this is only possible**
> **when he chooses to remember that he is *like* his Father.**
> **Can anxiety be One with Love, Peace, Joy?**

Jesus reminded me on Christmas Day 2008 that I have never, ever, seen him being anxious. 1Jn.3:2 says *we shall be like him when we see him as he is*. Is there one amongst us who does not experience anxiety? Assuredly, we would not be involuntarily embodied if we did not get anxious.

> Anxiety is, always, a free choice; it has always been, and will remain, a free choice. Anyone can choose, at any moment, to *cease* feeling anxious. It is not the will of Papa that His Son be anxious, and His Son's will is always identical to his Father's Will, because he is like his Father: perfect. And so is his will.
>
> It is inevitable that Papa's Son will, in due season, choose to return to his Father, but this is only possible when he chooses to remember that he is *like* his Father. Can anxiety be One with Love, Peace, Joy? Allowing, choosing for the ego to be in control of his mind can serve only to delay the inevitable. Can this be said to be the choice of a sane mind?

---

1. Jesus told Helen Schucman: "The word 'sin' should be changed to 'lack of love', because 'sin' is a man-made word with threat connotations which he made up himself. No REAL threat is involved anywhere."

45: Being the Light *and* the Saviour of the World

Have no doubt, my son, that the reality you experience is the Kingdom of Heaven ... it is the Father's good pleasure – and mine also – that you should receive the Kingdom.

–Jesus, January 9, 1994

JESUS REMINDS US in the first paragraph of Chapter 1 in *A Course in Miracles*:

> There is no order of difficulty in miracles. One is not "harder" or "bigger" than another. They are all the same. All expressions of love are maximal.

He further reminds us that we (all) are the Light of the world *and* the saviours of the world. Most of the fragments of the Sonship continue to perceive themselves as spiritually little and limited, due to the adopted, upside-down belief that we are sinners, guilty, and therefore, deserving of our lot ... So how can it be possible to be the Light of the world? And as for saviours ... *Blasphemy! Apostasy! Heresy!* But, not so fast; not only is there no order of difficulty, or magnitude, in miracles, there is no order of magnitude of our Light *or* our capacity for saving the world, though it may appear so to a mind yoked to the ego's script.

Let us, then, consider how the Spirit of Truth might reinterpret the situation. Although our Light *seems* dim, because we have been hiding it under a bushel, that bushel is made up; it does not exist, and therefore cannot *actually* dim the Light that we all *are*, because Papa imbued His Son with that Light at his creation. It is in Truth, therefore, undimmable and inextinguishable. Jesus demonstrated this, and all that he was/is, we also are. That is not a fable, a fantasy, but the simple, eternal Truth of our Being as Papa's beloved Son. *If only we can believe,* it becomes our *reality,* our *experience.* This is inevitable *because* it is true and the Truth *is* in us, however hard we have tried to veil it.

So, when we choose to *allow* our Light to shine into the world, though it may *seem* dim, even undiscernible, to us – because we are looking with eyes that cannot see the Truth of our Being – it *is* illuminating, irradiating the world nevertheless. How can that be possible, when it does not *appear* to be so to the rational mind? First, let us remember that the rational mind is the split-off-from-Truth part of our mind, and can only 'rationalise' what seems to be real to the bodily senses. So, what it *believes* to be real – illusion – is all it can see; *it cannot see what it does not believe.*

If we desire to *see* the Truth, then *first* we must be willing to *believe,* for it is our unbelief that veils the Truth from our vision. Papa hides *nothing* from His Son; why would He? He gave us everything, and what He gives He *never* takes away. But we can, in our game of make-believe, *pretend* that we cannot see, and to give some 'rationale' to that aspect of the game of make-believe called spiritual blindness, we pretend we have 'sinned', rebelled against God, so He, in a fit of anger, banished His Son from Heaven, into outer darkness, thus rationalising our blindness. Some convoluted rationale!

If we believe outer darkness is real, we would have to believe either that *we* made that outer darkness or *God* did. But Papa is the *Light,* and can create only in His own likeness, not a dimmed-down version (so says Jesus, and he, assuredly, ought to know), so He *couldn't* have made outer darkness, even if He had wanted to (as if …). That therefore leaves us, His Son in fragmented form, as the only other possible fabricant of outer darkness. *We* made outer darkness so we could banish *ourself,* hide ourself from Him there!

The fable just gets more absurd, more impossible, more implausible, more comical.

But there is yet a third, and even more absurd possibility: that Papa is limited, and His Light, the Light that He IS, only reaches so far until it dims and eventually fades into twilight and then into total 'outer' darkness. For that to be so we have to believe the omnipotent, omniscient, omnipresent Creator has created somewhere He does not – *cannot* – go, cannot Be. But the Light that is Life, is Love, is Truth, *is* God – eternally – is *within*. Within, where the Kingdom is to be found, is *everywhere* and has no limits; forever. Everywhere *real*, but not *anywhere* unreal because unreality is nowhere; ever. In Matthew 5:16, Jesus says:

> *Let your light so shine before men, that they may see your good works, and glorify your Father which is in heaven.*

At some moments during any given day we all let our Light shine before men. It may seem, outwardly, like so minor a matter that it is inconsequential, and most would not consider it to be letting our Light – the Light that is the Creator Spirit within us all – shine before men. Like, holding a door open for another to pass through; smiling – at a stranger *or* a loved one, it makes no difference – from the heart; singing for joy; feeling compassion for the world … the list is endless. We can grow that list within us by choosing to be more *focused* on kingdomly thoughts and feelings. Yet we will only so choose in response to *innate desire* for restoration to the Light.

Then, as we become more focused, so does our awareness of the Light within us grow, until we realise that that Light was *always* there; *never* dim other than to our own, self-occluded sight. But it was our *sight* that was dim, veiled, *not* the Light Itself. And, the more we become aware of Its brightness, and that It is *within* us – not something else somewhere outside ourself – the more It affirms that, just as Jesus taught us in the long ago, we truly *are* the Light of the world, and the Light that we are is *limitless*. Then we will be drawn to *allow* our Light to shine, to glorify Its heavenly Source within us, and *Know* Its joy.

Thus we could say, "I am the Light of the world (just as Jesus tells me) and so I *choose* to let the Light that I *Am* shine into the world (not hide it under a bushel)."

What, then, about being the *saviours* of the world? Surely, that is a very different story from being the Light? The Light may be bright within us, but the world can't see it, except in the relatively few, such as Mother Teresa of Calcutta (Kolkata). Well, exactly the same *principle* applies to being the saviour of the world as to being the Light of the world. In fact, it is the Light within us that IS the saviour of the world, in just the same way as is the Light that is Jesus. Okay, but how does that work in us to save the world in *practise*? First, it is not the planet, but humanity that is to be saved.

Humanity is saved – or, specifically, *Awakened* from the dream of fear and death to the Reality of eternal, unbounded, ineffable Love and Life – by the remembering *of* and restoration *to* its eternal *Oneness*. Separation is a state of mind; a false belief that has fabricated an illusion called time and place that is then *perceived* as reality. However, reality is Love, and Love is of eternity, not of time. And that Love is within, just as is the Light; for Love and Light are one and the same. As we let the *Light* within us shine by accepting, *not resisting*, Its reality, so, to save the world, do we allow the *Love* within us to irradiate ourself and the world of humanity and every living thing around us – our brothers in the Sonship of God.

Forgiving ourself for misperceptions about ourself and our brothers is freeing ourself *and* our brothers from the shackles that bind us to the illusion of separation. Love is *unifying*, and thus, Love expressed through forgiveness and blessing ends separation, thereby saving the world. There is no order of difficulty or magnitude in saving. Every expression of Loving-, forgiving- and blessing-saving is maximal. Just as separation is a state of mind, so is Love, and its attendant unity, a state of mind; *Christ Mind*. It is within us all, Calling to each of us. Let us respond with open hearts to the exhortation in Isaiah 60:1:

Arise, shine; for thy Light is come, and the glory of the LORD is risen upon [or, more accurately, *within*] thee.

Diary of a Christ Communicant

P.M. April 19, 2011

**As the leavening of the third and final, completion, or
Kingdom, measure of meal – which equates with the
Aquarian Age – gets into its stride, it becomes possible,
even for those who only *begin* to waken, to see the raising process. And marvel – and rejoice – at its perfection.**

The ego has continually tried to derail Jesus' six-thousand years
long Great Rescue Programme, right from its inception. For
example, Abraham perceiving Papa wanted him to sacrifice his son,
Isaac. This would have been an end to the vehicle through which
the Messiah was to incarnate: Israel; virgin to God.

But Jesus *Knew* this would be the case; that is the nature
of the ego, so it was inevitable. But the empowerment
of the Great Rescue Programme, and its Chief Executive
Officer, was always going to be able to thwart the ego's
disorganised, haphazard, willy-nilly, opportunistic
endeavours.

Jesus had the advantage over the ego of a) having all
the resources of eternity at his disposal – an immeasurably
greater capability than the ego's puny, time and place,
shambolic efforts, and b) he Knew the end from the
beginning.

From inception of the Great Rescue Programme, before
Abraham, he who is known as Jesus was always standing
at the end of time, looking on at the replay, *Knowing* the
outcome. This is why he is completely unflappable. His
Plan is totally organised in every detail, and cohesive; ego's
is reactionary and uncoordinated. The result is inevitable;
no contest. Jesus is not contesting anything because there
is nothing (ego) to contest. He simply proceeds, one step,
one phase at a time, and all is unfolding perfectly. This is
for the benefit of his brethren, not just his own, because

they have blinded themselves to the Light of Eternal Truth, so they have to journey in blind trust, one faltering step at a time. This is why it is of such comfort and benefit to hold his hand every step of the Way.

And now, as the leavening of the third and final, completion, or *Kingdom*, measure of meal – which equates with the Aquarian Age – gets into its stride, it becomes possible, even for those who only *begin* to waken, to see the raising process. And marvel – and rejoice – at its perfection.

46: The Power in Jesus' Name

My son, in Truth it is not I who set you free but you yourself, by your heart's desire for the Spirit of Truth ... By your commitment you can help me to attract the attention of those who are ready in their heart to open the door to Him.

–Jesus, January 30, 1994

I T IS NOT HARD TO OBSERVE that there is frequent use, in books, articles, social networking ..., of the word *universe* as the source of abundance, blessing, fulfilment of our desires and aspirations. What, *exactly*, one might enquire, is intended by use of this term? That will depend on where the user is on the Path to remembrance of reality. If we believe time and place is reality, our journey back to spiritual wakefulness is barely begun. This means that our mind is still confused about our true Identity, and whether we are separate or all One, with Jesus, in the Sonship of the Father, the Creator Spirit.

It will serve us well to consider what we mean if we use the term 'Universe' instead of 'The Creator Spirit', or 'God', or 'Papa' (or whatever). The reason is, there are, seemingly, *two* universes. One is real, entirely benign, perfect, changeless, and is our true Home. We can think of it as Heaven, Papa, eternity, and it is *within*. The other is *without*, made up, illusory, of entirely malign intent, deceiving, constantly changing, destructive, temporal, and always, therefore – without fail – ending in 'death'. So, if/when we speak of 'the Universe' as being our providential source, we might want to be clear about *which* Universe we have in mind.

It seems doubtful Papa would have a problem with His little ones thinking/speaking of Him as 'the Universe', but if we use that term because we are *embarrassed* to say Creator, heavenly Father, God, Papa … then some more in-depth examination of our state of mind would not go amiss. It is time to re-embrace our *true* Source, honour, acknowledge, respect, acclaim, celebrate 'Him' and our relationship with Him. Unwillingness for this, but desiring to acknowledge the universe as supplier of abundance could mean we are inadvertently following the ego's script, a recipe for disappointment.

Using the masculine pronoun – as in Papa, Father, etc. – to address our Creator *is* poetic, but somehow, 'He', 'Him', 'His' seems more consistent with respect and veneration than 'It'! And if Jesus spoke of the Creator using masculine terms to identify the Giver of Life, abundance, blessing, fulfilment, peace, joy … so be it. That should be good enough for us, since we can readily acknowledge he knows more than the present state of remembrance of most of the rest of us, his brethren. And seeking to use controversy as a delaying manoeuvre to our return to Oneness can serve no-one.

In our seeming state of separation, we have been deceived for millennia into the perception that the Creator is a God of anger, wrath and judgement. The responses to that have been varied: to appease with countless blood – or other – sacrifices; entreating for mercy; 'hiding' from that wrathful god … But the God of *Love* Calls us Home to Oneness with Him in eternity, and the Great Awakening to remembrance is now gathering momentum. That remembrance is bringing back to our intuitive awareness an acknowledgement of the 'something beyond' our little, limited, mortal 'id-entity'.

At the same time we are renouncing the lie that we are sinful, unworthy of God's unconditional Love. But there is a dichotomy, in which part of us acknowledges 'a higher power' but is unwilling to attribute it as being the god of institutionalised religion: 'Father'. Who wants a father that is a constant threat to our very existence, unless we make blood sacrifice to him and confess we are wretched, unworthy, there is no health in us, so need to constantly supplicate for clemency? For that matter, what father wants a son with such an attitude when his intent is for him to inherit his estate?

Papa wants his Son to *recognise* (know *again*) and *accept* his Pedigree, rejoicing in it with thanksgiving. This is because the Source of our Being – of ALL Being – *Loves* His creation. Love is embracing, inclusive, tender, caring. Love, simply, IS; It has a name: I AM. Love, Papa, I AM calls His creation by His Name. We *also* are I AM. Yet the unserviceableness of substituting *universe* as the Source of All, *our* source, is that most people think of the universe as *out there*. But Papa is *within*. There *is* no 'out there'. Out there is impersonal because it is *not* Love; it is separate. It engenders fear, doubt, insecurity...

We appear to be in a state of separation, symbolised by arbitrary, given names with which, in our state of forgetfulness, we identify. Those names are an ego ploy to reinforce forgetfulness of our One, *true* Identity, yet, when we are willing, the Spirit of Truth can reinterpret those names for us. Names, therefore, can be perceived as powerful symbols for good *or* for evil, depending on the intention of our life. Here is an extract from the *Diary of a Christ Communicant* dated December 29, 1996 which brings clarity to this perception:

Beloved Jesus, my emerging awareness of your power to accomplish, the power in your very Name, is so staggering I feel almost overawed by it.

> Names are but symbols. Some names in time and place are symbols of power for destruction, for fear, just as are some words. This has no meaning in Heaven, where all is peace, joy and Love unending. Your name is rising in tempo and power as your desire for the Kingdom and the illumination it brings you refines your vibration and further increases your power. My name, whether Jesus Christ of Nazareth or Yeshua Messiah, is power to fulfil according to *my* desire and commitment. My desire and

commitment for the Kingdom and to all my little ones – my flock – is absolute; and so, therefore, is the power of my name.

In the hearts and minds and lives of those who Love me it is power of strength, protection, inspiration, enlightenment, upliftment and fulfilment. In those who reject me it is power to bring disintegration of false structures. This is why the enemy [ego] tries to stop the use of my name in the hearts, minds and mouths of my flock, save in scorn, contempt, derision or profanity.

Your one-pointed commitment to my name – and therefore, to me – is your power and your protection because Papa has given me this power for all my brethren in response to my desire and commitment. This power is freely available to all who will receive of it.

All in Papa's creation is perfectly ordered and structured according to His *Principles of Life*. To enter into His Most Holy Place it is necessary to be *aligned* – attuned, at-One – with this. You cannot accomplish this of yourself, but by your *desire* He will accomplish it for you. Peace and joy is yours in response and according to your desire for it. All *is* well.

In *A Course in Miracles* Jesus tells us that the Truth needs no defence. The Truth is its *own* defence because Truth is unassailable. When we choose to *live* the Truth it sets us free because our alignment, our Atonement with it makes *us* unassailable. Just as it did Jesus, even while they were nailing him to the cross. Crucifying is not practised at this phase of the Great Rescue Programme, yet most of us are still crucifying *ourself*, slowly, unwittingly, by our adherence to, and defence of, the *ego's* script. We can become unassailable from within in an instant, regardless of what *appears* to be happening without. *Because we are like Jesus.* It is merely a matter of our free choice, which is only *actually* free according to our willingness to believe.

47: Loving Beyond All Illusory Barriers

It is necessary that my little ones be nurtured with unconditional Love and care and compassion, and that they be taught the Living Truth, by which Knowledge shall they be led forward; and wisdom shall give them stature; and Love shall make them whole.

–Jesus, February 27, 1994

I HAVE HEARD IT SAID that we should not attempt to commune, or have conscious fellowship, with our loved ones who have laid aside their body and now find themselves in the etheric counterpart of the Earth, because this keeps them tied to the Earth; holds them back and delays or prevents their onward progress toward the Light, the final destiny of us all. To use a technical term, this is poppycock! There are two sound reasons for refuting this perception. One is that the departed loved one may be a few paces *behind* where we are on our journey of spiritual Awakening to the eternity of Heaven.

The other is that the departed loved one may be a few paces *ahead* of us. Let us, then, examine the first reason first. If a loved one is behind us and we are in a position to help them forward, would it be a Love-based decision to choose not to help them? We do not need two guesses at an answer to that question. That loved one may not have been approachable on matters of esoteric consideration during their Earth-life embodiment. This is due to fear, though it will often be disguised simply as disbelief, or claiming superior 'knowledge', such as adherence to doctrines and dogmas of one sect or another.

But when someone finds themself in a place, or, more meaningfully, *a state of mind*, that clearly demonstrates things post-disembodiment are not what was anticipated, they are likely to be more amenable to some help – words of guidance, enlightenment, Love, blessing … – than was previously the case. Approaching such a soul, who will very likely be feeling lost, lonely, vulnerable, fearful, despondent … with an air of condescension or dismissal will serve no-one. Approaching with Love, compassion, understanding, desire to help, will benefit them *and* us to move forward on the journey back to Oneness.

How, then, does one commune, or fellowship, with a disembodied brother? Exactly the same way as if they were embodied is the answer. Whether embodied or disembodied, *all* commun(icat)ion between brothers is mind-to-mind, irrespective of the medium used – telephone, internet, pen and paper, face to face … We simply focus our mind on the brother and send them our thoughts; silently or vocally makes no difference; sincerity is all that is required. It is a case of attunement, or At-*One*-ment. Brothers in spirit receive our thoughts and feelings directed to them without difficulty, regardless of in which mansion in Papa's House they seem to be.

How do we *receive* their thoughts and feelings directed to us? Again, it is a matter of attunement. We literally *imagine* their response, or what we *believe* they would say to us. Sceptics will say that is fanciful, a fairy-tale, made-up, unreal … If we subscribe to the ego's script there is, indeed, no reality to such imaginings because there is no reality to the ego. But when the Holy Spirit is our Commun(icat)ion Service Provider and our intent is to be truly helpful and Loving to all, then we are engaging the *creative* mind imagining (or *imaging* – whether visual or in words makes no difference because both are creative in their purpose and intent) that is our *God-given* right, and such exchanges are all *via* the Holy Spirit.

We may not necessarily be *aware* of such communications from our loved ones in spirit straight away. We have believed for so long that we are a body, and our bodily senses are the only mechanism for receiving (as well as sending) communication, that most of the fragmented Sonship is still stuck in that misperception. It takes desire, practise and commitment. Sitting quietly in an undisturbed place and sending *heartfelt* Love and blessings to the desired party is conducive to getting started with meaningful communion. Writing our thoughts is helpful, keeping notebook ready to write the response-thoughts that come into our mind.

We will do well to bear in mind that keeping such communing endeavours focused lovingly, caringly, sincerely, light-heartedly on matters of eternal, spiritual reality – rather than religious doctrines and dogmas or trivial, social chit-chat – will serve us and our brother beneficially.

The reason most of us are nervous, fearful, equivocal … about communing with disembodied souls – loved ones or otherwise – is belief in a 'veil of separation' that is, somehow, ludicrously, meaninglessly, 'sacrosanct'; that it has been placed there by God, and should not be crossed, opened or in any way tampered with. *There IS no veil*, least of all created by Papa. We made it up by believing it, so we can *easily* unmake it by *ceasing* to believe in it. What we believe is what becomes our reality, whether just in our mind or in form, *manifested* from our mind. When we stop believing, it ceases to be real for us, in mind *or* form.

Jesus made the dispelling of the veil of separation immeasurably easier for us at the departure of his soul from his body on the cross, at which point, so the record states, the temple veil was rent in two, from top to bottom (Mt. 27:51), symbolising the end of the illusory separation of man from God.

So, if a deceased loved one is behind us on the Path to the Light at the time of their demise, sending our heartfelt Love and blessings to them will automatically bring us to their awareness, however dark and dismal the place in which they initially find themself. Repeatedly, gently irradiating them with our Love and blessings – reassurances that asking for Help from Jesus and/or the Spirit of Truth – will almost always *rapidly* effect their rescue to a more congenial place, or, more meaningfully, state of mind. They will soon let us know of the change; their joy, peace and gratitude will come flooding through to our awareness. I have witnessed this rapid transformation many, many times, so *Know* it to be so of a certainty beyond all doubt.

If they are so deeply entrenched in unbelief, or guilt, or fear, it may take longer. So what? If we truly have Love in our heart and desire for their release and forward progress, we will *gladly* persevere in our outpourings for them. For that matter, we can continue in like manner for any and all *embodied* souls, to the same effect in due season. It matters not how long it seems to take, for time is nothing but an illusion. How else can ALL the fragments of the Sonship be restored to the Oneness that is our inescapable destiny?

When our brother has been brought, by the help of our Love and blessings, to a happier place – *state of mind*, actually – of being, their progress toward the Destination of us all can proceed exponentially quicker because the awareness of eternal reality is much more accessible in spirit than in the denseness of embodiment. That brother will then be in a place of greater understanding and empowerment, and because we have helped them, they will have a potent desire to help *us* forward during our continuing incarnate state as well as when our sojourn with a body is at an end.

Now to the second, sound reason for communing with our loved ones in spirit: if our departed brother is already a few paces *ahead* of us by the moment of their demise, and there is a cordial, even Loving feeling between us, they will naturally want to help us right from the outset, just as was the desire of their heart previously. How can we avail ourself of that lovingly, freely-given help if we shut ourself off from it by denying access to it because they are 'dead and gone', and therefore, 'beyond our reach'?

Whether a brother is seemingly ahead of us *or* behind, limiting ourself by keeping the shutter of unbelief closed benefits no-one.

According to Jesus in *A Course in Miracles* we are all here to be truly helpful. Can there be one amongst us who, regardless of their beliefs – or unbeliefs – would gainsay that? Also according to Jesus in the *Course*, giving and receiving are one and the same thing. Thus, helping a brother, whether embodied or disembodied (it makes no difference) is helping ourself. For in Truth we are all One. And the most releasing, empowering help we can give is forgiveness, Love and blessing. Open-endedly. Just like Jesus.

Diary of a Christ Communicant

P.M. April 20, 2011

> ***Knowing* and believing are not the same thing. *Knowing* is absolute and nothing can change it, because *Knowing* is of Truth, and Truth cannot be changed. People can choose to *believe* what is not Truth to be true, but believing it so does not make it so.**

Dear Spirit of Truth, Can you please speak about the difference between believing and *Knowing*?

> *Knowing* and believing are not the same thing. *Knowing* is absolute and nothing can change it, because *Knowing* is of Truth, and Truth cannot be changed. People can choose to *believe* what is not Truth to be true, but believing it so does not make it so. People can also *believe* Truth without *Knowing* it so.
>
> Only revelation *reveals* Truth for what it is, and it is revelation that brings *Knowing*. *Knowing* is certainty beyond all doubt. Revelation comes only from *within*. *Knowing* and Truth are One because They are of Eternity and therefore cannot be changed. Believing is of time and place because it *can* change, and therefore is not of Eternity, so cannot be Truth because it has been *adopted* as a belief, not *revealed*. Believing what is true can be verified by revelation and then it becomes *Known*, for that soul, as

unchangeable Truth.

Revelation is from Papa and can be placed in His little ones by an anointed messenger, such as Jesus and the Spirit of Truth, or any ascended Being under Christ authority who is a *clear* channel, or conduit for the Living Word, and thus, empowerment, from the Source. But this can only happen when the recipient is actually *ready* to receive it. Before then, his channels of receptivity are not sufficiently open.

Knowing can only be of Truth, and by living that Truth it brings freedom, peace, certainty – an end to all doubt – and joy. *Believing* to be true what is not true can but bring uncertainty, doubt, fanaticism, insanity and death.

48: Bringing Darkness to the Light

Unconditional Love is the stuff of which the Kingdom is created.
Take freely of it and fill your heart, soul, life, that it occupy all
parts of you, leaving space for no other contrary vibrations. Love
and bless unreservedly, that the Kingdom may flow unrestricted
through you into the Earth.

–Jesus, March 20, 1994

MANY YEARS AGO Jesus told me, "When all around is chaos and disarray, *then* rejoice, for the Kingdom is at hand, even at the doors." The inference to be drawn from this statement is that the breakdown of the old order codes of conduct for a society to seem to function sustainably is a *sign*, an indicator, a herald that there is a New Order at hand, even now in the process of emerging into the awareness of the world at large. The New Order is, as stated, the Kingdom of Heaven on Earth, or 'the real world' as Jesus calls it in the *Course*.

This New Order is one in which Love, compassion, honesty, Truth, forgiveness, sharing, the brotherhood of man, transparency, the remembrance that in reality all living things are One, that as we give so do we receive … is ubiquitous. And yet, to an upside-down mind his statement makes no sense. How, asks the unbelieving mind, can the Kingdom be at hand – even at the doors – when chaos and disarray in the form of lying, cheating, stealing, cruelty, war-mongering, corruption, murder … from the highest levels on down, is manifestly on the increase, with ever-diminishing shame or remorse?

An analogy can, perhaps, help to provide a comprehensible answer. The organism known as humanity has been suffering from a deep and pernicious malaise since the dawn of time. That malaise is spiritual darkness, caused by the belief in separation from the Light, aka the Creator Spirit, the Source of All. Yet there is an *increasing* awareness and acceptance that a great outpouring of Spirit is taking place, right now, on the Earth. Spirit is another word for Love, Light, Truth, God; They are all the same. Religion is not a cure for this malaise because religion is about *control through fear*.

Religion, which is *always* conditional, has *contributed* to the malaise and is part of it, inciting and fomenting guilt, fear, sacrifice, punishment, torture, mendacity, cover-ups ... much of which, particularly the promulgation of false doctrines, is still widely practised in the name of God today. Spirituality, as an expression of the Creator, on the other hand, is about freedom through *unconditional* Love, forgiveness, transparency ... The Light of eternal, Spiritual Truth is shining now, ever brighter, into the sick, confused mind of the fragmented Sonship of God and could be said to be acting like a poultice, drawing the malaise, the poison *to the surface*.

There, it is gathering, as pus gathers – when drawn to the surface by a poultice – in an abscess. When the malaise is dispersed throughout the body of the organism, and its symptoms *suppressed* – not healed – by the 'allopathic medicine' of fear-based religion, or by state lies, hidden agendas and oppression, it *seems* to be less threatening, less acute. But it *is* chronic, and only *correction* of its cause – the *apparent* absence of Light – can truly *heal* the organism of the condition. The correction of the absence of Light is, of course, the *application* of Light. That is being shone by Papa, under the perfect ministry of healer Jesus.

The malaise, the pus, *has* to be drawn to the surface, *fully* revealed, exposed, so it can be released, purged, and the organism healed – restored to wholeness, which is, of course, *Oneness*. This can be a painful process, because the malaise is being brought to the surface and seems to be concentrated into a localised *time* – now – just as an abscess is the poison in the organism concentrated into a localised *place*. But we all know that without the 'Light-poultice' the chronic malaise would continue indefinitely, gradually weakening the organism until it was no longer viable, and would succumb.

Of course that never would, never could be the outcome because the Great Rescue Programme is infallible and unstoppable. How could it be otherwise, with all-empowered-by-Love healer Jesus in charge of the procedure?

The malaise manifests in many forms, to which some have been referred above. Yet, amongst the most abhorrent is child abuse – not just by the Roman Catholic Church and other religious organisations, but so often by parents – in an array of forms, including sexual, physical, emotional, psychological... This nightmare symptom is coming to the surface, along with all the rest. Over time, Theresa and I have been contacted by a number of souls seeking help dealing with the trauma of parental abuse decades previously. I am prompted to share a deeply poignant example from a lady, now in her 50s, who, for confidentiality, is referred to here as 'TF':

> While reading your book ["*Seek ye First the Kingdom...*"] I came upon the section discussing paedophilia and a word I never heard of before 'pederasty', although I know only too well what it is.
>
> I read what Jesus had to say about it. [Here are some extracts from what Jesus says about offences against children in Matthew chapter 18: ... whoso shall offend one of these little ones which believe in me, it were better for him that a millstone were hanged about his neck, and *that* he were drowned in the depth of the sea. Woe unto the world because of offences! for it must needs be that offences come; but woe to that man by whom the offence cometh! ... Take heed that ye despise not one of these little ones; for I say unto you, That in heaven their angels do

always behold the face of my Father which is in heaven.]

It was not me who was so viciously and horrifically violated but my two younger twin brothers by the man who was supposed to protect them, our father. I was a helpless witness to these frequent and extremely vicious attacks on two small boys. I was only 4 years older and unable to stop him, although I tried. It was my job to protect them because my mother worked and I failed miserably.

I have had a lot of therapy around this. But I cannot forgive him. He died 20 years ago and never had to pay for his sins against these two small boys and I cannot let it go. **I want to let it go**. I want to believe that he is being held accountable in the afterlife. He *must* be held accountable! When I read that section in your book I hoped that knowing that he is being judged by God for his sins will be the final step to letting this go.

Please tell me what you think/know happens to people like him. I would like to live out the rest of my life free from the horrors of this psychopath I called my father. He was also physically extremely violent to all of us and the things that he spoke to us were pure hatred and evil.

I believe my being led to your book was for this purpose. To be finally released from these horrific flashbacks. New things coming up even at this age. So weary of seeing those little boys suffer and a mother who didn't care.

I have emboldened a key sentence in TF's message. She wants, she *desires*, to let it go. That is crucial, paramount; *all*, in fact, that is asked of us, so we can then hand all such to our Higher Self, the Holy Spirit, to effect the healing. Theresa and I connected with TF on Skype and were able to help her understand more deeply that Papa does not judge, for in the eternal reality there is nothing *to* judge. We are, in His sight, innocent, just like Jesus; that judgement *perpetuates* the illusory cycles of violence and abuse that signify and symbolise the fantasy of separation from Papa; that true forgiveness breaks those cycles. All of them. No exceptions – thus healing and leading us back to awareness of the Truth of our Oneness.

We are all responsible for our own thoughts and actions, and it cannot be any other way because we have inviolable free will. As we give, so do we receive. Thus, for souls who seem to be trapped in a cycle of violence and abuse, God will not judge them, but the consequences of their thoughts and deeds will deliver back to them – that is to say, any of us – what they have given out. That cycle – all cycles of time and place – must keep repeating until the lesson, the *opportunity* it keeps delivering, is recognised for what it really is: a chance to see the illusion for the no-thing it is, and forgive it, and let it go by releasing it – and oneself – into innocence.

Thus can those terrible – but, happily, *illusory* – cycles be broken, forever. TF broke the cycle by so *choosing*, and raised her offspring without abuse, but instead, with love, in conscious awareness of the duty of care that parents take on – whether they know it and apply it or not – when they bring souls into embodiment. My beloved Theresa did the same. For this, and all such, let us join with Heaven in a loud *Alleluia!!* Unforgiveness is a closed door in our heart that keeps us bound in servitude to darkness, guilt, fear, grievance and judgement. Heavy burdens indeed. True forgiveness releases us into Light, innocence, peace, Love and joy. Forever. Forgiveness is the poultice, the Light shining into our minds that withdraws, discharges the pus, heals the abscess and restores us to wholeness of Being.

Diary of a Christ Communicant

P.M. April 21, 2011

I Am One with *each* fragment of the Sonship, and therefore the connecting link between all. I can perfectly convey Love and blessing from the giver to any to whom they are sincerely sent.

One who is hurting is calling for Love, but often reacts defensively, *denying* their hurt, which may cause their rejection of our Love when we offer it direct. So in order to respond to their call for Love *with* Love, we can do it via You, Holy Spirit. That way, they will not be consciously aware of our offering, so cannot consciously reject it.

I Am One with *each* fragment of the Sonship, and therefore the connecting link between all. I can perfectly convey Love and blessing from the giver to any to whom they are sincerely sent. Ignore all the ego's scornful insinuations that this will not, does not work, just because its construct – the body and its limited and limiting senses – may discern no awareness of what I Am accomplishing with your Love and blessing.

Have no attachment to seeing results outwardly, for I work *within*, and results always work within *immediately*, though their outward appearance may seem to be delayed. But time is an illusion. Leave time out of your considerations and, instead, give thanks for the *eternal* order of Being, in which all is perfect, *always*.

Faith – steadfast and unswerving – is required in order to prevail and stand fast against the ego's derision. By faith shall all be revealed. Faith first, *then* sight.

49: The Rejoining of the Sonship

. . . fear not that the Creator Spirit is always in the midst, and those who Love Him and aspire toward Him will receive of His guiding and illuminating.

–*Jesus,* Easter Sunday, April 17, 1994

T HE GREAT RESCUE PROGRAMME, the final phase of what in *A Course in Miracles* Jesus calls the Atonement (i.e., the *Awakening* from fear to Love, darkness to Light), is now moving ever more powerfully and transformingly into its final phase. The destination is the restoration of the fragmented Sonship (one, *appearing* as many) to the *remembrance* of the Oneness – in unconditional, perfect Love – that we all really are. During this early stage of the final phase there is taking place, on a grand scale, a *reconnecting* of joyful, Kingdom-resonant, Loving, transparent relationships between souls who are *ready* for that rejoining.

Geographical distance is meaningless, irrelevant in this local, national and intercontinental reuniting. With the aid of modern communications technology such as the internet, social networking and Skype, the Holy Spirit is drawing back together, by miracles and synchronicities, those who already *belong* back together because their relationships – being healed and released from all karmic entanglements – are restored to Love. Healed relationships can be recognised as such by their shared, unequivocal Love for and devotion to the living Jesus and espousal of their lives to him and his Great Rescue Programme.

There are also many relationships that outwardly seem to be idyllic; that have worked superficially for, perhaps, decades, yet are now breaking down and the parties going their separate ways, often with considerable rancour. This is because such relationships are not founded on a sound, spiritually-committed footing. We are all citizens of eternity, sojourning in time; spiritual beings appearing to have a bodily experience. If relationships are not functioning from that precept, or willing to become so, now is the time, in many instances, for parting of the ways.

But that parting is not permanent. Papa created but *One* Son and it is inevitable he will be restored to Oneness in due season. There are no accidents, 'coincidences' or chance happenings in reality, although to our outward, flawed perception it may *seem* that way. People are drawn into relationship for one reason only: opportunity. If they belong together because their long-established (often over numerous embodiments together) association is founded on the rock of unconditional, eternal Love, that reconnection will provide opportunity for the Light they really *are* to shine even more brightly in the world.

If the 'foundation' of the relationship is the sand of a karmic entanglement (that also may go back through indeterminate 'previous' embodiments), then clearly the opportunity they have re-called into their presence is to *heal* that brokenness, to *rebuild it* on the rock. Because of the largely free hand such entangled relationships afford the ego, the opportunity reconnecting provides is likely to be missed, or wasted, again and again, often deepening the degree of brokenness each time. Yet the law of karma, or *opportunity*, means they are drawn together repeatedly until true forgiveness prevails.

It is inevitable that this will happen eventually because Oneness is the true nature of Papa's Son. I am intimately aware of this because my parents' marriage was just such an example. Theirs was not the most blissful relationship and there were frequent occasions when they rubbed each other up the wrong way over what, instead, could have been discerned as chances to fulfil their purpose in the connection: to forgive and rebuild, collapsing time by saving them some turns on the carousel of birth and death. Instead their misperceptions eroded away untold opportunities for a true healing.

But, by the Grace of God, from their greater vantage point in the etheric realms since their passing, they have now become aware of this. From the blessed experience of communing with them it has been my joy to have learned that they both are now fully clear about how the opportunities were missed and how to ensure they will not be missed again during their next embodiment. There is sincere and genuine closeness between them in their *re*cognition that in eternity all souls are connected as One, and their ongoing relationship remains an opportunity for healing and uniting.

In this enlarged understanding my mother has planned her next incarnation, and by seeking wise counsel from the Realms of Light, has selected the mother through whom she will make her next embodiment. That mother-to-be is presently a teenager, and part of our extended family of Loved-ones. Everyone has such an extended family, some of whom are embodied with us now and some are in spirit, Loving us and ever-mindful for our well-being and progress toward the Light of Home in Papa. At the last 'count' my dad was still planning his next embodiment, in close deliberation also with wise counsel.

The continuing, blessed, precious fellowship with our loved ones in spirit is not only possible but of immeasurable benefit to us and to them, in healing – rejoining – the Sonship. If a soul is not ready for healing with a brother before they lay aside their body, it is not 'too late' for the healing-through-true-forgiveness to occur. Again, Theresa and I are intimately aware of this because a *magnificent* healing between us and her dad took place after his passing, as described in *"Seek ye First the Kingdom..."*. Prior to that there was *seemingly* irreversible brokenness. But true forgiveness is the primary mechanism for rendering 'the impossible' possible.

The false doctrine forbidding communion between embodied and disembodied souls still lingers, and plays right into the ego's hands, fuelled by fear of the unknown. This may have served a temporary purpose in Old Testament times, but now we are able to place ourself in the care, guidance and protection of Jesus. By consciously so choosing, we are kept safe from the devices of darkness, while being restored to remembrance that we are, and have always been, an inextricable part of the Light. And by this remembrance, become willing to allow the Light that we *are* to shine into the darkness, for the highest good of all, embodied as well as disembodied; it makes no difference because there *is* no difference.

We are all One, and the rejoining back into that Oneness is being delayed unnecessarily by allowing ourself to believe we are separated, not just from Papa, but from our brothers, untold numbers of whom are 'beyond the veil'. Piffle! There *is* no veil. We made it up, and only *believe* it is real, so for us it *seems* real. It is not real for Papa, nor Jesus, nor the Holy Spirit, nor for untold loved ones, brothers, in the Realms of Light. So who is mistaken in their perceptions? One guess should do it.

Some of those brothers that we have deemed to be 'beyond the veil' are in a position to help us and some are in need of our help. By denying ourself access to, communion with, those brothers, we deny ourself opportunity to avail ourself of their help – not to speak of their Love and fellowship! – and also to be truly helpful to those there who are in need of help. Jesus counsels us in the *Course*:

> You can do much on behalf of your own healing and that of others if, in a situation calling for help, you think of it this way:
> *I am here **only** to be truly helpful.*
> *I am here to represent Him Who sent me …* [1]

He further states:

> God is praised whenever any mind learns [or, *remembers*] to be wholly helpful. This is impossible without being wholly harmless, because the two beliefs must coexist. *The*

truly helpful are invulnerable, because they are not protecting their egos and so nothing can hurt them. **Their helpfulness is their praise of God,** and He will return their praise of Him because they are like Him, and they can rejoice together. God goes out to them and through them, and there is great joy throughout the Kingdom.

Every mind that is changed adds to this joy with its individual willingness to share in it. **The truly helpful are God's miracle workers,** whom I direct until we are all united in the joy of the Kingdom. I will direct you to wherever you can be truly helpful, and to whoever can follow my guidance through you.[(2)]

Let us choose to leave no-one out, wherever they may seem to be, so Jesus *can* direct us to *wherever* we can be truly, *unreservedly* helpful.

Diary of a Christ Communicant

P.M. April 22, 2011

> **Time and place is about 'doing'; eternity is about Being. There is nothing to *do* in Heaven – it already is created, perfectly, by Papa – except experience, rejoice, participate in and thus, *extend*, the joy, peace and Love that is Heaven. For Heaven is what you ARE, not what you do.**

What, here, do we do that we imagine we will do in Heaven? If nothing, what we do here must be a *distraction* from Heaven, our true and only Home. So why do we distract ourself, blindly, mindlessly?

All that is needful is to open the eyes, the true, *inner-seeing* eyes, and see the distractions of time and place for what they are, and be an observer of them; a passerby, rather than a fully engaged participant. Time and place is about 'doing'; eternity is about Being. There is nothing to *do* in Heaven – it already is created, perfectly, by Papa – except experience, rejoice, participate in and thus, *extend*, the joy, peace and Love that is Heaven. For Heaven is what you ARE, not what you do. And creating is a process, an outcome, an *effect* of Being, not of doing.

Of course, each soul has things to do in time and he can still perform all that he desires, or is expected of him, diligently, to the best of his ability; for each soul brings varying gifts to his sojourn in time, each according to his abilities and potential. These can all be performed and developed, honed, perfected honestly, fairly, for the highest good of all.

And with that approach he is indeed bringing a little bit of Heaven with him and expanding it, extending it within the earthly experience, contributing meaningfully to *the Kingdom of Heaven on Earth*. For, as well you Know, it is entirely possible to BE kingdomly in one's demeanour and intent, irrespective of what one is *doing* at any and every moment. And in due season the Being enlarges and the doing diminishes in their respectively perceived import, until Heaven is all there IS.

---

1. *ACIM,* Chapter 2, p28, V. The Function of the Miracle Worker, A:18.(8),1–3.

2. *ACIM* Chapter 4, p71, VII Creation and Communication, 8.

50: Revelation:
The Key to Knowledge

Let your hearts be set upon your highest desires and the Lord shall accomplish them for you. Thus shall the Crown of your Glory be complete.

–A Christ-server from the Realms of Light, April 24, 1994

R EVELATION IS THE MECHANISM by which we are restored to Knowledge. The term *knowledge* is widely misunderstood and misused in time and place. It can only be applied correctly to that which is *eternally true*, unchanging, unchangeable; whose Source is Papa, the Creator Spirit. Yet it is used in referring to matters perceived about time and place, all of which is illusory, changes constantly according to the perspective of the perceiver, is entropic and passes away. All that can be acquired about such is *information*, since it is impossible to *Know* the unreal; the unreal doesn't exist.

Only the real can be *Known*. The real and the unreal are mutually exclusive. If we believe the unreal is real, we cannot Know the real. That which is real is of the Creator; there is no other source of reality, no other way reality can be *Known* except it is revealed by and from that Source. Revelation comes from *within*, the dwelling place of the Source of All, so it *cannot* be found in the without, though most of the fragmented Sonship of God still seeks unsuccessfully there for it, gathering information and mistakenly believing it to be Knowledge.

Knowledge comes only from Papa by our Atonement with Him *within*, so cannot be shared with, extended to, those who are willing to receive it by those who have received it from Papa until the willing recipient is *actually ready* to receive it. This is because until then his channels of receptivity are not fully open. Papa Knows. He gave everything to His Son at his creation, so we all *have* all Knowledge, but because we believe we are separate from Papa, we have *forgotten* that everything, including, of course, Knowledge, is *already* ours. But our brothers who are on their way to, or have arrived at, remembrance of Who they really Are *can* help those still in forgetfulness who *desire* to remember.

This help can be in the form of guidance as to *where* to seek (*the Kingdom of God is <u>within</u> you.* ~ Jesus [Lk. 17:21]) and *how* to attune with the Source. But anyone within the Sonship who has received Knowledge by revelation cannot impart the *Knowledge* to a brother because the brother must open himself to Papa to receive it *direct*. When that happens and Knowledge is given by revelation it is because he is *ready* to receive it. Then those brothers can *share* in the celebration, the Self-empowerment that Knowledge brings. It cannot be expressed in words, which are merely symbols.

We can, of course, be given the 'facts' of reality by a brother to whom revelation has brought Knowledge. But they will be simply words that we can accept or reject; they do not become part of our *Being* until we are ready, willing, to *receive* the revelation, direct from Papa, that will bring them to Life, to Knowingness, to certainty beyond all doubt, within us. Then, those words will become the *Living* Word, or Word of *Life* within us; part of our Being, *enlivening* us. No thought processes are involved and no linear time elapses with revelation. It is a free gift from Papa, which He gave to His Son at his creation, so it has always been with us. We cannot *take* it, appropriate it; it can only be *given* to us. And that giving is only given – *revealed* – when we have *received* it and accepted it back unto ourself for what it is.

When we allow to be removed from our upside-down mind the

veil of unbelief that has kept us blind, forgetful, in darkness ... there, *instantly*, is *Knowledge*, complete, intact, within us. One moment we do not seem to Know, and then *suddenly*, in the selfsame instant, we simply *Know*. This does not mean that ALL Knowledge is imparted, restored to us, in a single, revelatory instant; that would be too much for us, in our somnolent state, to take in. It would be deeply shocking, disorienting. Papa Knows this and because He Loves us totally, revelation is *commensurate with our receptivity*.

We can come (back) to readiness for receiving the free gift of revelation of Knowledge simply by truly, earnestly, steadfastly *desiring* it; by opening our mind to receive it and accept it unto ourself by adopting a *willingness* to believe – and thus dispelling the *unbelief* we hold about eternal reality and our indispensable part in it. That unbelief has kept us in the misperception that we are separate; somehow – absurdly – forgetful, unaware, unworthy. Yet, how can Papa's beloved Son be unworthy of the perfect, *unconditional* Love of his Father, Who can create only in His perfect likeness?

There is no other source of Knowledge than Papa, and until we are willing to acKnowledge that Truth we are wandering, lost, alone, fearful in the spiritual darkness that is the wilderness of forgetfulness. The ego would have us believe that to surrender our 'independence' from God back to Him in this way is to disempower ourself. Yet even with our Earth-mind perception we can recognise that 'Knowledge is power'. Information is 'power' also, but *solely* within the confines of illusion, time and place. But the temporal is in constant flux, so *illusory* power is 'here today, gone tomorrow'.

Such temporal 'power' is duplicitous because, not being eternal, its source can but be the ego. It is always power *over* rather than power *with*. In eternity there is *always* equality of Being, and power of one over another is, by definition, lacking equality, so has no part in Heaven, eternity, Papa. Such counterfeit power deceives, and always comes to the end of its cycle. Because it is *abuse* of power, it creates a karmic indebtedness, or imbalance, which has to be restored to equilibrium, whether in the 'present' or a subsequent embodiment. But even within our seemingly embodied state we can treat every brother with equality when we remember that in the Truth of eternity we *are* equal.

Knowledge can only be revealed (actually, *restored*) to us by Papa when He Knows we are ready for it. Knowledge is power, in eternity, but can be *applied* also in time (*All power is given unto me in heaven <u>and in earth</u>.* ~ Jesus [Mt.28:18]). That power is perfect, unconditional Love. Then, just as this quote from Jesus indicates, do we have ALL power. This empowerment is already ours, has always been and will always be ours because we are Papa's Son. He has not taken it away from us; why would He? How could He? To suggest He would, or could, is to imply He could have made a mistake. What He freely gives is *forever* given, and therefore *forever* ours because He does not make mistakes.

Unconditional, perfect Love is ours, right now, and empowers and enlightens us; for miracles; for being the Light of the world; for saving the world. Steadfast willingness to *accept* the Truth of our eternal Being opens our floodgates, that we may receive in abundance the revelation of all Knowing that Papa ceaselessly outpours upon His beloved Son, and be restored to full remembrance that we – all – *are* His beloved Son, in whom He is well pleased.

For any of us as yet to experience a revelatory moment, any attempt at explaining it may seem incomprehensible; gobbledegook. But the moment such an event takes place, it all becomes absolutely clear, makes *perfect* sense. Meanwhile, if we truly seek and earnestly desire to remember Who we really are, we can say:

Thank You, Holy Spirit, for healing my mind; for shining the Light of understanding there, and bringing me, one step at a time, to greater awareness and readiness to receive revelatory experience of my true, eternal Being in Papa.

Diary of a Christ Communicant

P.M. April 24, , Easter Day 2011

**Who in his right mind can believe that Papa, Who creat-
ed His Son in His own likeness, could have created him
to know and experience pain and suffering? The idea
is not worth countenancing. So for all who are ready to
hear it: do not entertain it longer.**

According to Jesus in *A Course in Miracles*, the innocent cannot experience pain or suffering. Thus his not *suffering* on the cross. Alleluia! *We* experience pain and suffering because we believe we are guilty and *deserve* punishment. He had long ago abandoned that false belief. When we choose to accept, and remember, that we are, just like Jesus, innocent in Papa's sight, we also will be incapable of experiencing pain and suffering.

Indeed so. And who in his right mind can believe that Papa, Who created His Son in His own likeness, could have created him to know and experience pain and suffering? The idea is so absurd that it is not worth countenancing. So for all who are ready to hear it: do not entertain it longer.

It is not real, it is not true, so holding onto such an idea, such a belief can only be insane and cause fear, doubt, uncertainty. It is a made-up idea as part of the masquerade to appear as other than one Is.

Yet to most of the fragments it still seems so real it is all very well to say, 'Let us abandon the idea forthwith'. It seems easier said than done.

This is simply because it has been believed for so long. But minds *can* be changed, and the realisation that time isn't real either can assist in this, if there is the motivation, the desire for remembrance of eternal reality and an end to time.

Simply choosing anew, changing our mind suddenly, doesn't seem to change what we are *experiencing* suddenly.

Only outwardly, to *conscious* perception. But it does, *immediately*, set in motion a complete reorganisation of the unconscious mind, and is cause for celebration! The unconscious turnaround – from following the ego's script of darkness, despair and 'death' to following the Light script that leads to endless joy, peace and Love – has thus been set in motion, *irreversibly*, even though lapses to old-order perceptions will still seem to occur. Accepting the 'inevitability' of this and choosing to ignore it will enable such recurrences to diminish into obscurity over time.

One step at a time the transformation begins to take place. Remember, only infinite patience brings immediate effects. Most of the slumbering Sonship has only *finite* patience, so the progress can but be at a pace that maintains a degree of comfort in an uncomfortable, upside-down world. But in eternity there is no rush, so it matters not at all. Rushing is, as well you now Know, the ego's way of trying to re-establish control.

Lastly, let all remember that no-one is *ever* alone. Help, *empowered* Help, is always at hand.

51: Seeing the Reality within the Crucifixion

You ask and I draw back the veil on your awareness. You ask when you are ready to remember. Do this – commune – in remembrance of me and I will gently, lovingly, restore the Living Word of Truth back into your mind . . .

–*Jesus,* May 23, 2010

ON EASTER SUNDAY MORNING I awoke to the sense of being in a place of awareness, like a platform, providing an elevated view – about thirty feet (nine metres) above the surrounding ground – of the events taking place in the world below me. This was not just a 'bodily' elevation but a *perceptual* elevation; a higher place of understanding of, perspective on, the events of which Easter is the anniversary of remembrance and celebration. I was in the Company of a group of others – perhaps a dozen, maybe more – from the Realms of Light, and also including Jesus himself, all of us in the Higher, Self, Son-of-God awareness. The vibration was entirely positive and peaceful; a peace that can come only from all-Knowing, of certainty beyond doubt that all was *entirely well*; of Knowing the end from the beginning; of Knowing that we are eternal, invulnerable, indestructible; that fear is an illusion, and therefore, along with illusory events that engender it, it does not exist in reality.

Jesus, with the rest of us, was observing the crucifixion of his body – and the subsequent events, including, of course, the resurrection – down below us, and there was free-flowing discussion amongst us, including Jesus, as if we were watching the playing-out of a planned occurrence within the Great Rescue Programme; this, of course, is exactly what it *was*. There was no emotion, no distress, simply satisfaction that all was proceeding according to plan, though all present knew that it certainly could not have been otherwise. The exchanges between those in the gathering – few as they were, since all present Knew exactly what was happening and the reality behind it – were as much telepathic (Mind-to-Mind communing) as spoken, though it made no difference, and were of a rejoiceful and thanksgiving nature, as of a job well done and a mission accomplished ('It is finished', Jn. 19:30).

If there was any sense of wonder, astonishment, amazement, it came only from the Earth-mind consciousness part of me, at the newness, for me, of such a perspective, and the recognition that this was/is actually the only *true* perspective: from the Kingdom of Heaven; the healed mind of Papa's beloved Son; reality.

From that awe-struck state of mind I said to him, "Jesus, my beloved brother; this morning I celebrate, in wonderment, honouring you in this, your magnificent feat, the blessed event of your resurrection, with all my inner being. And I observe the difference in my perspective on it now, after this experience, from previous years; how it has transformed my understanding of it from an Earth-mind viewpoint to an Eternal, heavenly perspective.

"I now see, clearly, for the first time, that this, the whole Easter event, was not 'special' to you, as it has always been seen by your brothers from their earthly perception of the event. I have always marvelled that you could have gone through the Last Supper, sharing all that you shared, giving all that you gave, without a hint of distraction, of fear; always focused on what you had to tell your friends. Now, this morning, I am experiencing it all from a fully awakened state of awareness, where the crucifixion and the process of resurrection is seen to be no more out of the ordinary than any other event, whether a miracle or a mundane happening."

He replied:

"My beloved, faithful, steadfast friend and brother; you remember I said *'I did it to get your attention.'* [See *"Seek ye First the Kingdom..."*, Vignette 11 for details.] It worked, did it not?

"You are right in your observation that there was nothing special or difficult about it for One who knows the Truth of Eternity, who knows Self, who *is* Self, and for whom time and place are no thing, do not exist.

"I knew my brothers would see these events as the great miracle that, to their perception, it was. That worked for the larger intent of holding their attention, their focus on me, throughout the second measure, *the Jesus Measure* as you have been inspired to call it. But now is the *Kingdom Measure* with us. This is the time, the moment, for a higher, leavened, raised up awareness, an expanded understanding of the progressive, unfolding nature of the Great Rescue Programme.

"You observe rightly that the sun goes forward but the moon goes backward;[1] that if one is not going forward, one is going backward. What purpose could be served by the continuance, *indefinitely*, of an incomplete, limited understanding of the Great Rescue Programme, and of the significant events that form its structure? One perspective, if incomplete, may be serviceable for a span – even the span of a whole measure and its leavening – but the sun (Son) goes forward to the leavening of the *whole*; until *all* are leavened, raised up to wakefulness, equality of Knowing, of Being, of remembrance.

"Now is the point of changeover between limitedness of understanding and *un*limitedness; where *nothing* is hidden that shall not be revealed. Of course, as you Know, nothing has ever been hidden; all is out in the open for all to see, to *Know*, to understand, just as has always, uninterruptedly been so... until the Son fell asleep a moment and dreamed a dream of forgetfulness. Forgetfulness of Who He Is: *One*. One, eternally, limitlessly, in Papa, our Father Creator.

"But it was always inevitable that the Son would awaken, and that the dream of illusions, of forgetfulness, would be over. How could it not be, since in reality it never began, never was, never *could* be real? The Son simply IS; Knows; is All, like His Father, with all the attributes of His Father, Who gave Him everything, *never* withheld anything.

"Now is the New Day dawning, and will never set. Now is the moment of awakening. To the forgetful, another two thousand years seems endless. I would remind such: time is an illusion; all is NOW. My brothers have – as they always have had – free choice to awaken *soon*, or to remain stay-a-beds a little longer, holding onto the dream of littleness and fear. Or they can arise early, and venture forth into the glory of the beginning of the New Day, when the sun (Son) starts to rise and cast His newly-remembered Light on all His brothers, to help them stir from their slumbers.

"I rejoice, beloved, to greet you, to embrace you, to share with you our exultation together in the glory of the Dawn. Let us pause a moment in the unspeakable ecstasy of the Light of Truth arising once more in the mind of our brothers who begin to join with us. Then, let us, together, lovingly, gently, tenderly, caringly, softly, continue upon our task of calling to those who begin to rouse from sleep. Let us always be care-full, in this labour of Love, not to shake them too hard, for the place between sleep and wakefulness can be a confusing state of mind.

"Yet still, the Dawn Chorus of ministering Angels calls to them deep in their unconscious minds, ensuring that awaken they shall, and rejoice at their remembering all once more. So arises the understanding that they, too, are not a body; that they, also, are eternal, invulnerable, indestructible; that they, too, can manipulate the stuff of dreams to their command – and then let them go completely, once they begin to remember who they ARE – from dreams of guilt and fear and death, to dreams of happiness, of Light, of waking to unlimitedness, from whence the transition to reality can be gently made.

"Resurrection can only be – or appear to be – after there has been death. Yet have I not stated from the beginning that there *is* no death, unless you are espoused to illusions, to dreams of unreality? Whosoever lives and believes in the Son – that *he* IS the Son – shall never, *can* never, die. Thus, ultimately, can there be no resurrection, but only an Awakening from the dream. Let our gentle call therefore be, *'Arise, shine; for thy Light is come, and the glory of the LORD is risen within thee.'*

"Peace and joy be with *all* my brothers."

Having seen Jesus, in early 1997, as he appeared shortly after the crucifixion, entirely unaffected by that event (see *"Seek ye First the Kingdom..."*, Vignette 27 for details), it is now clear, from the true, leavened perspective, how that was possible.

As always, we are at free choice to continue to think and believe in littleness, thus limiting ourself to, imprisoning ourself within, such thoughts and beliefs, *or* to raise our vision and accept the Assistance, freely offered, to escape forever from littleness, by him of whom it is written:

> The Spirit of the Lord is upon me, because he hath anointed me to preach the gospel ['Good News'] to the poor; he hath sent me to heal the brokenhearted, to preach deliverance to the captives, and recovering of sight to the blind, to set at liberty them that are bruised, to preach the acceptable year of the Lord (Lk. 4:18, 19).

Diary of a Christ Communicant

Holy Communion October 31, 1993

> **My son, it is the Father's good pleasure to give the Kingdom to His little ones... It does, however, depend on the willingness of those little ones to *receive* these good gifts.**

Beloved Lord Jesus, I know that even though the energies are at somewhat of a low ebb and our awareness of Inner Plane activity is also, you have explained that much is accomplished by our *heart's desire* for the coming of the Kingdom of Heaven on Earth.

My son, it is the Father's good pleasure to give the Kingdom to His little ones, even as it is the good pleasure of earthly parents to give of their best to their little ones of Earth-life incarnation. It has no bearing on whether the little ones behave well *all* the time. It does, however, depend on the willingness of those little ones to *receive* these good gifts. Can a parent give a good gift to his or her little one when the little one is unwilling to receive it? Nevertheless, the parent, in his greater wisdom, knows the gift is good and will benefit the little one, so he must create conditions in which the little one shall become aware that the gift is more desirable and beneficial to accept than to continue in the circumstances whereby he does not benefit from the gift.

When the little one, by and by, recognises that his life is less fortunate without it, he will come to his father and say, I am sorry I was unwilling to receive what it was your desire to give me; this was ungrateful and ungracious of me; I will do my best to make amends and live in such a way as to demonstrate the change of understanding and gratitude for your giving.

And this, Beloved, is all the Father Creator Wills for His little ones, that their eyes be opened to the great gift. If the little ones will not gladly receive, He will not vent His wrath, for His Love is unconditional. Rather, He will seek ways to bring the awareness of His children to the desirableness of His gift.

Master, you have a way of making it so simple.

And so it is, my son! Peace be with you.

---

1. The sun is a symbol of Spirit-operated Mind and creativity; the moon is a symbol of psychic consciousness, not under Christ-Mind or God-Mind control, but rather, under ego-mind control.

52: One Problem: Guilt.
One Solution: Forgiveness.

*. . . this which you do in my name is reality in the eternal
awareness, and your performing it in Earth-life ritual communion
is an attuning with the living reality. This brings the reality
into focus at your Earth-conscious level of awareness and builds,
manifests, the structure in the outer.*

–*Jesus,* September 12, 1993

A S MANY OF US ARE AWARE, in 1965, Dr. Helen Schucman started receiving dictation from Jesus for the most important document ever to bless humanity, by a quantum factor. Helen devoted seven years of her life to this work, with the encouragement and support of her colleague, Dr. William Thetford. It has been said that she underwent preparation for this remarkable feat during several prior incarnations. The dictation was completed in 1972, but it took a further four years of dedicated collaboration with other people before it first became available to the world at large in 1976.

In the ensuing years *A Course in Miracles* has transformed the understanding of millions of Light-seekers around the world – and continues to transform millions more – about the nature of reality, eternal Truth, who we all are and our Awakening and restoration to our place in eternity, in the Heart of God. It is certain that that transformation will continue until *A Course in Miracles* has completed the objectives set in it by Jesus. For his all-empowerment-by-Love makes his commitment to and endeavours for the spiritual

Awakening of the fragmented Sonship of God inevitable.

Helen's faculty for hearing Jesus' speaking started to develop before the dictation of the *Course* began, and it continued after the work was finished in 1972. She wrote much beautiful poetry, published in a work entitled *The Gifts of God*. She said she was the *scribe* of the *Course* but the *inspired author* of the poems. In addition to dictating *A Course in Miracles*, there were many other communications from Jesus to Helen. Some, although given after the scribing of the *Course* was finished, were, and remain, of profound importance for the entire Sonship of God. Happily, these survive in the 'Urtext'.

Urtext is a word deriving from the German, meaning *original text*. One communication from Jesus to Helen after the editing of the *Course* was completed has come to my attention from the Urtext. For me it has incalculable significance for us all as a statement of the core message of the *Course*. Here it is:

Was There a Physical Resurrection?

My body disappeared because I had no illusion about it. The last one had gone. It was laid in the tomb, but there was nothing left to bury. It did not disintegrate because the unreal cannot die. It merely became what it always was [nothing; no-thing]. And that is what "rolling the stone away" [Mt. 28:2] means. The body disappears, and no longer hides what lies beyond. It merely ceases to interfere with vision. To roll the stone away is to see beyond the tomb, beyond death, and to understand the body's nothingness. What is understood as nothing <u>must</u> disappear.

I did assume a human form with human attributes afterwards, to speak to those who were to prove the body's worthlessness to the world. This has been much misunderstood. I came to tell them that death is illusion, and the mind that made the body can make another since form itself is an illusion. They did not understand. But now I talk to you and give you the same message. The death of an illusion means nothing. It disappears when you awaken and decide to dream no more. **And you still do have the power to make this decision as I did.**

God holds out His hand to His Son to help him rise and return to Him. I can help because the world is illusion, and I have overcome the world. Look past the tomb, the body, the illusion. Have faith in nothing but the spirit and the guidance God gives you. He could not have created the body *because* **it is a limit. He must have created the spirit because it is immortal. Can those who are created like Him be limited? The body is the symbol of the world.** *Leave it behind.* **It cannot enter Heaven. But I can take you there anytime you choose. Together we can watch the world disappear and its symbol vanish as it does so.** And then, and then … I cannot speak of that. [Is not this because the ineffable glory of what awaits us all when we Awaken to our Oneness in Papa is *beyond* words, and thus, unspeakable?]

A body cannot stay without illusions, and the last one to be overcome is death. This is the message of the crucifixion: there is no order of difficulty in miracles. This is the message of the resurrection: Illusions are illusions. Truth is true. *Illusions vanish. Only Truth remains.*

These lessons needed to be taught but once, for when the stone of death is rolled away, what can be seen except an empty tomb? And that is what you see who follow me into the sunlight and away from death, past all illusions, on to Heaven's gate, where God will come Himself to take you Home.

This magnificent message tells us two key things: 1) the empowerment (and thus, trustworthiness) of his *fully Awake* Mind, and 2) this empowerment is also *our* God-given heritage. All that is required is for us to *claim* it, *receive* it and *accept* unto ourself (again) what Papa freely, lovingly, unceasingly holds out to us. The guilt, fear, misery, pain, mortality (I could go on!) we chose – in place of eternal joy, peace and Love – can be gone without unwarranted delay, *if only we can believe*. Only our unbelief – 'the stone of death' – stands in the way. NOTHING else. Because unbelief engenders judgement. And there is no judgement in heaven.

Jesus did not suffer on the cross. He was not really there. His animated body certainly *seemed* to be 'there' to outward appearances, but in Mind and Spirit he was far, *far* beyond that place of awareness – with Papa, incapable of experiencing pain because innocence *cannot* experience pain. It is only belief that we are guilty that causes our experience of pain because we believe guilt should be punished. As Pursah says to Gary Renard in *The Disappearance of the Universe*, pages 138 and 139:

> Because of the power of the mind, you need to appreciate the power of your *belief*. It was your belief in the idea that you could be separate from God – your taking it seriously – that gave it so much seeming power and realism. As the *Course* says:

> **Freedom from illusions lies only in not believing them.**[1]

I would certainly recommend that this above statement by Jesus be read six times to help assimilate its full impact and implication.

And on page 140 Pursah says:

> As long as you believe in the reality of the physical universe, then everything you perceive will be a constant reminder to you that you've committed the act of separating yourself from God.

As Jesus also reminds us in *A Course in Miracles*:

> The Truth about you is so lofty that nothing unworthy of God is worthy of you. Choose, then, what you want **in these terms**, and accept nothing that you would not offer to God as wholly fitting for Him.[2]

And:

> If you want to be like me I will help you, *knowing* that
> we are alike. If you want to be different, I will wait until
> you change your mind. I can teach you, but only you can
> choose to listen to my teaching. How else can it be, if God's
> Kingdom is freedom?[3]

There is but one problem besetting humanity, not the myriad that
appear to be the case. That problem is the seemingly fixed belief
in the separation; that bodies, and *all* the temporal, are real. That
belief fills our unconscious mind with a sense of guilt, blocking,
or supplanting, awareness – and thus, experience – of the true,
eternal, unified, blissful estate of Papa's Son. Just a little willingness
to set aside that fixed belief is all that is required in order to allow
the Holy Spirit – *our own, inner Self* – to shine the Light of eternal
Truth into our mind, restoring it to awareness, remembrance of our
eternal, luminescent Being. Forgiveness is the key that facilitates
that willingness.

Diary of a Christ Communicant

A.M. February 25, 2011

> **In time and place there is an ebb and flow. Go with the
> flow. Do not resist, for you are resisting nothing. If you
> resist, you are making something of nothing. Only in
> surrender can I uphold you, for then you have surren-
> dered all gods, or idols, that you would have otherwise
> made and served before Me.**

The awareness available to us through our bodily senses indicates
how we, Papa's limitless Son, have placed limitation upon ourself.

Papa, I want *all* of You, and I feel as if I have only *part* of You.
And I want You to have *all* of me.

> My beloved, you *have* all of Me, for I have given Myself
> to you, unreservedly. And I *have* all of you, for you are
> My Idea, and ideas never leave their source. Your Source

is Me; I Am All *in* all. Regardless of any appearances to the contrary, this is the unchangeable Truth. That which changes is not real, for it passes away and is gone, leaving only reality. Reality remains, for it is eternal. All that is needed is *already* provided, complete and whole.

All this is already Known to you. So *re*-mind yourself of it when it seems as if unreality would carry you away again. Remember, My son, in time and place there is an ebb and flow. Go with the flow. Do not resist, for you are resisting nothing. If you resist, you are making something of nothing. Only in surrender can I uphold you, for then you have surrendered all gods, or idols, that you would have otherwise made and served before Me.

Place them upon My altar, which is your heart, to demonstrate to yourself your faith that I Am Who *you* truly are, and all else is made up, and therefore due only to fail and disappear. Have no fear, for fear is the god of darkness when there is only Light, which is Love, which is Life, which is Truth. Come to Me as a little child comes to his daddy when he is fearful of shadows, and knows he is safe in his daddy's arms.

There is nothing else to do, for all is done. No defences are needed against the Truth, for living, *Being* the Truth shall set you free. And Truth needs no defences, for it is indestructible. Truth cannot be hidden, though My Son can pretend to hide himself from Truth.

Papa, we – or rather, ego – complicates, but You simplify magnificently.

Finis

---

1. *ACIM*, Chapter 8, p154, VIII, 16:5.
2. *ACIM*, Chapter 9, p177, VII, 8:4,5.
3. *ACIM* Chapter 8, p145, IV, 6:3–6.

Afterword

As I write this Afterword, in 2016, it is my inner understanding that there are to be follow-on volumes. This is not in the remit of persona Brian to determine, but the Spirit of Truth, with Which Brian is a willing collaborator. As stated in the Introduction, *the Great Rescue Programme*, or *Great Awakening* from a dream of 'death' back to eternal, boundless Life, Love, peace and joy – inestimably exceeding human understanding – is, from our perspective in linear time, a progressive, unfolding process, moving infallibly and unstoppably toward Its liberating, limitless conclusion.

And so our Oneness with It moves along too, because we are all integral, intrinsic parts of It. Hence this follow-on book from *"Seek ye First the Kingdom..."*, to help us keep in step and up with the progress. The progress continues far beyond publication of *this* volume, so, all the while I am prompted from within to continue as a communication mechanism for helping us to continue keeping in step and up with the progress, I will continue to be a willing participant, and share the results with all who are willing to receive them. If our commitment is to live in the holy instant of *now* – the only moment there is – it could not contribute serviceably to wonder how 'long' that collaboration be!

A few years after I first began writing weekly *Messages of Encouragement* I began to get anxious about whether I could continue. I felt I was running out of ideas. What was I supposed to be writing *about*? After all, I was writing to, or for, people around the world I had never met, hardly knew. How was I to know what they wanted to hear about? And what one may have wanted to hear about, perhaps others would not, and vice-versa.

This was in danger of becoming a downward, negative spiral. Happily, I knew that I could take all my thoughts, doubts, concerns to Jesus or, in this instance, the Holy Spirit, and this I did. I gave Him an ear full, complaining that here I was, out on a limb that I had never intended to embark upon and now could see no way forward; that I was on the verge of becoming fresh out of ideas.

He knew this was coming, of course, and His answer was instantaneous – which in Truth they *always* are. When we don't *hear* them instantaneously it is more to do with our *unwillingness* to hear them – usually engendered by fear, or some other ego block to our receptivity. This situation was not causing me fear of *Him*, but of my own inadequacy to continue what I had begun, perhaps out of over-eagerness, and was now 'painting myself into a corner'.

His reply took me completely by surprise and changed everything in a flash. He said, "You're not writing for them; you're writing for *you*. If anyone else benefits from what you're writing, that's a bonus." This was a thunderbolt, but a very *beneficent* thunderbolt. Suddenly, I was free from having to 'perform' to the expectations of others. In a way, it was like stage fright.

If the performer is too focused on the audience out there beyond the footlights he might panic and freeze, forget his scripted lines and go totally blank. But by ignoring the audience, pretending they are not there, that he is his own audience, so any improvisation – a change of words, ideas, direction – will make sense to himself first, and anyone else hearing would make their own interpretation anyway, so it didn't matter.

Now, all at once, I was free to write about the mystical, esoteric, spiritual, arcane, metaphysical, synchronistic aspects of our eternal Being that were of interest to *me!* I *Knew* – because Jesus tells us in the Bible, "Ask, and it shall be given you; seek, and ye shall find; knock, and it shall be opened unto you ..." (Mt. 7:7) – from decades of experience that if a subject arose in my mind of import to my spiritual growth and understanding, and I *asked* for his input, guidance, explanation, the answer *would* be given.

Often the answer was a direct, spoken response; at other times the inspiration would flow in such a way as to be undiscernible whether what flowed into my mind was Jesus'/Holy Spirit's speaking or simply my own thought processes. As our Awakening progresses, any dividing line we may have previously perceived between Their Mind and ours fades, until we realise there actually *is* no dividing line; there is only *Universal Mind* and we are all part of That. Either way, the clarity that would arise was unquestionably inspiration, so by whatever mechanism the answer was delivered, the Source was Higher Mind communicating the answer. This all demonstrated our connectedness to, our Oneness within our ultimate Source – Papa.

Such is the lovingly given endowment that is freely available to us all, and which we deny ourself only by our unbelief. As the Great Awakening proceeds, may we all be blessed with a greater willingness to listen to the Voice for Papa that is *already*, ceaselessly speaking to us in our mind, waiting with infinite patience for us to actually listen, hear and respond, thus establishing a precious Holy Communion, remembering that communion means common – i.e., shared – union.

–*Brian Longhurst*

Author's Note:
About the Cover Illustration

The publisher of this work has suggested that I provide an explanation of the story behind the cover illustration, and this I am very pleased to do. Here it is:

My friend, Michael Roads, is renowned for his 'Five-Day Intensives', during which he leads attendees on 'inner exercises'. These are intended to help free the mind from self-imposed limitations and allow an unrestricted view of Self, Life, relationships, opening up a greater sense of spiritual purpose and direction. Theresa and I have attended these events when Michael, accompanied by his darling wife, Carolyn, comes to England, and I have undergone a number of mystical experiences during them.

On one inner exercise Michael invited the group to imagine a ride on a butterfly, to see where it would take each of us. A butterfly soon appeared to me and I immediately realised this was Jesus. He invited me to climb on his back, which I was, needless to say, overjoyed to do. He soared into the air and we quickly reached a considerable elevation. Although our direction was forward, he weaved from side to side, tilting, or banking, thus enabling my view first of one side and then the other as we progressed, giving me a broad vista of the journey. It was altogether a very gentle motion and I felt no concern at all for my safety, high above the ground. To my slight surprise no noteworthy panoramas appeared to particularly attract my attention.

This in no way detracted from the event; I was having the time – the ride – of my life as butterfly-Jesus' passenger. Linear time has very little to do with mystical experiences such as this, but it seemed as if this journey took the equivalent of several minutes. In due course he alighted and I descended from his back, with a sense of elation filling and overflowing my heart and soul. He resumed his Jesus-bodily form and we sat side by side on an outcrop of rock on a high hill, overlooking the world below. He looked at me as if to say, "Well, did you enjoy the journey?" The smile on my face, the joy upwelling and spilling over from within me told him all he needed by way of a reply.

We sat there for a few more moments, simply absorbing the togetherness, exulting in the shared companionship, then he looked at me again with such Love, joy, gentleness, and yet with a sense of purpose in his countenance, and said, "*NOW*, we can go *anywhere* together!" He placed what seemed to me an inordinate emphasis on the word 'now', the purpose and meaning of which escaped me. Immediately he finished saying this we shot vertically up at breath-taking speed – 'warp speed', one might say – right into the Heart of Papa, in the very heights of Heaven.

One might be prompted to enquire what His Heart 'looks' like. I have no specific answer to that – especially one that could begin to be comprehended by a finite, limited mind, for how can the finite comprehend the infinite? But how our exalted Destination was *represented* to me visually was somewhat like photographs I have seen of the Orion Nebula taken through the Hubble Space Telescope, though much brighter, and *alive*. I experienced moving right into the *midst* of this... what words can describe this, other than an *ineffable state of Infinite Being; of Life Itself; of Holy Stillness; Quietness and yet absolute Communion; Transcendence; Divine Presence, celestial peace; joy far beyond finite capacity to experience* – and yet, all-embracing comfortableness, gentleness, acceptance ...

I was aware of becoming part *of* It, One *with* It, and It was – IS – Eternal, perfect Love. Limitedness, littleness – all the apparent traits of embodied, mortal humanness – cannot exist in this Presence, this state of Ultimate Being. To ascend to It permanently, eternally can be possible only by surrendering all the attributes, quirks, idiosyncrasies of the human persona; a total abandonment, *renouncing* of the ego. However incomprehensible that may seem to our Earth-mind consciousness, we have the perfect model for that in Jesus. He may have appeared in human form two thousand years ago, but his mind was – and is – in entire Oneness with this state of Being. And this state of Being is the final, eternal Destiny of us all, to which Jesus came to restore us.

This awareness was, in linear time terms, fleeting, yet completely, totally vivid, etched into my mind, my memory forever. Then I was back in my bodily awareness, feeling the indescribable vastness of the contrast between the two states of awareness.

I have pondered this majestic, magnificent event innumerable times since, and one aspect has puzzled me on every occasion; that I had no awareness of any landscape details as I soared high above the ground on butterfly-Jesus' back. Then, while sharing this experience with our kindred-spirit friend, Deborah, in the autumn of 2015, the answer was suddenly, instantaneously with me. The soaring along, banking from side to side was Jesus showing me, *symbolically* – how else could it be portrayed? – that this represented the fifty years of my one-on-one journey with him since the 1960s, in which he has so lovingly, patiently, light-heartedly, caringly, perfectly led me from spiritual infancy to active, purposeful progress toward the Light of our eternal Home in our Father Creator. This explained his heavy emphasis on the word *now* – after five decades of his preparing me, leading me forward, one step at a time, toward Awakening.

This event, this experience, symbolises the journey and destination of us *all*, each in our own way. We may each begin from a different, separate starting point – consciously, anyway – but our common destination is One because Oneness is the eternal Truth of our Being.

Glossary of Terms

ACIM. The acronynm for the book, *A Course in Miracles,* scribed by Helen Schucman, PhD, and transcribed by William Thetford, PhD. *A Course in Miracles,* Second Edition, was used as reference in *Finding the Kingdom Within.* It contains the Combined Volume, Text, Workbook for Students and Manual for Teachers. Foundation for Inner Peace, Publisher, 1992.

Act(s). Incarnation(s).

Aforetime. Before incarnating.

Agapé. Spiritual love.

ASK(ing) Ask(ing), Seek(ing), Knock(ing). This is from Mt. 7:7, 8, in which Jesus says: "*Ask,* and it shall be given you; *seek,* and ye shall find; *knock,* and it shall be opened unto you: For every one that asketh receiveth; and he that seeketh findeth; and to him that knocketh it shall be opened."

Atonement. *Atonement* can have two very distinctly different meanings. In theological circles, and pronounced 'a-*tone*-ment', it means blood sacrifice. First, in Mosaic tradition, of animals, and then in orthodox Christian belief, of Jesus, intended as reconciliation of man to God for sins committed – *and thus, made real* – by the *death* of Jesus on the cross. In the context that it is used here and in *A Course in Miracles* it is pronounced 'At-*One*-ment', having its roots in Anglo-Saxon, meaning *making 'at one'* or *restoration to oneness.* This is accomplished not by Jesus' *death* but by his *Life.* For detailed explanation of this, see "*Seek ye First the Kingdom…*", Part Two, Vignette 12: The False Doctrine of Sacrifice as the Path to Salvation. See also, *True Forgiveness.*

Big Me. The same as Holy Breath, or Holy Spirit. See *Message of Encouragement* dated June 18th 2008 at honest2goodness.org.uk for explanation.

BLASER. Blessing(s) Amplified by Stimulated Emission of Radiation (of heartfelt, unconditional Love and goodwill). This works most powerfully if repeated three times, such as "I bless you, bless you, bless you", ensuring optimum focus and sincerity is engaged in the endeavour.

Breath, The. The same as the Holy Breath, or Holy Spirit, or Spirit of Truth.

Carousel. A revolution of the carousel of birth and death means an incarnation.

CGP. Care, guidance and protection.

DCC. Diary of a Christ Communicant. The written records of Jesus' (and other souls from the Realms of Light) speaking to Brian Longhurst over the decades since 1967. For details visit: www.honest2goodness.org.uk/Diary.htm

FLI. Freely, lovingly, immediately.

Fragments. The broken, apparently separated parts of the Sonship of God; humanity.

FTOC. Faith, Trust, Obedience (to the Voice for God, our Higher Self, within us) and Commitment.

Great Rescue Programme. The six-thousand-year long plan of Jesus for restoring us to our true home in the Eternity of Heaven. This is described by Jesus (Mt. 13:33) as the parable of the three measures of meal (see *"Seek ye First the Kingdom..."* ch. 10, for a full explanation of the parable), and is also the final, or completion phase of the Atonement, as described in *A Course in Miracles*.

Holy Breath, The. Holy Spirit; also known as the Spirit of Truth, or simply, 'the Breath'.

HTG. Honest to Goodness. The blanket name given to Brian Longhurst from Spirit to cover all the writing given/inspired/received by him from There.

IPS. Inner Plane Servers (of the sanctuary of Christ Communion).

KOH. Kingdom of Heaven.

KOHOE. Kingdom of Heaven on Earth.

LSD. Light of Spiritual Discernment.

MoE(s). Message(s) of Encouragement.

NTI. Abbreviation for "The Holy Spirit's Interpretation of the New Testament", copyright Regina Dawn Akers 2008.

Olga Park. My spiritual mentor from 1965, as described in *"Seek ye First the Kingdom..."*, from chapter 2.

OTAF. Opportunity to Transform Adversity into Fulfilment.

Papa. God; the Creator Spirit; our heavenly Father. For full explanation of this, see *"Seek ye First the Kingdom..."* chapter 8.

pB. persona Brian (or persona anyone, using their initial).

PCB. Pray (for), Commit (into the care of Jesus/Holy Spirit), and Bless (our brethren and/or ourself).

PLF(s). Principle(s) of Life of the Father. The term used by Jesus to describe the cosmic, esoteric, immutable laws by which God's Creation operates. God is in the Principles, but 'the devil (ego) is in the detail', always seeking to distract us from the Way.

SAA. Surrender (our ego-leasehold on our life into the care of Jesus and/or the Holy Spirit), Accept (that, having Surrendered, *whatever* happens is within Their control) and Allow (whatever happens to happen without our resisting it, trusting that all is according to Their empowered, benign control over our life).

SFGS. *"Synchronicity, for Goodness' Sake."* This was the original title of Brian Longhurst's first book, but changed in 2011 to *"Seek ye First the Kingdom..."* (also known as SYFK).

SYFK. *"Seek ye First the Kingdom..."*

SMCC. Society/Service of Mystical Communion with Christ. A devotional instrument, or mechanism, for attuning with the living Jesus on the Christ-desire wavelength.

Synchronicity. The simultaneous occurrence of events which appear significantly related but have no [*outwardly*] discernible causal connection (New Oxford Dictionary of English ([1 vol., 1998]).

T&p. Time and place.

Three measures of meal. See 'GRP'.

True forgiveness. [True] Forgiveness recognises that what you *thought* your brother did to you has not [actually] occurred. It does not pardon sins and [therefore] make them real. It sees [instead, that] there *was* no sin. And in that view are all *your* sins forgiven. *What is sin except a false idea about God's Son?* [True] Forgiveness merely sees its falsity, and therefore **lets it go**. *What then is free to take its place is now the Will of God.* (From *A Course in Miracles*, Workbook, 2nd edition, page 401.)

Voice for God. The Holy Spirit, or Holy/Whole Self; our inner connection to God and our One, Christ-Self while we seem to be outwardly separated from Them.

About the Author

Brian Longhurst has been aware of the reality of the spirit realms since childhood. Born in England, he moved to Canada as a young man, where he began what was to become an enduring, personal relationship with Jesus, who manifested in glory to him when Brian was twenty-two years of age. Jesus told him he had come to lead him back to God. From then, his encounters with the living Jesus began in earnest, with a decades-long journey of spiritual awakening. His first book, *"Seek ye First the Kingdom..."*, published in 2012, recounts that journey.

After marrying, Brian returned to live in England. He now resides in Gloucestershire with his wife, Theresa.

Read More . . .

More writings of Brian Longhurst, including his Messages of Encouragement (MoEs), Diary of a Christ Communicant, and a Forum page, in which all are invited to share their Christ-awarenesses, or ask questions about Eternal Reality, are available at:

www.honest2goodness.org.uk

Recommended by Brian:
Any who feel inspired to enter in and climb the inner stairway to the Upper Room of personal, one-on-one Communion with the living Jesus will find this website most beneficial:

www.members.shaw.ca/communion/

Visit Brian's author page at:
www.SixDegreesPublishing.com

Made in the USA
Monee, IL
07 July 2026

56544769R00198